Independence

The Creation of a National Park

Independence

The Creation of a National Park

Constance M. Greiff

Foreword by Charles B. Hosmer, Jr.

upp

University of Pennsylvania Press
Philadelphia   1987

This work was published with the support of the Independence
Hall Association.

The National Park Service, United States Department of the
Interior, has generously provided illustrations and photographs
from its collection.

Library of Congress Cataloging-in-Publication Data

Greiff, Constance M.
  Independence: the creation of a national park.

  Bibliography: p.
  Includes index.
  1. Independence National Historical Park (Pa.)—
History. I. Title.
F158.65.I3G74 1987   974.8′11   86-30747
ISBN 0-8122-8047-4

Contents

Illustrations

Foreword

P reservationists today tend to believe that efforts to save historic buildings in America began in the recent past. This book shows conclusively that generations of patriotic Americans have attempted to preserve and interpret key historic sites, particularly those connected with the founding of the nation. The story of the Independence Square neighborhood gives us a synopsis of the shifts in restoration and preservation theory over a century and a half. In the nineteenth century Independence Hall and Mount Vernon were perhaps America's most cherished patriotic shrines. Both the Centennial and the Bicentennial focused on old Philadelphia, and the treatment of the key structures around Independence Hall permits a dramatic comparison between post–Civil War America and the nation that emerged from the Civil Rights movement and the Vietnam War.

The reader of this book will meet a cast of characters who contributed to the interpretation of our history: Judge Edwin O. Lewis, the architect Charles E. Peterson, Superintendent Hobie Cawood, and National Park Service professionals in all fields who helped to develop our most complex urban historical park. The Philadelphia story involved leadership and ideas from local figures, municipal government, and the staff of the National Park Service. Vast expenditures for staffing, land acquisition, demolition, restoration, and interpretation made everyone associated with the program a politician as well as a historian. Many different philosophies and planning concepts had to be welded together to create and administer the park.

There were historical precedents for the Philadelphia project in the history of preservation in the United States. In 1926, twenty-five years before the creation of Independence National Historical Park, John D. Rockefeller, Jr., began a vast historical undertaking in Williamsburg, Virginia. He financed the restoration and reconstruction of large elements of an eighteenth-century town, employing the talents of architects, archeologists, landscape architects, engineers, and historians. Charles Peterson, who was to play a key role later in Philadelphia, began his career as a restoration architect at Colonial National Historical Park in Yorktown, Virginia. He was in constant contact with the staff in nearby Williamsburg, noting their research techniques and their interdisciplinary collaboration in the preparation of restoration plans.

Peterson then moved on to St. Louis, where he was a researcher for the Jefferson National Expansion Memorial in the late 1930s. This was the first large urban historical project carried out by the National Park Service. It was not, however, an ideal preparation for Peterson's work at Independence. The

St. Louis assignment required him to study a large number of nineteenth-century commercial buildings slated for eventual demolition so that a memorial could be constructed on the levee above the Mississippi River. Only two major historic buildings survived the land clearance program, and Peterson's effort to save and restore an old fur trade warehouse for the park eventually failed. The St. Louis project gave Peterson a respect for commercial structures of the Victorian era and extensive experience in carrying out survey and research activities in an urban setting. But these attitudes created tensions in Philadelphia when he set out to save the Jayne Building in the 1950s.

Constance Greiff portrays the heroes of the long story of Independence Park, and Peterson is one of the seminal figures in the history of preservation and restoration nationally. One of the strengths of this account is her picture of Peterson's role as a teacher and manager of the professionals who were to play important roles in preservation after the 1950s. The standards set by Peterson in his office were put into practice by Lee Nelson and Penny Batcheler when the actual renovation of Independence Hall took place.

Throughout the 1930s and 1940s, National Park Service historians made most of the important decisions regarding the development of historical parks, although architects might suggest specific changes in restoration plans. At Colonial National Historical Park, for example, historians administered the areas at Yorktown and Jamestown, and their decision to reconstruct earthworks and buildings brought those parks into the educational program of the Department of the Interior. At around the same time, Charles Peterson was spending federal emergency relief money to hire architects all over the country to make measured drawings of old buildings that were in danger. The historians had a decisive voice in the process of surveying and adding historical areas to the park system. Although the architects began to assert themselves in the decision-making process in the 1950s, the Philadelphia program was a historical one, and the principal goal for the planners was to teach the values of the founding fathers. The buildings within the park would be treated as documents from the past.

Throughout this book we are exposed to philosophical battles between groups of professionals, each of which believed that it had found the most direct path to historical truth. At times we find the historians and architects debating the future of the nineteenth-century buildings in the park area and the very mission of the project. Judge Lewis had one vision of Independence National Historical Park, whereas the architects and historians believed that the visitor deserved a different picture of the area. The debates over the development of Franklin Court, for example, show the considerations that led the park professionals to adopt architectural innovation instead of the conjectural reconstruction that almost certainly would have been carried out in the 1930s and 1940s. The detailed account here gives us the precedents for each decision the staff made.

Some readers might ask why it is important for us to know about office politics within the National Park Service. Many visitors to our national historical parks believe that our public officials have managed to select with unerring instinct the most important historic buildings in the nation for preservation, and that restoration has been a comparatively simple matter of consulting information at hand and returning a structure to its original appearance. On the contrary, the story of the various renovations and restorations of Independence Hall is a saga of changing tastes, improved professional standards, patience, cooperation between professionals, and shifting interpretive goals. One could conclude that there will someday be a sequel to this book giving us an account of how Independence Park changed in the latter years of the twentieth century. The reader will gain from the present account an appreciation of the knowledge and sincerity of the people who lavished their skill, time, and money on the buildings that have survived from the founding of the nation. After reading this book, no one will look at the Liberty Bell in its new pavilion without respect for the efforts of Hobie Cawood and his staff in preparing for the influx of Bicentennial visitors. Only those who know the history of the move can appreciate the agony involved in winning the support of city officials for transporting the nation's most evocative historical relic at midnight from the hallway of Independence Hall across Chestnut Street to its new home. Similar dramatic moments marked every step of planning and construction.

Yet the development of this park was only a part of the vast historical program carried out by the National Park Service. In the 1930s architects and historians wrote historic structures reports on the restoration of the Ford Mansion at Morristown, New Jersey. Just before World War II an architect, an archeologist, and a historian collaborated in a research enterprise that culminated in the reconstruction of the McLean House at Appomattox Court House, Virginia. The documents involved in the McLean reconstruction were subjected to the same thorough testing that was later used at Independence. The National Park Service Advisory Board adopted its standards for restoration well before the project at Independence had even started. When Edward Riley and Charles Peterson began the research effort at Philadelphia in 1951, there were clear precedents for them to follow, even if they faced unique problems in locating the sources that would be most helpful to them.

National trends in preservation thinking were not clearly reflected in the programs that developed at Independence National Historical Park. When the architects were drawing up plans for the treatment of Congress Hall and Independence Hall, most preservationists in America were developing municipal zoning ordinances. When the historians in Philadelphia were researching the history of each building in the park, their colleagues in Washington were beginning thematic studies for the National Landmarks program. In the 1960s when the debates over demolition and restoration in Philadelphia were at their peak, legislators in Washington were drafting the Historic Preservation Act of 1966, and National Park Service administrators were preparing to hire the original staff of the Office of Archeology and Historic Preservation. Independence alumni like Ernest Connally and William Murtagh had just been chosen to administer the new program that created the National Register of Historic Places. While Richard Nixon was signing the 1971 executive order that required federal officials in all executive departments to protect historic buildings that came under their care, officials in Philadelphia were dealing with Franklin Court, the Liberty Bell, the Visitor Center, and preparations for the crowds that were expected to come with the Bicentennial. The triumphant completion of the Philadelphia park complex in 1976 coincided with passage of the most influential piece of preservation legislation of the decade—the tax act that granted important advantages to developers who renovated historic commercial structures. If the preservation of the Jayne Building had been considered in the 1970s, it might have survived. Moreover, the mall facing Independence Hall would have been more difficult to clear in the 1970s as a result of the new legislation and the National Register process that was already operating.

The jokes that are often made about the quality of work done by committees do not seem to apply to the development of Independence Park. Greiff makes it clear that each painful decision made in Philadelphia was the work of dedicated individuals who attempted to influence the course of events with the needs of posterity in mind. It would be no exaggeration to say that some day we will need another portrait gallery there—an exhibition that will show us the men and women who contributed so much to the preservation and interpretation of the buildings of the Independence National Historical Park. Until that happens, this book should serve as a fitting tribute to their efforts.

Charles B. Hosmer, Jr.

Acknowledgments

T he history of recent events is a salutary reminder of how much of the past is lost when only a written record remains. Documents may establish what happened, but are less reliable for explaining why and how it happened. This is especially the case since long-distance telephoning became convenient and relatively inexpensive. At Independence the decline in the flow of correspondence and memoranda after the installation of the Federal Telephone System in the early 1960s is startling.

It is therefore fortunate that it was possible to write this volume soon after the events described, and not just on the basis of the written word, but with access to the thoughts and memories of many of the participants. Some of these were recorded for oral history projects in 1969–70 and 1976–77. Others were shared with me during a series of interviews conducted as part of the research for this book. I am grateful to all those who consented to be interviewed.

Of these, several people with long associations with Independence National Historical Park and retentive memories must be singled out. George A. Palmer, who retired as deputy regional director of the Mid-Atlantic Region in 1973, has retained a lively interest in the National Park Service, the region, and Independence. He conceived the idea of this book, carried out the post-Bicentennial oral history project, and has been an unfailing and accurate source of information about National Park Service policies and personalities. Charles E. Peterson, who was assigned to Philadelphia to assist in the preparation of the report that persuaded Congress to establish the park, became its first resident architect and directed many of its restorations. He shared not only his reminiscences, but also correspondence and memoranda from his personal files. Martin I. Yoelson, who served at Independence from 1951 until his retirement as chief of the Office of History in 1982, shared his encyclopedic knowledge of materials relating not only to the creation and development of the park, but also to its eighteenth-century history. Penelope Hartshorne Batcheler, who, as a historical architect, has dealt with the park's buildings since 1955, answered with patience frequent questions about planning decisions, particularly those concerning Franklin Court, and about restoration procedures. All four read the manuscript and made valuable contributions and necessary corrections.

The current staff of the park provided full cooperation at all times. Superintendent Hobart G. Cawood and Assistant Superintendent Bernard Goodman provided insights into the park's operating procedures. David

Dutcher, who succeeded Yoelson as chief of the Office of History, served, after the latter's departure, as administrator of the project, and as my primary liaison with the park. I am also grateful to the park librarian, Shirley Mays, who assisted me in finding various materials, and to Thomas Davies, who took several modern photographs of the park specifically for this publication.

This book would not have been possible without the help of my research assistant, Robert W. Craig, who located, copied, and organized the voluminous National Park Service files on which it is based. A succession of administrative assistants, Cheryl Grek, Susan Borosko, and Sophia Coscia, transcribed interviews and made seemingly endless revisions and corrections to the manuscript.

This published version represents a distillation of a longer manuscript. I owe a debt of gratitude to Mark Carroll, editor for professional publications of the National Park Service, for his sensitive editorial suggestions.

Finally, I wish to thank the Eastern National Park and Monument Association and Independence National Historical Park for their generous financial support for this work.

One
Welcome to Independence

For Americans—indeed, for all people—there are no more potent symbols of individual freedom than Independence Hall and the Liberty Bell. Since 1951 this building and this long-silent tocsin have been maintained by the American people as part of Independence National Historical Park. The park includes three square blocks in the City of Philadelphia where the dream of a free country of independent citizens became fact. Here were written the two documents—the Declaration of Independence and the Constitution—on which the foundations of our country rest. Here, from 1790 to 1800, when Philadelphia was the nation's capital, the principle of governance based on the rights of individual citizens was first tested. Through a series of events, that in retrospect seem almost miraculous, many of the buildings in which these events took place were preserved. Through years of devotion and effort on the part of the City of Philadelphia, the National Park Service, and countless private citizens, these places have been restored for the enjoyment and enlightenment of the millions who come to Independence.

Independence National Historical Park is many things to many people. It is, of course, as it was intended to be, a national shrine. The events that took place here two centuries ago, and the buildings and objects associated with them, are what attract visitors from every state in the union and almost every country around the globe. This place where our nation began arouses deep feelings. The attentive silence of the crowds in the Assembly Room is a testament to this emotion. So is the awe on the faces of children as they touch the Liberty Bell. But Independence is more than an object of reverence. It is also a place to be reminded of the ideals that formed the basis for the founding of the United States, and on which its continued survival depends. And as they tour the park, visitors are made aware that the formation of this nation was the work of men, imperfect like themselves, who transcended their faults and foibles to create an enduring democracy, the oldest in the world and a model for free men everywhere.

The purpose of Independence is serious, but the mood in the park is not necessarily solemn. Independence can be the setting for ceremony, or for protest, or for celebration. It is a site that often appears on the itineraries of visiting heads of state and other dignitaries. With luck, the weather on the day of their visit will be fine, and the flags on Independence Mall will be

1. *Independence Square from the northwest. Flanking Independence Hall are the open arcades and east and west wing buildings reconstructed in 1896. Congress Hall is to the far right; the flank of Old City Hall and the rear of Philosophical Hall are to the far left. Behind the latter is visible the balustraded roof of Library Hall, reconstructed by the American Philosophical Society. In this photograph taken in 1974, the soon-to-be demolished Irwin Building and its neighbor at the northwest corner of Walnut and Fourth Streets are still visible at the left rear.*

snapping in the breeze. The motorcade will come down Chestnut Street with more flags flying, flanked by motorcycle-mounted Philadelphia police. On the front steps of Independence Hall the superintendent, assistant superintendent, and other members of the park staff will be waiting in uniform to receive the distinguished guests. They will conduct them on a tour of the Assembly Room and to the Liberty Bell, and around more of the park if requested. How much these visits are enjoyed by the dignitaries is sometimes difficult to judge, but they are certainly enjoyed by the spectators. Like parades they offer a good measure of spectacle, enlivened by the excitement of press and television coverage, and spiced with a bit of pageantry and ritual.

2. In the spring the park sprouts flowers and children. Here children from a neighboring nursery school take advantage of an early spring day to fly a kite on the lawn behind Carpenters' Hall.

Other events are less sedate. Philadelphians and tourists tend to congregate at Independence on many occasions. Some are scheduled, such as the annual Fourth of July celebration, culminating in a massive fireworks display. Others are unplanned. The biggest crowd ever gathered at the park came together spontaneously when the Philadelphia Flyers won the Stanley Cup. That was a joyful, if somewhat raucous, gathering; at other times the mood of the crowd has been less pleasant. Independence was the site of frequent protests and demonstrations by activists on both sides of the issue during the Vietnam war. It is a source of pride to the staff that none of these incidents became ugly.

Independence is also an urban park, a green oasis in the midst of a busy city. In pleasant weather mothers wheel baby carriages and strollers through the park, and toddlers roll on the lawns. In the gardens people read in the shade of the trees, feed the birds, or sit talking with friends. Office workers buy lunch from sidewalk vendors on the streets around the park and eat in

3

Independence Square. When the days become warm, sunbathers stretch out on the mall or other grassy areas. At all times of year, people move through the park as they go from home to office, from office to shop. For Independence is not an isolated shrine, but, as it has always been, part of a living city.

The park, of course, changes with the seasons, but you can always feel the city around you. The tall buildings on two sides are more obvious in winter when the trees are bare. Except on summer weekends, you can hear the pulse of traffic. The river at the park's back is also a constant presence. The light is aqueous; there is always a hint of moisture in the air, and sometimes a tang of salt, for the Delaware River is tidal at Philadelphia. Independence has other characteristic scents as well: in winter the smell of the roasting chestnuts and hot pretzels sold by the sidewalk vendors, and in warm weather the mingled perfume of flowers and, reminiscent of the eighteenth century, the faintly sweet odor of horse dung, caught in the interstices of the brick sidewalks. On a weekend, when there is little automobile traffic, the clop of the horses' hooves can be heard distinctly, as they draw tourist-laden carriages along the streets around the park. In spring the high-pitched babble of young voices fills the air, as school buses disgorge the hundreds of thousands of children who visit the park for class trips. In summer there are other sights and sounds, the exotic tongues of foreign visitors, or the voices of actors performing in a playlet or puppet show illuminating some aspect of the park's past.

If you come to Independence—as most visitors do—by car or bus, you will probably arrive from the east, just as travelers did in the eighteenth century. Now the park is easily accessible by interstate highway. Then the journey was often long and sometimes arduous, made by ships, which tied up at the wharves that lined the Delaware River and Dock Creek, or by horse or on foot on roads so rough that even a long voyage was the preferred mode of travel.

The weary traveler found rest and sustenance in the taverns near Philadelphia's waterfront, of which the most elegant was the City Tavern, on Second Street near Walnut. When John Adams arrived from Boston to attend the first Continental Congress, he noted that "dirty, dusty and fatigued as we were, we could not resist the importunity to go to the tavern, the most genteel one in America." At the tavern John Adams and his fellow delegates, other distinguished visitors, and Philadelphia's men of affairs could find refreshment for all occasions and all seasons.

As you enter the park today, the reconstructed City Tavern welcomes visitors as it did two hundred years ago. Inside you will see the kind of setting in which many of the country's founders met one another for the first time in 1774 and began to debate the course of action they would follow when they sat as the first Continental Congress. You can also dine on dishes that would have been familiar to them and try the drinks with which they slaked their thirst. In the days when no central heating warded off winter's damp chill

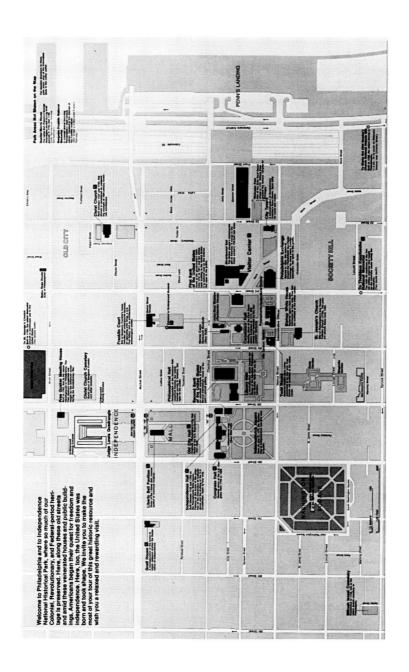

Map of Indepenence National Historic Park.

3. *The Visitor Center, with its controversial tower, as seen from Dock Street. Reflected in the glass facade is the Merchants' Exchange. Beyond, to the left, is the First Bank of the United States.*

and no air conditioning alleviated Philadelphia's summer heat, hot toddies and cooling punches offered the best relief from the weather's vagaries.

Across from the City Tavern, on the east side of Second Street, is Welcome Park. Honoring William Penn, the park was developed on the site of the Slate Roof House, which the Proprietor rented during his second residence in Philadelphia from 1699 to 1701. Pause to look at the paving, which lays out at your feet the original plan of the city as drawn by Penn's surveyor, Thomas Holme. In the center of the park a small replica of the statue of William Penn that tops City Hall overlooks this version of the Philadelphia Penn knew. Graphics mounted on a wall bordering the park illuminate Penn's career as statesman, soldier, and religious leader.

An alley on the north side of the City Tavern leads further into the park. As you follow it up to the curve of Dock Street, the Merchants' Exchange is on your left. Designed by William Strickland, Philadelphia's most notable nineteenth-century architect, it was built between 1832 and 1834. Here Philadelphia's merchants and traders awaited the return of ships from Europe, the West Indies, and China. Here they traded shares in their ventures, and purchased insurance for their ships and cargoes. From the magnificent curved portico, jutting toward the river, Philadelphia's businessmen could see the masts of the vessels tied up in the river, just as the sailor, anxious for port, could glimpse the sun striking the gilded weathervane that topped the

6

elegant Grecian cupola. Today, restored on the exterior, and rehabilitated on the interior for modern office use, the Merchants' Exchange serves as headquarters for the Mid-Atlantic Regional Office of the National Park Service.

On your right is the Visitor Center, a contemporary brick and glass building. In its tall tower hangs the Bicentennial Bell, a gift from the British people, formed in the same foundry that cast the original Liberty Bell. Inside the Visitor Center you will find information on all aspects of the park, as well as on other historical and nonhistorical places in Philadelphia. This is the place to examine the schedule of special events and to make arrangements for guided tours. The Visitor Center also houses a theater in which the film "Independence" is shown at frequent intervals. Filmed under the guidance of the director John Huston, the movie recreates, in the words of the participants, the stirring events that took place here. You can see the startled expression on Ben Franklin's face as John Adams tells him, at the gates of Carpenters' Court, that the colonies will eventually sever themselves from the mother country. You watch the delegates to the Second Continental Congress pound the green-baize-covered tables in the Assembly Room of Independence Hall in response to Richard Henry Lee's rousing call for independence. And finally, in 1787, you hear the relief in Franklin's voice as, referring to the chair in which George Washington presided over the Constitutional Convention, he expresses the belief that the emblem carried on its crest represents a rising, not a setting, sun. The movie was filmed at Independence, at the sites, on the grounds, and in the buildings where the events took place two hundred years ago.

If you have only a limited amount of time to spend at Independence, the most direct approach to the main section of the park is to cross Third Street in mid-block. There, directly across from the Visitor Center, is the First Bank of the United States with its graceful portico. Chartered by Congress in 1791 to serve as a national bank, the First Bank was the precursor of the Federal Reserve system. The bank occupied rented quarters in Carpenters' Hall before completing this marble-fronted brick edifice in 1797. Shortly after the federal government failed to renew the bank's charter in 1811, Stephen Girard bought the property. Except for a brief hiatus, the building remained a component of the Girard Bank until 1929. Restored to its eighteenth-century appearance on the exterior, the building retains the magnificent interior rotunda installed by the Girard Bank in 1901–2. The first floor is now used for special exhibits and other events; the second for park offices; the third houses the park's library.

To the left of the First Bank are gently contoured tree-shaded lawns. The deep swale, crossed by a little bridge and often filled with water after a heavy rain, is a reminder that Dock Creek once flowed into the Delaware River from this area. Much of the park, like this area, is in lawn, some twelve acres of it. Shade and ornament are provided by almost two thousand trees and a wide variety of shrubs, most of them species known in Philadelphia in the eighteenth century. Among the more unusual trees are Stewartia, Franklinia (discovered by Philadelphia's noted colonial botanist and horticulturist, John Bartram, and named in honor of his friend, Benjamin Franklin), and the William Penn maple, with its upright, rather than spreading, branches. Rising above the lawns in many parts of this area of the park, especially along the city streets that form its boundaries, are low brick walls surrounding beds of ivy. These mark, like gravesites, the locations of some of the more important lost buildings of the colonial and federal eras. If you stretch your imagination, you can see the area as it was then, a tightly built urban landscape. The streets were lined with houses, inns, shops, and other businesses, and peopled with shopkeepers, sailors, housewives, merchants, and citizens on public business.

The pathways you follow through the park are the same ones they walked, for they follow the old patterns. By the middle of the eighteenth century, Philadelphia's squares, the blocks of land bounded by the major thoroughfares, had been divided and interlaced with minor streets, alleys, and walkways. At Independence the old routes for vehicular traffic are paved, as they were originally, with cobblestones and flagstone gutters, although no vehicles now travel them.

As you walk west, the backs of the buildings along Walnut Street form a wall, sheltering this part of the park from the city's busy traffic. Ahead is Carpenters' Hall, a Georgian building of jewellike precision and symmetry. Despite its small size, it has a commanding presence that proclaims its function as an institutional building. Carpenters' Hall was erected on a piece of ground now known as Carpenters' Court between 1770 and 1774 by the Carpenters' Company of the City and County of Philadelphia. The Carpenters' Company, founded in 1724 by the master builders of Philadelphia, is the oldest surviving trade association in the United States. The organization still owns and maintains the building, opening the first floor to the public on a regular basis. In 1774 the Carpenters' Company offered use of this space in their new meeting hall to the delegates to the First Continental Congress. When you enter through the fanlit doorway, you will thus see the space where Congress sat during the first debates on the course to be followed by the newly united colonies. The first floor of Carpenters' Hall now houses displays related to the history of Carpenters' Court as the location of the Revolutionary Quartermaster's offices and, later, the United States' first war department. Other exhibits feature old carpenters' tools and a remarkably detailed scale model of the building's construction.

Carpenters' Hall, with its cruciform plan and its perfectly proportioned facades on all four sides, seems to have been designed to be seen as it is now, out in the open. In fact, the Carpenters' Company placed it on an interior lot, hemmed in by other buildings, reserving the valuable street frontage for sale or lease. In 1775 the Carpenters' Company sold its Chestnut Street frontage on the east side of the alley leading to Carpenters' Hall. The purchaser, Joseph Pemberton, a Quaker merchant, built one of Philadelphia's most elegant houses on the site. In 1791 the Carpenters' Company leased Carpenters' Hall to the First Bank and erected a building known as New Hall on the west side of their alley. The Pemberton House and New Hall have been reconstructed, the former as an army-navy museum, the latter as a marine corps museum. Together they recreate the enclosed character of the Chestnut Street approach to Carpenters' Court.

To the west of Carpenters' Hall stands the imposing bulk of the Second Bank of the United States. The classical grandeur of its design, executed in pale gray marble, forms a striking contrast to the smaller, more delicate Carpenters' Hall. The Second Bank was chartered in 1816. Although the federal government had rejected the concept of a national banking system in failing to renew the charter of the First Bank in 1811, the financial dislocations attendant on the War of 1812 and its aftermath rekindled enthusiasm for such a system. Like its predecessor, the bank first leased Carpenters' Hall. In 1818 the Second Bank announced an architectural competition for its new building. The winner was William Strickland, a young Philadelphia architect who would later design the Merchants' Exchange. This massive and impressive structure, based on the Parthenon, is one of the earliest and most magnificent buildings in the Greek Revival style in the United States. The Second Bank, completed in 1824, set a precedent for classically styled banks that would be followed well into the twentieth century.

By the late 1820s and early 1830s, however, political sentiment had once more turned against the concept of a national bank. In 1832 President Andrew Jackson vetoed the bill rechartering the Second Bank and withdrew the federal government's deposits. It was reorganized as a state bank, but in 1839, in the midst of one of the country's worst recessions, the bank was bankrupt. Reorganized again, it continued to operate until 1845, when the federal government acquired the property for use as the Philadelphia Custom House. The building was transferred to the National Park Service in 1939, making it in a sense the oldest component of the park. The interior is now a gallery of portraits of the signers of the Declaration of Independence and other notable figures of the revolutionary and federal periods.

Behind the Second Bank the cobblestones of Library Street lead past the rear extension of the American Philosophical Society's library. Like many of Philadelphia's enduring institutions, the Philosophical Society traces its founding to Benjamin Franklin. It was organized in 1743 as a forum for the pursuit of scientific and technological knowledge. The front of the society's building, facing Fifth Street, is a replica of Library Hall, originally built by the Library Company of Philadelphia. Like the American Philosophical Society, the Library Company originated in the fertile mind of Franklin. He organized it in 1731, making it the oldest subscription library in North America. For many years after its founding, the Library Company rented space in buildings in the area, among them Carpenters' Hall and Independence Hall. In 1789 a young physician and amateur architect, William Thornton, won the architectural competition for the design of Library Hall. Four years later he would also win the competition for designing the United States Capitol in Washington. Library Hall was completed in 1790 and occupied by the Library Company until 1880, when the Library sold it and moved to larger quarters. The old building was demolished in 1884. Although the replica, reconstructed in 1959, stands on federally owned park land, the building was erected and is maintained by the American Philosophical Society, a private institution. The library is open to the society's members and visiting scholars.

Crossing Fifth Street, you enter Independence Square. The square and the buildings on it are the heart of the park, the ultimate reason for its being. The centerpiece, Independence Hall, is probably the most revered building in the United States and a universally recognized symbol of political liberty. Although its soaring tower dominates the square, its power does not derive primarily from its architectural presence, but rather from its hold on the imagination of free people everywhere. Within its walls a remarkable group of citizens of diverse background and calling came together to debate and then create a new force in the civilized world, a government, just in purpose, deriving its powers from the consent of the governed. The ideas set forth in the two documents adopted in this building, the Declaration of Independence and the Constitution of the United States, survive, after two hundred years, with a power undiminished by time.

Independence Hall was erected between 1732 and 1736 as the State House of the Province of Pennsylvania. On the first floor was a broad hallway, flanked by the meeting room of the Pennsylvania Assembly and the Supreme Court Room. On the second floor the Long Gallery occupied the entire north front. Behind it were a Committee Room for the Assembly and a room for the governor and his provincial council. In 1751 a tower containing a majestic staircase was added to the south side. Almost from the day it was built, Independence Hall began to undergo alterations and additions to accommodate changing functions. In 1972 the National Park Service completed restoration of the building's interior and such exterior features as the colossal tall-case clock. Years of research to identify eighteenth-century features and to recreate those that had been destroyed preceded the restoration. If you take the tour of Independence Hall, which starts in the East Wing, you will once again see the interior as the delegates to the Continental Congresses and the Constitutional Convention saw it. When you enter the broad hallway through the Chestnut Street door, open archways give access to the Supreme Court Room. Here are bench and bar—the dais where the judges sat in their scarlet robes and the railing that separated spectators from participants in the trial—as they were in the eighteenth century.

Across the hall, and separated from it by a wall rather than an open arcade, is the Assembly Room. Facing the door and raised on a platform is the chair from which George Washington presided over the Constitutional

4. *The restored west facade of Independence Hall, including the tall-case clock, seen from a window in Congress Hall.*

Convention. On the table in front of the presiding officer's chair sits the silver inkwell believed to have been used by the delegates when they signed the Declaration and the Constitution. Ranged across the room from north to south are baize-covered tables like those at which the delegates sat in geographical order. The chairs are not original, but in collecting chairs like those used at the time, the park has assembled the finest known collection of signed Philadelphia Windsors. Especially on a drowsy summer day, with the sun slanting through the windows, it is easy to people this room with ghosts in perukes and knee breeches, to hear the rustle of papers, and the voices raised in impassioned debate.

Upstairs in Independence Hall the mood is less serious. A table in the Long Room is set as it might have been for a dinner or other entertainment. The room is cleared for dancing, and a harpsichord stands ready to provide the music. In the southwest corner, the Governor's Council Chamber, fitted with fine Philadelphia and English furnishings, stands ready to receive visitors, as it did in the days when Governor Thomas Penn welcomed delegations of Indians and other Pennsylvania citizens.

During the revolutionary period, Pennsylvania had turned over the Assembly Room to the Continental Congress. However, when the federal government chose Philadelphia to be its temporary seat from 1790 to 1800, while the new capital city at Washington, D.C., was under construction, the government of Pennsylvania retained possession of Independence Hall and its wings. The nation's business was conducted in two new buildings at either end of Independence Hall. The Philadelphia County Courthouse, better known as Congress Hall, was built in 1787–89 at the corner of Chestnut and Sixth Streets. The building was hastily enlarged in 1793 to accommodate an expanded House of Representatives. Its near twin, Old City Hall at the corner of Fifth Street, was completed in 1791. During the last decade of the eighteenth century, the United States Supreme Court sat in the large courtroom on the building's first floor. This was the only time in our nation's history that all levels of government—federal, state, county, and municipal—were housed in the same building complex.

You enter Congress Hall, as members of the House of Representatives did, from the east side. In this chamber the congressmen forged laws for the new republic, while spectators watched from behind the bar or from the gallery along the north side of the room. The discussions were often impassioned, occasionally breaking into physical violence. The senators entered through the Chestnut Street door, proceeding up the graceful staircase to their second-floor meeting hall, where, in succession, Vice-Presidents John Adams and Thomas Jefferson presided over a somewhat more dignified assembly. Facing the vice-president were the senators, comfortably disposed in the armchairs made for their use by the cabinetmaker Thomas Affleck. Many of these, erroneously known as the "signers' chairs," were collected over the years and were displayed in Independence Hall when the National Park Service took over its management; others were acquired by the park service.

Balancing Congress Hall on the east side of the square is Old City Hall. In the courtroom at the rear you may watch a brief program explaining the founding of the nation's judicial system. It was in Philadelphia that the Supreme Court established its role as interpreter of the Constitution. Behind Old City Hall along Fifth Street is the headquarters of the American Philosophical Society. It stands on land purchased by the society in 1785, and was completed in 1790. Restored by the society in 1953, it is an important element of Independence Square.

Across Chestnut Street, north of Independence Square, lie the three blocks of Independence Mall. The mall was created by the state of Pennsylvania but is now part of the federal park. It is plentifully supplied with such amenities as trees, plazas, and fountains. Most importantly, its first block is the site of what is, to most visitors, the most highly valued object in the park, the Liberty Bell. Housed in a glass pavilion, in full view of Independence Hall, the bell can be viewed from all sides, and visitors are encouraged to touch it.

The bell is undoubtedly our nation's greatest talisman, instantly recognized throughout the world as a symbol of America's freedom. Despite the bell's present fame, its beginnings were not auspicious. Cast at London's Whitechapel Bell Foundry in 1752, it cracked on its first testing in Philadelphia. After two recastings it was finally hung in the State House tower, but its sound was so unsatisfactory that a second bell was ordered, which tolled the hours. The old bell, however, still rang to summon members to meetings of the Pennsylvania Assembly and to mark important occasions. Thus, along with the city's other bells, it pealed to announce the public proclamation of the Declaration of Independence on July 8, 1776. The bell is believed to have cracked again in 1835, tolling for the death of Chief Justice John Marshall. Although repairs were attempted, they were not successful, and it was silenced forever after ringing on Washington's birthday in 1846.

By that time, however, the bell had acquired a new life, almost a new identity, as the Liberty Bell. In 1839 a Boston abolitionist group gave the bell its name, inspired not only by its role in hailing the Declaration, but also by its prophetic biblical inscription, "Proclaim liberty throughout all the land unto all the inhabitants thereof." In the next decade other abolitionists and popular historians retold, and sometimes embroidered, the Liberty Bell's story. In 1852, the hundredth anniversary of the bell, it was taken down from the tower. For the next 124 years it was exhibited in various locations on the first floor of Independence Hall, where visitors could see and touch it. With the approach of the Bicentennial, however, the park's management realized that the millions of visitors who want to get close to the bell could not be accommodated in Independence Hall. With appropriate ceremony the bell was moved to its present location at the stroke of midnight as 1975 ended and 1976 began.

The Liberty Bell has survived several potential disasters. In 1753 it was almost returned to England for credit toward the purchase of the second bell. In 1777 the bell was spirited away from Philadelphia and hidden in Allentown to prevent its capture by the British army. In 1828 it was given as scrap to the contractor who was casting a new bell. When he found that the cost of removing it exceeded its scrap value, he returned it as a gift to the city of Philadelphia. In 1846 a proposal to recast it came to naught.

Now the Liberty Bell is the most venerated object in the park, a national icon. It is not as beautiful as some other things that were in Independence Hall in those momentous days two hundred years ago, and it is irreparably damaged. Perhaps that is part of its almost mystical appeal. Like our democracy it is fragile and imperfect, but it has weathered threats, and it has endured.

The remaining major area of the park is slightly separated from the rest of the streets of Philadelphia. This is Franklin Court, which runs between Chestnut and Market Streets, midway between Third and Fourth Streets. Benjamin Franklin was Philadelphia's presiding genius in the eighteenth century, the founder of its major civic and intellectual institutions. He was also a scientific innovator of world renown, a profound political thinker and writer of persuasive eloquence, and an active participant in this country's founding. Yet until the development of the park, he was the only major figure of the period with no tangible memorial. Washington's Mount Vernon, Jefferson's Monticello, the Adams Homestead, had all been preserved, so that future generations could understand their owners as living men, appreciate their interests, and experience their tastes. Establishing a similar site for Franklin became a major purpose of the park. Now, at Franklin Court, you can begin to comprehend this perhaps most complicated of the founding fathers in his own milieu.

The best approach to Franklin Court is from Market Street. Like the Carpenters' Company with its hall, Franklin chose to build for himself on an interior lot, reserving the more valuable street frontage for rental properties. In the last years of his life, from 1786 to 1787, he devoted much of his attention to erecting three new brick buildings on Market Street. One of them replaced the house where he had boarded with his future wife's family, the Reads, when he first came to Philadelphia. The exteriors of these three, along with two other buildings in the row, have been restored or reconstructed to their eighteenth-century appearance. The building on the site of the Read House, at 316 Market, houses the B. Free Franklin post office, in recognition of Franklin's role, as colonial postmaster general, in organizing the reliable postal service that helped to unite the thirteen colonies. Another of the

5. *Even in mid-winter a steady stream of visitors comes to see the Liberty Bell in its glass pavilion opposite Independence Hall.*

buildings, 318 Market, commemorates Franklin the builder. The interior is devoted to a fascinating display of the types of evidence, archeological and architectural, that formed the basis for the park's restorations, and in particular that of Franklin Court. The third of Franklin's buildings is the "Aurora" print shop. Franklin, of course, had made his mark as a printer and publisher, and in the last years of his life, his development of Franklin Court included construction of this shop for his grandson and namesake, Benjamin Franklin Bache.

An arched opening in the center of the Market Street row provided a carriageway giving access to the interior of Franklin Court. In this sheltered spot Franklin built his house. It was erected between 1763 and 1765. When it was completed, Franklin's wife and daughter moved into it, but Franklin himself was in London. On his final return to Philadelphia in 1785, Franklin, in retirement, added to the house, improved the garden with walks, flowering shrubs, and trees, and erected the Bache print shop within the court. He lived in the house until his death in 1790, but his family occupied it only rarely after that, and it was demolished in 1812. Franklin's papers yielded an astonishing amount of information about the house, including floor plans, uses of the rooms, and even many of the interior color schemes. Surprisingly, however, no pictorial representation could be found. Lacking an accurate view of the exterior, the National Park Service reluctantly decided not to reconstruct the house. In an imaginative design for the court, colored paving outlines the floor plan of house and shop, and steel frames delineate their bulk. Paths and plantings suggest the secluded garden Franklin so enjoyed, and a mulberry tree, like the one under which he enjoyed sitting and receiving visitors, once more spreads its shade.

What you see on the surface is only about half of what there is to see at Franklin Court, for much of it remains, or has been newly constructed, underground. At 318 Market Street old underground storage vaults and pits are revealed in the building's cellar. Within the space frame marking the site of Franklin's house, you can peer through viewing tubes at what the archeologists found of surviving foundations and other features. At the west side of the court, an entrance gives access to the long ramp down to an underground museum. A corridor, lined with objects that actually belonged to Franklin or are like those used by him, leads to a large installation interpreting the many facets of this man of many accomplishments. You may use a bank of telephones to "call up" a host of famous figures, past and present, to hear what they have to say about Franklin. You may also elicit Franklin's own opinions on a variety of topics ranging from politics to sex and marriage, summoned up at your touch for display on a video screen. Stand at the railed-in enclosure in the center of the room and watch "Franklin on the World Stage," in which mechanical figures perform a series of playlets illuminating his role as this country's first diplomat. Displays around the room portray

6. Visitors inside the frame of the "ghost house" at Franklin Court peer down at the foundations of Benjamin Franklin's house, visible beneath the ground through viewing ports.

Franklin as founder of institutions, printer-publisher, and inventor. The museum also includes a small theater. Since this is the site of Franklin's home, the brief film shown here concentrates on his domestic life. Nevertheless, the scope of the movie is not narrow. Franklin participated in epic events, and their effects on his family make the issues of the era more meaningful to us. Nowhere at the park is it clearer that the Revolution was in fact a civil war than in the poignant portrayal of the deterioration of the relationship between 17

7. Eighteenth- and early-nineteenth-century buildings on Walnut Street, restored and reconstructed, with the Bishop White House in the foreground.

Franklin and his illegitimate, but acknowledged, son, William, the Loyalist governor of New Jersey.

It is possible to see these major elements of Independence in a day or even less. Those with more time to explore may wish to recapture the flavor of the eighteenth-century Philadelphia that the nation's founders knew. Once again the best place to start is the Visitor Center. You may wish to check there to see the schedule for tours of buildings in the southern part of the park, and to inquire about other sites in adjacent Society Hill.

From the Visitor Center stroll toward Walnut Street, passing the Merchants' Exchange again and then turn west. Here on the north side of Walnut an eighteenth-century streetscape of Philadelphia rowhouses has been recreated from what was, thirty years ago, a motley collection of old and new buildings.

Two of the buildings are meticulous restorations. The Bishop White House, at the east end of the row, was built by William White in 1786–87. Bishop White was rector of Christ Church and St. Peter's Church, first Protestant Episcopal bishop of Pennsylvania, chaplain of the Continental Congress, and a strong supporter of liberty and religious freedom. He lived in this house until his death in 1836. At the west end of the row, with its entrance on Fourth Street, is the Todd House. Built in 1775, it was purchased in 1791 by an up-and-coming young Philadelphia lawyer, John Todd, Jr., and his vivacious wife, Dolley Payne. Two years later John Todd was dead, a victim of one of the yellow fever epidemics that swept Philadelphia in the late eighteenth century. His twenty-three-year-old widow stayed on in the house with her young son. Here Senator Aaron Burr brought his friend, Congressman James Madison, to meet the widow Todd. Madison was twenty years older than Dolley, but his wooing was swift, and within six months after John Todd's death, his widow became Dolley Madison. Both houses, furnished as they were at the time of their famous occupants' residence, are open for guided tours.

Other buildings in the row include the Kidd, Fling, and McIlvaine Houses. The Kidd and Fling Houses are occupied by an institution long associated with the area, the Pennsylvania Horticultural Society, founded in 1824. The Horticultural Society welcomes visitors to its exhibit room and interested readers to its specialized library. The McIlvaine House has become part of park headquarters and also houses the offices of the Friends of Independence National Historical Park, a volunteer support group.

The remaining buildings in the row are reconstructions, erected to fill in the street scene and to provide structural stability for the Bishop White and Todd Houses. Those adjacent to the Todd House are used as offices by the Eastern National Park and Monument Association and the Carl Schurz Foundation. The building at Number 313 Walnut, next to the Bishop White House, is park headquarters. The block also includes two formal gardens, one at the Third Street corner, maintained by the park, and the other in mid-block, maintained by the Horticultural Society.

Penn's plans envisaged Philadelphia as a "Greene Countrie Towne," with free-standing houses set in ample grounds. From the beginning, however, Philadelphia acquired a very different configuration. The Delaware River was so vital to the area's trade and commerce that the inhabitants clustered close to its banks. They followed the custom of cities and towns in the countries from which they had come, erecting buildings that were close together or in rows. By the late eighteenth century, Philadelphia had grown so populous, and land values near the river had risen so high, that the rowhouse had become the prevailing form, with the land at the back of the houses occupied by stables, necessaries, and other buildings. However, a few of the wealthier merchants dwelt in substantial mansions and maintained formal gardens. The Horticultural Society's garden reflects the type of planting that might have ornamented the home of a prosperous Philadelphian of the period. You can observe another aspect of period gardening behind the Todd House, where a kitchen garden of the era has been recreated. The vegetables are those Dolley Todd would have harvested, to serve immediately or preserve for winter use. Interspersed among them are plants that served as natural pesticides in the days before chemical sprays were known—onions, garlic, and marigolds.

In the next block of Walnut Street, a finger of the park reaches southward, forming a green walkway inviting you to Society Hill, the restored neighborhood that stretches from Walnut to South Street. In mid-block the greenway widens to form the Rose Garden. This is a quiet oasis at all times of the year, but is at its most beautiful in May and June. Then dozens of roses are in bloom, filling the air with their fragrance. There are fifty-six varieties of roses, one for each signer of the Declaration of Independence, given by the Daughters of the American Revolution. All are species known in the eighteenth century. In season the display of the roses is augmented by the brilliance of spring bulbs and perennials. From the Rose Garden a walk bordered by the tall, upright forms of columnar English oaks leads to Locust Street, where the National Park Service has rehabilitated a group of late eighteenth-century houses as residences for park personnel. Along the south side of the street the Magnolia Garden offers another serene retreat from the surrounding city.

If you have the time, you will want to explore Society Hill further. Society Hill derives its name not from the position or influence of its inhabitants, but from the Free Society of Traders, a joint stock company that purchased land from William Penn in 1632. Their strip of land ran between Spruce and Pine Streets from the Delaware to the Schuylkill. The company dissolved in 1723, but the name has been rediscovered and is now applied to an area bounded by Walnut, Front, South, and Sixth Streets. Society Hill was indeed a fashionable part of Philadelphia from the early eighteenth century to the middle of the nineteenth century. It then entered a period of decline as the commercial activity along the waterfront spread, and as new residential areas were opened to the west. Revitalized beginning in the late 1950s, it is once again one of Philadelphia's most desirable neighborhoods.

Society Hill's peaceful tree-shaded streets are lined with brick rowhouses, punctuated with free-standing structures—churches, schools, a market. Many of the buildings are architecturally and historically distinguished. About eight hundred of them date from the eighteenth and nineteenth centuries. Blended with the old structures are contemporary buildings to serve the new residential and commercial needs of the community. You may wish to stroll through Society Hill on your own, savoring the pleasures of discovering a handsome fanlight, a skillfully wrought iron railing, or a glimpse of a hidden garden.

In addition to the areas close to Independence Square, Independence National Historical Park encompasses some relatively far-flung sites. The Deshler-Morris House is in Germantown. In the eighteenth century Germantown, now a part of Philadelphia, was a country village eight miles outside the city. The Deshler-Morris House, like many others in its vicinity, was built as a summer residence. Constructed by David Deshler in 1772–73, it belonged to Col. Isaac Franks in the years when Philadelphia was the nation's capital. Washington rented the house during the fall of 1793 to escape the yellow fever epidemic then ravaging Philadelphia. He liked it so well that he returned the following year. Although owned by the National Park Service, the house is shown to the public by the Germantown Historical Society. The reconstructed Graff House, at the corner of Market and Seventh Streets, is also part of the park. It was in the home of Jacob Graff, Jr., built the year before, that Thomas Jefferson rented two rooms, a parlor and a bedroom, in the spring of 1776. To these rooms Jefferson retreated to pen the draft of the Declaration of Independence. Two hundred years later the National Park Service undertook the reconstruction of the house, with funds provided by the Independence Hall Association, a private support group.

Financial and other forms of cooperation with private and public institutions played a key role in the development of Independence and continue to be an important factor in the park's operation. Thus, four sites in the park's neighborhood, which are still privately owned and administered, are considered part of the park because their owners and the National Park Service have signed formal agreements to ensure their continued preservation. All four are religious sites, illuminating the diversity that flourished in Pennsylvania under the guarantees of religious liberty conferred by William Penn. Christ Church, on Second Street just north of Market, is the oldest Anglican church in Philadelphia. Its congregation formed in 1695 and erected the present building between 1727 and 1754. It is a notable example of Georgian architecture, with a superbly proportioned Palladian window dominating the east end. Washington and Adams worshiped here during their sojourns in Philadelphia. Two signers of the Declaration of Independence are buried in its churchyard, and five more, including Benjamin Franklin, in Christ Church Cemetery at the corner of Fifth and Arch Streets.

The second church with a special relationship to the park is St. Joseph's Catholic Church, near Fourth Street on Willing's Alley, which lies between Locust and Walnut Streets. St. Joseph's is the oldest Catholic parish in Philadelphia and, indeed, in the United States outside Maryland, which was founded as a Catholic colony. Its parishioners have included Commodore John Barry, the Irish-American father of the United States Navy, whose statue stands in the middle of Independence Square, and Joseph Bonaparte, the brother of Napoleon. The present building was erected in 1839 on the site of St. Joseph's two earlier churches. The third of the churches is St. George's Methodist Church on Fourth Street between Vine and Race Streets, which traces its founding to 1769. The National Park Service has purchased and cleared land adjacent to all three buildings to enhance their settings and buffer them from fires. The fourth religious site is Mikveh Israel Cemetery on Spruce Street between Eighth and Ninth Streets. Set aside as a burial ground for Jews in 1738, the cemetery later became the property of Congregation Kaal Kadosh Mikveh Israel, the oldest synagogue in Philadelphia. Haym Salomon, who helped finance the Revolution, is buried here.

Without its tissue of cooperative agreements, Independence National Historical Park could not exist. Independence Hall and the Liberty Bell, for example, are part of the park because of such an agreement with their owner, the City of Philadelphia. "Cooperative agreement" is a term applied by the National Park Service to legal instruments pertaining to a wide variety of circumstances. Some, such as those that apply to the churches, simply formalize the intent of the park service and another institution or individual to work together toward a common purpose, in this case the preservation of these historic places. Other cooperative agreements are more closely akin to contracts or leases. They govern the National Park Service's use of property that does not belong to the federal government, or conversely, the use of federally owned property that is occupied by a private institution.

The key agreement with the City of Philadelphia provides that the city retains ownership of Independence Square, the buildings on it, the Liberty Bell, and various paintings and furnishings. The National Park Service is responsible for restoring and maintaining the city's property and exhibiting it to the public. The agreement, which became effective in 1951, runs for ninety-nine years. It excepts from National Park Service control the headquarters of the American Philosophical Society and the land on which it stands, which the society purchased from Pennsylvania in 1785. However, the society is associated with the park under an agreement whereby it committed itself to restoring its headquarters building to its eighteenth-century appearance and was permitted to erect its library, replicating the exterior of the original building of the Library Company, on federally owned land. Another essential privately owned component of the park, Carpenters' Hall, is covered by an agreement akin to those pertaining to the churches. Although Carpenters' Hall is within the heart of the park, the building and the land it stands on remain the property of the Carpenters' Company. This private group continues to maintain and operate its building, as it has for over two hundred years, but has entered into a formal agreement with the National Park Service to cooperate in its preservation. The buildings flanking Carpenters' Hall, New Hall and Pemberton House, were developed and are operated under cooperative agreements with, respectively, the United States Marine Corps and the Association of the United States Army and Navy League. Under another operating agreement the Germantown Historical Society shows the Deshler-Morris House to the public. Still other cooperative agreements cover tenancies of park-owned buildings or lands, sometimes with the provision that the tenants maintain the interior or other aspects of the property. Such agreements allow the use of the Kidd and Fling Houses and adjoining garden on Walnut Street by the Pennsylvania Horticultural Society and of the Free Quaker Meeting House at Fifth and Arch Streets by the Junior League of Philadelphia. Because of the cooperative agreements, the development and operation of Independence have required a continuous interaction between the National Park Service and dozens of public and private groups.

The intricacy of the cooperative agreements that make Independence possible is only a reflection of the complexity of managing a large national park in the middle of one of the largest cities in the United States. Independence consists of forty-two acres of land and buildings, including eighteen acres of plantings, most of it prime inner-city real estate. It must be maintained to the high standards the American people expect at a national shrine, and it must be open to the public 365 days a year. Large parts of the park that contribute to its smooth operation are never seen by the visitor. Indeed, many of the park's support mechanisms are literally underground. The comfort of visitors and protection of the buildings and their contents from the atmospheric conditions of a modern city, fire, and theft require sophisticated heating, cooling, air-cleaning, and warning systems. To accommodate them, a continuous cellar under the buildings on Independence Square is a maze of pipes, machinery, and controls. Under the sidewalk in front of Independence Hall is a vault dug to hold the condenser for the air-conditioning system for the adjacent buildings. Across Chestnut Street, under the first block of the mall, is a 10,000-gallon reservoir, a precaution against failure of the city's water supply in case of fire. Large chambers under the other two blocks of the mall contain the machinery and controls for fountains, plus an underground garage operated by the city.

Many of the people who keep the park running also work out of the visitor's sight. It takes over 200 National Park Service employees to run the park year round. That number is supplemented by 75 to 100 temporary workers—or, in park service parlance, "seasonals"—during the peak summer season. In 1976, the Bicentennial year, the staff swelled to approximately 400. Even so, visitors would not receive as much attention as they do if it were not for the VIPs—Volunteers in the Park—150 to 250 of whom put in regularly scheduled tours of duty. Wearing bright vests with the National Park Service emblem, they help staff the information desk at the Visitor Center, give guided tours, and assist in interpretation. Other parks also have volunteers, but no other unit in the National Park System can boast so large and so dedicated a corps.

Primary responsibility for the visitor's experience of the park rests with the rangers and park technicians of the Division of Interpretation and Visitors Services. The ranger is the basic building block of the National Park Service, dressed in the instantly recognizable green uniform and "Smokey Bear" hat. Most supervisors in the National Park Service have come up through the ranger ranks. In the process of doing so, the supervisor has probably done all the jobs, dirty and routine as well as interesting or glamorous, that it takes to run a park. He knows his business. The pronoun "he" could have been used entirely accurately twenty years ago, when the ranger corps was a white male preserve. Today the ranks include women and people of varied racial and ethnic backgrounds. Rangers are college-trained, often with graduate degrees in the natural sciences, archeology, or history. At Independence the last is the preferred discipline. Rangers are responsible for the education of visitors and for their safety and that of the park's resources, or, to use park service vocabulary, for interpretation and protection. At Independence these two functions occupy about half the park's staff. Park technicians, as part of the uniformed force, supplement the rangers as guides and guards. Although this entry-level position does not require a degree, most technicians are college-educated. Their objective, usually achieved, is to become rangers.

The other half of the Independence staff is less visible to the average visitor. They work behind the scenes or are out of uniform during their daily rounds but are no less vital to the park's operation. Overseeing the entire operation is the superintendent, who is responsible for everything that happens at the park, from planning for its future to snow removal. At large parks like Independence, the superintendent is backed up by an assistant superintendent. One or the other is on call 24 hours a day, 365 days a year.

The superintendent and his assistant are also responsible for fiscal management, personnel, contract administration, the conduct of operations in accordance with National Park Service regulations and directives, and reporting to and maintaining liaison with the regional office, Washington headquarters, and other units of the park service. About a dozen people carry out these functions for Independence and its satellites. At Independence the administrative load is heavier than it might otherwise be because the superintendent is responsible for administering three other National Park Service properties in Philadelphia. The first of these is Gloria Dei Church, about nine blocks south of park headquarters at Christian Street and Delaware Avenue. Gloria Dei, which is a National Historic Site, was erected as a Swedish church in 1700 and is sometimes called Old Swedes' Church, although it has been Protestant Episcopal since the mid-nineteenth century. Although its location is now somewhat isolated, it is still an active church. The congregation maintains the building, but the National Park Service is responsible for the grounds. Closer to Independence geographically and chronologically is the Thaddeus Kosciuszko National Memorial at Pine and Third Streets. In this restored brick townhouse, originally built in 1775, Kosciuszko rented rooms from November 1797 until May 1798. Kosciuszko, trained as an army officer in his native Poland, had served as a volunteer with the Continental Army. The third property administered through Independence is the Edgar Allan Poe National Historic Site at Seventh and Spring Garden Streets. Poe lived in Philadelphia from 1838 to 1844. These were the years during which, while employed as an editor, he began to compose mysteries, publishing such enduring tales as "The Gold Bug," "The Fall of the House of Usher," and "The Murders in the Rue Morgue." Of the several houses he rented during this period, this is the only one that survives.

Because of its size and the complexity and importance of its resources, Independence has a large group of professional specialists on its roster. The specialists are clustered in two groups, the Office of History and Historic Architecture and the Division of Museum Operations. Although most of the basic research tasks at the park have been accomplished, historical study continues. Questions from visitors and staff must be answered, and new scholarly findings must be integrated into the park's interpretive program. The Office of History also maintains a specialized research library for use by park staff and scholars. The library contains 7,000 volumes, mostly dealing with the history of the revolutionary and federal periods and of Philadelphia, 12,000 photographs and 5,000 slides documenting the history of the park, and most importantly, 150,000 cards, indexed by subject, the fruit of approximately 200 man-years of historical research. In addition to a librarian and historians, the staff includes historical architects, since the preservation of the historical fabric of Independence requires continuing skilled oversight. The architects are also responsible for the architectural study collection. These building fragments and materials, mostly dating to the eighteenth century, were assembled in the course of background research for the park's restorations. They are an invaluable—indeed, unique—source of information on early building techniques and technology.

Other collections within the park are the responsibility of the Museum Division. As a result of more than twenty years of collecting, the park is a notable museum of eighteenth-century furnishings, largely Philadelphia-made, period decorative arts, and paintings. Few of these objects were acquired with federal funds. The core of the collection was turned over to the park for safekeeping by the city of Philadelphia; other materials were privately donated or purchased with donated funds. The acquisition phase is largely over, but the curatorial staff continues to refine the collections, both in quality and in appropriateness for interpretive purposes. Conservation is an ongoing necessity. Paintings, fine woods, fragile fabrics, and paper all require skilled care if they are to be preserved for future generations. This is an undertaking of some magnitude, since the park's holdings include 18,000 objects and 250,000 fragments and other items in the archeological study collection.

Another of the park's major activities is maintenance of the grounds and the buildings and their contents. Indeed, well over half the Independence budget is devoted to this purpose. More than 3 million people visit the park every year; over 4 million came during the Bicentennial. Most treat the park with great respect. Nevertheless, the task of housekeeping, plus the wear and tear of heavy use, requires intense and unremitting effort, which is especially difficult because of the park's schedule. Unlike most museums and historic sites, Independence never fully closes, and Independence Hall and the Liberty Bell Pavilion are open daily. Cleaning and routine maintenance must be carried out during the hours when the historic buildings are closed. Major repairs and maintenance often go on before an audience of visitors. During the interior restoration of Independence Hall, parts of the building remained open at all times, and visitors observed the architects and skilled craftsmen at work.

Many skills are represented on the Independence maintenance staff. If the plumbing, air-conditioning, or other systems break down, repairs must be made immediately. So the roster includes air-conditioning specialists, an electrician, and pipefitters. The care of historic buildings requires constant attention to maintenance and repair, and particular skills. Not every workman can patch eighteenth-century wood or plaster moldings, or set a replacement brick with a proper joint. The painters, carpenters, and mason who carry out both major and minor work are backed by years of on-the-job training. Often it is these craftsmen, who live with the buildings on an intimate day-to-day basis, who call the attention of park management to the need for repairs. It was, for example, a master carpenter with over twenty years' experience at the park who noted in 1979 that the tower of Independence Hall required major maintenance, a project that was executed in the spring of 1982.

Maintaining the grounds is also an unceasing task. The park horticulturist supervises a staff of gardeners and laborers, who care for planted areas and walkways. Independence uses six hundred pounds of grass seed, a ton of fertilizer, and several hundred tons of mulch every year. During periods of intense use, such as occurred during the Bicentennial, this level of care may prove insufficient, and areas of the lawns will require resodding. Air pollution in the inner city is hard on trees and shrubs, which require more attention than they would in a more rural atmosphere. Although the growing season is obviously the busiest, and the regular staff must be supplemented with seasonals and volunteers, winter has its own demands. The park horticulturist and the grounds crew are always on call twenty-four hours a day, but it is usually in winter that the alarm is given. When there are storms, walks must be cleared, not only for park visitors, but also for local residents and workers in the nearby office buildings. If a winter storm starts during the night, snow removal begins at four or five o'clock in the morning, so that the walks can be cleared and salted or sanded by the time people go to work. Salt must be used sparingly because of potential damage to plantings and historic buildings. The test of the park's smooth administration is that the visitor is scarcely aware of the extraordinary effort it takes to keep this mini-city open and in top condition every day of the year.

Independence today looks serene and beautiful. Rosy-red brick buildings sit amid green lawns, criss-crossed by neat brick and cobbled paths. Trees shade well-tended gardens. The setting looks immutable and inevitable, as if this is the way it has always been and was meant to be. Yet the appearance is deceiving. Independence National Historical Park is, in fact, the product of three hundred years of change and over forty years of unremitting effort and debate, some of it far from peaceful.

Two
Dreams for a Park

In the two hundred years that followed the founding of Philadelphia, the area now encompassed by Independence National Historical Park changed greatly, from a virtual wilderness to a densely developed, decaying urban neighborhood. William Penn first saw the wooded site where he intended to plant a new city in the fall of 1682. Penn's venture in Pennsylvania was a curious blend of religious utopianism and real estate speculation. Penn's idealism led him to retain a surveyor to lay out a model city. It stretched from the Delaware to the Schuylkill. Laid out as a rectangular grid, its straight streets defined large squares and five public spaces. It was a vision of Philadelphia as a country town of ample open space, "in which each hath room enough for House, Garden and Small Orchard." He hoped to provide a haven for fellow dissenters and at the same time enlarge his family's fortune.

When Penn received the grant of Pennsylvania from Charles II in 1681, he was already familiar with the resources and needs of the New World through his participation in the proprietorships of East and West New Jersey. Through personal tours and publications, he moved quickly to promote Pennsylvania to prospective immigrants, offering the twin enticements of personal liberty and economic opportunity. Penn's promotional campaign achieved its goal of attracting settlers, although his hopes for financial aggrandizement proved vain. In 1692 alone, twenty-three ships brought immigrants to Pennsylvania, many of whom remained in Philadelphia. By the time Penn returned to England in 1694, there were "Three hundred and fifty-seven Houses; divers of them large, well built, with good Cellars, three stories, and some with Balconies."

By the beginning of the new century, Philadelphia was established as a thriving town. Estimates that the number of houses had risen to 1,400 by 1690 and more than 2,000 by 1698 were probably exaggerated; nevertheless, Philadelphia's population had outstripped that of every city in the colonies but Boston. Two Quaker meeting houses had been joined by several other churches: the Swede's church south of the town and, within its bounds, buildings for Anglican, Presbyterian, and Baptist congregations. However, the Proprietor's idealistic vision for the city had not been realized. Penn had expected development to begin along the fronts and move inland toward the center square, where the major public buildings would be located. Instead the early buildings were tightly packed along the Delaware from Spruce to Vine Streets. Warehouses, stores, and residences elbowed one another along Bank and Front Streets. The Philadelphia that Benjamin Franklin saw when he disembarked at the public dock at the foot of High Street in 1723 was a long, narrow town, strung out along the river, its streets and alleys closely hemmed with buildings. The skyline was low, unpunctuated by towers or spires, although a few of the town's wealthy merchants lived in what can only be described as suburban splendor on its outskirts from Third to Seventh Street.

Fifty years later, the delegates to the First and Second Continental Congresses arrived in a Philadelphia that could no longer be called a town, but had become a city. "Philadelphia," an English visitor wrote as early as 1755, "is London in miniature." By 1774 Philadelphia, with a population approaching 25,000, had surpassed Boston as the western hemisphere's largest port, and was, indeed, the second largest city in the English-speaking world. To its advantages of size and wealth were added those of location, midway between the northern and southern colonies, and political moderation. It was the obvious place for the representatives of the colonies to assemble to discuss common concerns and debate a course of action.

With the agricultural wealth of Pennsylvania and southern New Jersey passing through their storehouses, Philadelphia's merchants had become rich through trade with the other colonies, the West Indies, and Europe. The city reflected their wealth. Philadelphia had become a city predominantly of brick dwelling houses, which a French visitor admired because they "display a regular and noble appearance superior to that of our French houses." The finest houses were on Front and Second Streets, although no street was entirely residential. On Front Street the merchants maintained their wholesale operations, and Second Street was the fashionable shopping area, which "at midday with its crowds of pedestrians and its variety of elegant shops presents a sight that one wishes might be seen on the Rue Saint Honore."

The city boasted a number of amenities. Many of the streets were paved with cobbles taken from the Delaware River at Trenton and were supplied with flagstone cartways and gutters. There were brick sidewalks, some streetlights, a night watch, and several fire companies. Although the open squares provided in the original plan had not yet been landscaped, large private gardens provided the welcome relief of greenery. Delegates such as John Adams also visited, and were impressed by, the city's public buildings, including a jail and a hospital. Of course Carpenters' Hall, at the end of its alley off Chestnut Street between Third and Fourth, was well known to the delegates who met there in 1774. The State House, site of the momentous deliberations of 1776, dominated the block of Chestnut between Fifth and Sixth Streets. It was undoubtedly the most impressive public building in the colonies, with the mass of its main building topped by a lofty bell tower and

8. *Independence Hall as it looked to the delegates to the Continental Congress in 1776. This engraving appeared as an inset on John Reed's "Map of Philadelphia and Vicinity" of 1774, republished by Charles L. Warner in 1870. Park historians and architects consider it the most accurate eighteenth-century view of the building. It shows the original tower, taken down in 1781, and the flanking wings, larger than the reconstructions erected in 1896. Linking the hall and the wings are the enclosed arcades, with staircases giving access to the second floor of the wings.*

joined to the lower flanking office buildings by arcades containing handsome staircases.

There was much to be admired, and Adams found that the "Regularity and Elegance of this City are very striking." Nevertheless, the atmosphere of the city was not entirely pleasant. In the 1770s Dock Creek was still an open sewer west of Third Street, and there were several tanneries along its banks, one behind Carpenters' Hall. When the delegates sat in the State House in the summer of 1776, they could hardly have been unaware of the slaughter-house across Fifth Street between the back of the Norris garden and Walnut Street.

Those members of the Continental Congress who returned to serve in various capacities during the decade from 1790 to 1800, when Philadelphia was the seat of the federal government, must have found much in the city that was unfamiliar. For, with the burst of postrevolutionary prosperity, Philadelphia had expanded rapidly. Writing in 1793, Matthew Carey observed: **31**

"From the period of the adoption of the federal government at which time America was at the lowest ebb of distress, her situation [was] universally restored. . . . In this prosperity . . . Philadelphia participated in an eminent degree. Numbers of new houses, in almost every street, built in a very neat, elegant stile, adorned, at the same time that they greatly enlarged the city." Some old landmarks had disappeared in the neighborhood of the State House; others had been altered; new ones made their appearance during the decade. Dock Creek had been filled to Third Street and was lined with new buildings. The Carpenters' Company had erected their New Hall on the west side of their court in 1790. The State House had undergone major changes. Its steeple had been removed in 1781, and the stair tower was now capped by a low hipped roof. More importantly, two handsome edifices flanked the wing buildings: one to the east to serve as City Hall; one to the west for the county offices, better known because of its function during the decade as Congress Hall. Behind City Hall was the new brick building of the American Philosophical Society. The State House Yard had been landscaped in the new romantic taste, with artificial mounds and declivities, serpentine paths, informally disposed clumps of elms and willows, and benches for the enjoyment of the public. Across Fifth Street from the State House Yard, the slaughterhouse was gone. The graceful new building of the Library Company occupied part of what had been the Norris garden. Nearer to Walnut Street were the Philadelphia Dispensary and Surgeons' Hall, the remainder of the block still being occupied by somewhat ramshackle wooden buildings.

As the seat of the federal government, Philadelphia consolidated its position as the financial, as well as the political, capital of the United States. Toward the end of the decade new landmarks proclaimed the city's role as a banking center. The largest was the First Bank of the United States, with its colossal marble portico, on Third Street south of Chestnut, on the site of what had been the terraced garden of a house called Clarke Hall. Smaller, but perhaps even more imposing, was the Bank of Pennsylvania, erected on Second Street just north of the City Tavern in 1799. Designed by Benjamin Henry Latrobe, it was a classical building of great elegance. Twin porticos, each with six Ionic columns, fronted it on the east and west, and its domed banking room was expressed on the exterior, crowned by a glazed lantern.

The atmosphere of Philadelphia on the eve of a new century is lovingly captured in the series of watercolors and prints executed by William and Thomas Birch between 1798 and 1800. The renderings are somewhat idealized; nevertheless, the streetscapes are reasonably accurate. The straight streets are lined with decorous brick buildings, picked out with restrained light-colored trim of wood or stone. At intervals a more imposing building breaks the rows: the First Bank of the United States and the Bank of Pennsylvania; the new theater at the northwest corner of Chestnut and Sixth Streets; and, on Market Street, the colonnaded portico of the new Presbyterian church and Cooke's Building at the corner of Third Street, with its fanlit shop windows and plethora of Palladian openings on the upper floors. Despite its elegance, Cooke's overlooks the more earthy scene of the Market Shambles, where freshly butchered meat hangs on hooks in open stalls and Philadelphia's housewives shop for produce brought from the country. The streets pulse with life. Farmers' wagons in from the country, gentlemen's carriages, and troops of cavalry clop along the cobbled way. There are barrowmen and vendors; shoppers and entertainers. Ladies and gentlemen promenade, and groups of Indians see the sights. Dogs and children frolic, while their elders go about their work. It is a cosmopolitan scene, and one in which activity of every sort is packed within a narrow compass.

In 1850 a pair of pioneering photographers, William and Frederick Langenheim, hauled their daguerreotype camera to the top of the tower of Independence Hall and made panoramic views of the surrounding area. Their photographs show a city that had greatly expanded since the decade when it served as the nation's capital. Independence Hall was no longer at its western edge. Now the rows of buildings stretched westward toward the Schuylkill and far to the south. Yet the scale of the city was still much the same. Philadelphia remained a city of relatively low buildings, where only the spires of the churches punctuated the skyline. What the panorama, with its view of rooftops, failed to show was how much the function of the area around Independence Hall had changed, and how these changes in use had altered the appearance of the neighborhood at street level. Residences, shops, countinghouses, and taverns no longer intermingled in buildings that differed little in appearance from one another. The residential character of the blocks around Independence Square was almost gone, and the elegant retail shops had also followed the flight of fashion westward.

In the fifty years following the departure of the federal government for Washington, the face of old Philadelphia had been transformed. Some sections had become backwaters. The area around Independence Square had become the financial district, evolving from decorous rows of brick to a close-packed area of marble, brownstone, and granite. In the next fifty years this trend would continue, with taller buildings replacing both landmarks of the Proprietor's city and many of their successors. By the beginning of the twentieth century, many sites in the neighborhood had held four or five buildings in succession. Such old institutions as the Library Company and the Mercantile Library had left the neighborhood, although others, such as the Philosophical Society, remained.

The Independence Square neighborhood was still the center of the banking, insurance, and publishing industries. But with the completion of the new City Hall at Center Square in 1901, the financial community would follow the city's government westward. In the surrounding neighborhood, the pace of change would slow, although it would not cease. For the most part the change was not for the better. Small businesses replaced larger ones in what were fast becoming decaying buildings. Only around Independence

Square did publishing and insurance firms, still securely anchored in the area, continue to build. By the Sesquicentennial of the Declaration of Independence, the square was surrounded on three sides by tall office buildings.

Through all the decades of change, numerous buildings survived that had witnessed the genesis of the nation and the early days of the Republic. Some lasted because of the sentiment or conservatism of their owners; others because there was no demand for the land on which they stood. The Independence Hall group, Carpenters' Hall, the First and Second Banks of the United States, Christ Church, and other colonial churches were engulfed by the later city, while to the south, hundreds of half-forgotten early buildings in Society Hill succumbed slowly to decay. Except for Independence Square and Washington Square to its southwest, parking lots provided the only open space. As the government of the City of Philadelphia finally left Independence Square, groups of Philadelphians from all walks of life began to concern themselves with the future of the historic buildings and their surroundings.

Even while the area around them changed, two buildings increasingly were viewed as shrines: Independence Hall and Carpenters' Hall. Other historic buildings in the area survived through chance or because they continued to serve a purpose akin to that for which they were designed. In contrast, Independence Hall and Carpenters' Hall were the objects of pioneering historic preservation efforts. Carpenters' Hall, removed from commercial use and opened to the public in 1857, was refurbished on several occasions in the late nineteenth and early twentieth centuries; Independence Hall underwent a long series of alterations and restorations in its gradual transformation from Pennsylvania State House to national shrine.

In 1799 the government of Pennsylvania followed the movement of the state's population westward to Lancaster. A year later the federal government left Philadelphia for Washington. After over half a century, the complex on Independence Square was no longer the hub of political life for state or nation. Although state and city courts continued to sit in the Supreme Court Room, the Assembly Room and second floor of Independence Hall stood empty and unused. In an early example of what is now called adaptive use, the Pennsylvania legislature in 1802 granted the painter Charles Willson Peale permission to occupy these spaces as a museum. One of his sons, Rembrandt Peale, set up his studio in the Assembly Room. The elder Peale fitted up the second floor to display his portraits of prominent national figures and his natural history collection. This included such awe-inspiring specimens as a stuffed grizzly bear and an "Ourang Outang," and the skeleton of a mammoth, as well as 760 varieties of birds and 4,000 insects. To house them Peale carried out one of the first "restorations" of the building, returning the Long Gallery and the southern rooms to their original arrangement.

Peale was a sympathetic tenant for the building, but he also supported the first, and most destructive, of the major nineteenth-century alterations. In 1812 the Pennsylvania legislature authorized the Philadelphia County Commissioners to demolish the wing buildings and their connecting piazzas, or arcades, in order to erect fireproof buildings for the storage of records. Because the fireproof buildings were considerably larger than the old wings, their construction necessitated razing the library and committee rooms and the colossal clock case on the west wall of the old State House. Meanwhile, the state government, having once again moved west, this time to Harrisburg, and needing to pay for the construction of a new capitol, determined to sell the State House Square and the buildings on it. A proposal to subdivide the land into building lots met with howls from the citizens of Philadelphia. The bill that finally cleared the legislature in 1816 offered an alternative: the City of Philadelphia could purchase the property for $70,000. On June 29, 1818, the city took possession of its new property.

While the legal arrangements for the transfer were in process, the legislature vested control of the building in the Philadelphia County Commissioners, who in 1816 embarked on an elaborate program of alterations to Independence Hall. Decorative plasterwork was added to the interior; on the exterior the original simple front doorway was replaced by one with a more elaborate Corinthian surround, and the marble trim was painted. The change that aroused public sentiment, however, was a wanton act of destruction, the motives for which have never been ascertained. The paneling and other architectural woodwork of the Assembly Room were stripped from the walls, dismantled, and sold. The outrage expressed at this act reveals the aura of veneration that already clung to that space, if not to the entire building, and the desire to preserve the room's appearance for future generations. Almost forty years later John Binns still described the commissioners' action as a "sacrilegious outrage."

In the next decade two events caused the city to attempt to rectify the commissioners' mistake: the visit of the Marquis de Lafayette in 1824 and the fiftieth anniversary of the signing of the Declaration in 1826. Having redecorated the Assembly Room, by then referred to as the Hall of Independence, for Lafayette's use as a levee room, the city decided to restore it to its original appearance. Another part of the building, however, claimed attention first. This was the tower, the wooden steeple of which had been removed in 1781. In 1828 the city councils commissioned William Strickland to design a replacement. Although the new steeple was of the same size and general form as the original, it differed considerably in detail. It was designed to accommodate a four-faced clock and was adorned with a free interpretation of classical ornament in the early nineteenth-century taste. Nevertheless, the councilmen clearly viewed the steeple as a restoration.

Three years later, in 1831, the English-born architect John Haviland was commissioned to study the Assembly Room. His report of March 29, 1831, made it clear that restoration was the aim, stating, "In compliance with your request, I have examined 'the Hall of the Declaration of Independence,' with a view of reinstating it with its original architectural embellishments." Surprisingly enough, although only fifteen years had elapsed since the destruction of its original finishes, the fact that Haviland's work was inaccurate in many particulars elicited no known comment from the many Philadelphians who must have been familiar with the room before it was denuded.

As Philadelphia grew, its government required expanded offices. In 1854 the Common Council and Select Council of the expanded city moved into the second floor of Independence Hall. By this time, despite the need for space, the Assembly Room had clearly become a shrine. The Liberty Bell, removed from the tower in 1852, stood there, surmounted by the stuffed bald eagle from Peale's museum. A life-size statue of Washington by William Rush presided over the scene, and the walls were lined with portraits of distinguished figures of the revolutionary and federal eras, purchased from Peale's estate.

Despite this growth of reverence, the Independence Square group had another narrow escape at the end of the next decade. In 1868 the city councils voted to erect new municipal buildings on Independence Square. John McArthur, Jr., who would later become architect of the City Hall on Center Square, produced designs in much the same style as that structure. Bold and flamboyant Second Empire pavilions, scaled to the boulevards of Paris, would surround the square on three sides. Independence Hall would remain forlorn and dwarfed, between the two terminal buildings on Chestnut Street. Over the next few years, the councils rethought the matter and decided to build on Center Square. The approaching Centennial of the Declaration may have influenced this reversal. Soon after ground was broken for the new City Hall, the city councils confirmed the sacred status of the Assembly Room by setting it aside forever as a shrine in 1872. A committee, chaired by Col. Frank M. Etting, commenced work on refurnishing and restoration; in the course of this work four columns were erroneously installed in the Assembly Room. The project expanded to include removal of the paint that had been applied to the exterior marble trim and repair of woodwork in the hallway and stair tower. Etting's committee also dealt with the Supreme Court Room. Covering the bench and other trappings of the judiciary, they fitted the space out as a "National Museum" displaying furnishings, relics, and portraits related to the early history of Pennsylvania and the nation. For the first time the entire first floor of Independence Hall was opened for the enjoyment and education of the public.

In 1895, as the city government prepared to complete its move to the new City Hall, attention turned again to the fate of Independence Hall. In 1896 the Daughters of the American Revolution received authorization from the city to restore, at their own expense, the building's second floor. This was the start of a restoration program that eventually extended to the entire building. The DAR retained T. Mellon Rogers as architect, and Rogers continued in this capacity for the city's restoration of the remainder of the building. The work extended from the interior to the exterior and also involved substantial structural reinforcement. Most dramatically, the fireproof buildings constructed in 1812 were razed, and wings and arcades resembling the originals were constructed in their place. Unfortunately, although old views were consulted, Rogers seems to have made no attempt to seek out historical documentation or architectural evidence for his work, but apparently based it on a personal vision of eighteenth-century taste. As a result, much of the "restoration" was far from accurate. The wing buildings, for example, differed in dimension and detail from the originals. An even more damaging result of this approach was the destruction of original features, such as the cornice of the Supreme Court Room. These unfortunate actions had one happy result. Rogers's restoration precipitated so much criticism, especially from the Philadelphia Chapter of the American Institute of Architects, that the city asked the organization to appoint a subcommittee to advise on Independence Square. Over the next quarter of a century, the committee, under the chairmanship of Horace Wells Sellers, superintended restoration work on all the buildings in the row. In 1912–13 the committee made studies and prepared plans for the restoration of Congress Hall; in 1917 it carried out similar tasks for Old City Hall, although the work on the building was not completed until 1922; from 1921 to 1923 their work on the second floor of Independence Hall eradicated most of T. Mellon Rogers's "ice-cream saloon" colonial. The AIA restorations were landmarks in the field; the architects made careful measurements and subjected the buildings to rigorous architectural analysis. Much of their work at Congress Hall and Old City Hall was so accurate that the National Park Service left it undisturbed in its subsequent restoration of the buildings.

Thus, in the century that followed Lafayette's visit in 1824, the public reverence for the site spread from the Assembly Room to all of Independence Hall and then to its flanking buildings. There was a concomitant growth of interest in the grounds in which the buildings stood. As a public park, Independence Square was subject to continuing rearrangement and maintenance of the landscaping. There was a major effort during the Etting restoration of 1875–76, and in 1915–16, when the mid-nineteenth-century courthouse that had been erected behind Congress Hall was removed, the city undertook extensive relandscaping, producing the design of the square that remains today. Like the city's restoration of Independence Hall, the plan for the square depended on contemporary perceptions of eighteenth-century landscape design rather than on historical documentation. Nevertheless, the desire to provide the buildings on Independence Square with an appropriate setting was powerful, and would recur in different forms and under different auspices for the next fifty years.

With such a setting provided at the rear of the buildings to the south, attention focused on the northern approach. As the AIA completed its restoration of Congress Hall and prepared to make plans for restoring Old City Hall, two Philadelphia architects. Albert Kelsey and D. Knickerbacker Boyd, presented a preliminary study for a "new setting" for Independence Hall, a relatively modest public open space on the north side of Chestnut Street, running halfway to Market Street. It included a Classical Revival pavilion and formal gardens. Additional impetus to these plans came from three coincidental events of 1926: the Sesquicentennial of the Declaration of Independence, the opening of the Benjamin Franklin Bridge, linking Philadelphia with New Jersey, and publication of the first regional plan for the Philadelphia area. A variety of plans was put forward over the next decade, some sensible, some not. Among the latter was a proposal from Dr. Seneca Egbert, professor of hygiene at the medical school of the University of Pennsylvania. It called for clearance of the three blocks from Chestnut to Race Street between Fifth and Sixth Streets. Half of the first block would be developed by the City of Philadelphia and the United States government. The space at the north end, at the entrance to the Benjamin Franklin Bridge, would be allocated to the State of Pennsylvania. In between, a concourse to be developed by the city would be flanked by plots allocated to each of the other twelve original states. Egbert hoped that each state would erect a replica of one of its historic buildings of the colonial era to serve as a museum and archives of its role in the founding of the nation. Egbert was a physician, not an architect or planner; had his vision been realized, the result could have been ludicrous in design and scale. One aspect of his concept, however, did command serious attention: the creation of a three-block mall north of Chestnut Street. In a prophetic interview in 1935, George E. Nitzche, recorder at the University of Pennsylvania, suggested that the three blocks to the north be transformed into a national park, so that Independence Hall could have "a setting worthy of its pre-eminence."

At about the same time, a prominent Philadelphia architect, Roy F. Larson, began, in his words, to "play with" a setting for Independence Hall. He was expanding on the work of a senior partner in his firm, the noted architect Paul Phillipe Cret. Cret was among those who had produced schemes for a small park across Chestnut Street from Independence Hall in the mid-1920s. Larson enlarged Cret's design, not only to the north, but also, in a modest way, to the east of Independence Square. Larson was not the first to consider an enhanced setting for the historic buildings east of Independence Square. In the 1930s interest in the area was undoubtedly sparked by the building of the new federal Custom House at the southwest corner of Chestnut and Second Streets. In 1933 A. Raymond Raff, in his dual capacity as Collector of the Port and president of the Carpenters' Company, proposed a series of improvements for the neighborhood around the Custom House, among which was a "Congress Plaza," which would have created a formal landscaped park along Third Street west of the Custom House. West of Third Street three buildings—the First Bank of the United States, Carpenters' Hall, and the Second Bank of the United States—would be preserved. The buildings between them and along Chestnut Street would be removed and replaced by plantings. Another scheme, put forward by Emerson C. Custis, whose real estate office was in the Merchants' Exchange, would have created office buildings around the Custom House and a mall running from the new development to Independence Hall. Although the First and Second Banks and Carpenters' Hall would remain, banks, insurance companies, and other businesses were expected to construct new buildings running back from Chestnut and Walnut Streets to the mall.

Few of these early schemes dealt with the issue of implementation. Those that did assumed that the projects would be privately funded or would be carried out through the initiative of the City of Philadelphia. When the Depression of the 1930s appeared to preclude financial support from either private philanthropy or the municipality, proponents of enhancement of the historic scene turned to a new potential source of assistance: the federal government.

A series of events in the early 1930s increased the National Park Service's role in historic preservation. Although components of the National Park System had previously included what were classified as historic sites, most of these were actually prehistoric Native American ruins in the southwest. In 1930, however, two historic areas in Virginia were added to the system: Colonial National Monument at Yorktown and the George Washington Birthplace at Wakefield. In 1933 the country's first National Historical Park was created at Morristown, New Jersey. That same year a reorganization dramatically increased the National Park Service's stewardship of federally owned historic properties. It incorporated into the National Park System the national capital parks, which included such buildings as Ford's Theater and the Custis-Lee Mansion; the national memorials, giving the Service custody of such monuments as the Statue of Liberty and the Lincoln Memorial; the national military parks, which included twenty-three Revolutionary and Civil War battlefields; national military cemeteries; and national monuments. The reorganization almost quadrupled the number of historic areas administered by the National Park Service. Its role as the agency charged with the federal government's historic preservation responsibilities, and the acquisition and management of historic properties, was recognized and expanded by passage of the Historic Sites Act of 1935. The act placed the National Park Service in the forefront of preservation activity by authorizing it to engage in research and educational and service programs. Most importantly for the future of Independence, the act provided that the Secretary of the Interior, through the National Park Service, could "contract and make cooperative agreements with States, municipal subdivisions, associations, or individuals . . . to protect, preserve, maintain, or operate any historic building, site, object, or property used in connection therewith for public use, regardless as to whether the title thereto is in the United States."

Philadelphians were quick to recognize the opportunities afforded by the 1935 act. Even before the act was passed, Sen. Joseph E. Guffey drafted a bill calling for the creation of a national monument at Carpenters' Hall. George Nitzche recommended that Guffey's bill be amended to provide for the inclusion of Independence Hall and other adjacent historic structures. Proposals for a larger park continued to be discussed. In 1939 Struthers Burt contacted the National Park Service about a project aimed at razing nonhistoric structures within a radius of three or more city blocks of Independence Hall. Burt had returned to Philadelphia after living for many years in Wyoming. He was well known to the National Park Service for his role in interesting the Rockefellers in purchasing land at Jackson Hole, Wyoming, to add to Grand Teton National Park. His suggestion produced a flurry of activity, but Burt became discouraged, believing that Philadelphians would never provide sufficient support. Fiske Kimball, the respected director of the Philadelphia Art Museum and an influential member of the National Park Service Advisory Board, doubted that the necessary components of a park could be assembled. He thought it unlikely that the city or the Carpenters' Company would yield control of their buildings, and viewed the mall scheme as liable to abuse by real estate speculators.

Nevertheless, by the late 1930s the National Park Service had established a foothold in Philadelphia through ownership of the Second Bank of the United States. For ninety years after 1845 the building had served as the United States Custom House for Philadelphia. With completion of the new Custom House, the building had become redundant, and in early 1938 the Treasury Department put it up for sale. Kimball fired off telegrams to the National Park Service director, Arno B. Cammerer, and Secretary of the Interior Harold Ickes. Characterizing the building as "the masterpiece of the Greek Revival in America" and its possible loss as an "artistic calamity," he urged acquisition by the National Park Service if no other public or quasi-public use could be found. The National Park Service historian who was sent to Philadelphia to evaluate the building, Alvin P. Stauffer, pointed out that in addition to its architectural distinction, the bank was a reminder of the landmark struggle between Andrew Jackson and Nicholas Biddle over the federal government's financial policies. Stauffer's superior, Ronald F. Lee, chief historian of the National Park Service, recommended to Cammerer its transfer from the Treasury Department and drafted a letter for Ickes's signature requesting a delay in its disposition. Cammerer agreed with Lee's appraisal, on condition that maintenance of the building could be assured.

Within a few weeks the major components of a feasible plan began to emerge. Fiske Kimball had found that the Carl Schurz Memorial Foundation, a nonprofit group dedicated to preserving the cultural heritage of German-Americans, would maintain the building to house its offices and library. The Works Progress Administration would fund its restoration and renovation.

On the strength of these commitments, the Department of the Interior applied for transfer of the property from the Treasury Department in January 1939, a transfer duly made in April of the same year. After some delay, the Department of the Interior entered into a cooperative agreement with the Carl Schurz Foundation on December 18, 1939. The building would be restored, under the direction of National Park Service architects, by the WPA, using $100,000 in federal funds and $15,000 contributed by the foundation, which would maintain it and allow reasonable public access. By the fall of 1940, the work had been accomplished and the foundation had moved in. With protection of the Second Bank assured, the National Park Service set its sights on the Independence Hall group. In April 1941 Director Newton Drury, former Director Cammerer, and Chief Historian Lee met with Philadelphia's Mayor Lamberton to discuss a cooperative agreement for the city-owned buildings. Although the park service drafted such an agreement, the city did not sign it. The idea, initiated by the National Park Service and unsupported by any strong constituency of Philadelphians, had been presented without sufficient preparation.

The approach of war, however, renewed local interest in protecting Independence Hall and the adjacent historic buildings. Fear of possible damage from fire-bombing, coupled with an upsurge of patriotism, inspired an outburst of activity in late 1941 and 1942. Despite Struthers Burt's misgivings, Philadelphians from several walks of life began to garner support for a national park. One of these early activists was Isidor Ostroff, who represented the Fifth Ward, which included Independence Square and Society Hill, in the Pennsylvania legislature. Ostroff, a Democrat in a city long dominated by a Republican machine, had been elected on President Roosevelt's coattails in the landslide of 1936. Ostroff, who practiced law in Philadelphia, was frankly emotional in his patriotism. As the son of an immigrant, he was proud to represent what he considered the most sacred district in all the United States because it included Independence Hall. However, Ostroff was dismayed by the severely dilapidated housing stock in the Fifth Ward, parts of which had become a virtual skid row. As he read the various proposals for a park around Independence Hall, he began to view a federal takeover as the key to revitalization of the neighborhood. In the fall of 1941, he persuaded the Democratic committeemen in the Fifth Ward to circulate a petition to Congress. The petition, addressed to Rep. Leon Sacks, asked that Congress pass appropriate legislation to create a national historical park in an area bounded by Second, Sixth, Sansom, and Chestnut Streets. The Fifth Ward was then sparsely populated; Ostroff had won the 1936 election with about 2,500 votes. He managed to garner about 1,200 signatures on the petition. Sacks duly introduced a bill, H.R. 6925, on January 21, 1942, asking Congress to create a commission to study such a park. In a country reeling from the shock of Pearl Harbor, the bill went nowhere.

9. *Judge Edwin O. Lewis. In large part, Independence National Historical Park came into being because of the persuasiveness and persistence of Judge Lewis, first as president of the Independence Hall Association, and later as chairman of the Philadelphia National Shrines Park Commission and the Independence National Historical Park Advisory Commission.*

The onset of the war appeared to put a stop to the National Park Service's attempts to expand its toehold in Philadelphia. On March 28, 1942, President Roosevelt signed a letter designating Gloria Dei (Old Swedes' Church) as a national historic site, the prerequisite for entering into a cooperative agreement for the building's preservation. At the same time he put a virtual stop to the designation process for the duration of the war. The secretary of the interior entered into a cooperative agreement with the Corporation of Gloria Dei Church on May 1, 1942. Under its terms, the corporation agreed to preserve the church and other buildings and the burying ground, to seek National Park Service approval before making repairs or alterations to the buildings, to "advise with" the park service about decorations and furnishings, and to allow public access.

Meanwhile, the idea of a national park at Independence had attracted a champion far more influential than Ostroff: Judge Edwin O. Lewis. A courtly Virginian, Lewis was an imposing presence, articulate, persuasive, and personable. Even those who disagreed with him usually found him likable. Charles E. Peterson, the National Park Service's leading expert on historic buildings, would, in the 1950s, often be at loggerheads with Lewis about the fate of nineteenth-century architecture within the park's boundaries. On a personal level, however, their relationship was cordial. Lewis, a consummate politician, maintained contact with a broad spectrum of people in the arts, business, and politics. He was also persistent and determined that any project for which he was responsible would be a success.

Like an earlier Philadelphia benefactor, Benjamin Franklin, Lewis was not a native of the city. Like Franklin, he came to Philadelphia as a young man to work as a printer. Like Franklin, he became active in various social and political circles, and was a tireless worker for the civic good of his adopted city. Edwin O. Lewis was born in Richmond, Virginia, where, at the age of fifteen, he learned to operate a linotype machine. In 1896, when he was sixteen years old, he came, by steamboat, to Philadelphia. He worked nights as a linotype operator, first at the *Philadelphia Press* and then at the *Public Ledger,* both in the Independence Hall neighborhood, and later at the *North American* at Broad and Sansom Streets. The newspapers were his liberal education.

However, the newspapers did not provide Lewis with enough formal education to enter law school. So for a year he attended a tutoring school, which met in the old courthouse behind Congress Hall. He worked at night and went to classes during the day. He went through the University of Pennsylvania Law School in the same manner. It was a grueling schedule, but Lewis seemed to thrive on it. Obtaining his degree in 1902, Lewis began to practice law and quickly became involved in local politics, first as a Democrat, then as secretary of the independent City Party, and eventually as a Republican. In 1907 he was elected to the City Council, serving two years, and from 1912 to 1916 was first assistant city solicitor. After a brief period out of politics, he returned to office as a judge in 1923 and by the late 1930s was president judge of Common Pleas Court number 2 for Philadelphia County. When the Japanese bombed Pearl Harbor on December 7, 1941, Lewis was president of the Pennsylvania Chapter of the Sons of the American Revolution. Concerned with the potential danger to Independence Hall from enemy bombing, and the certainty of continuing deterioration, he appointed a committee of architects to consider the problem. He named D. Knickerbacker Boyd as chairman of the committee.

David Knickerbacker Boyd, FAIA, was an architect perhaps as well known for his services to the profession as for the buildings he designed. Credited

with being one of the first to espouse the set-back principle for the design of
tall buildings, he had served as consultant to various federal departments and
state and municipal governments, as well as to the Russell Sage Foundation.
A former president of the Philadelphia Chapter and Pennsylvania Association
of the AIA, he had also been secretary and vice-president of the national
body. In addition to his architectural activities as a professional and volunteer, he was interested in patriotic and historical affairs and was a long-time
member of the Society of the Cincinnati and the Sons of the American
Revolution.

His involvement with Independence Hall went back to 1915, when he
had collaborated on a design for a park fronting the building across Chestnut
Street. Boyd's personal qualities would be useful in his new assignment.
According to his daughter he combined great tact, and the ability to defuse
controversial situations with wit, with the intensity and drive to see a project
through to completion. Boyd also had the time to devote to the project
because his architectural practice had suffered during the Depression.

The Sons of the American Revolution Committee on the Protection of
Historic Buildings held its first meeting on December 22, 1941. Boyd moved
quickly to solicit support from various historical and civic groups, and several
subcommittees were established. In the early months of the committee's
existence, he also persuaded the Insurance Company of North America to
underwrite a protective mechanism costing $15,000 for the Liberty Bell. The
scheme called for mounting the bell on an elevator, which, in the event of an
air raid, would lower the bell into a steel and concrete underground vault. In
the course of the committee's meetings and discussions, it became clear that
the group's interest in Independence Hall and the buildings around it
probably outstripped that of the Sons of the American Revolution. The issue
that most disturbed the parent organization appears to have been lobbying.
The committee had discussed creating sentiment for a national park connected with the Independence Hall group. Rep. Leon Sacks, who had introduced in January a bill appropriating funds for a commission to define the
boundaries of a park, had asked for support. The response of the board of
managers of the Sons was to disassociate itself from the committee's work
with a vote of thanks to all concerned.

Boyd and Lewis were not willing to let the matter drop. Acting in a
personal capacity, rather than as chairman of the committee, Boyd issued
invitations to a meeting to be held at the library of the Philadelphia Chapter
of the AIA in the Architects Building on May 21, 1942. The fifty-one people
invited were carefully chosen. They included politicians, architects, representatives of city government, business groups, and historical and cultural institutions. The purpose of the meeting, as stated in the invitation, was to discuss
means of protecting Philadelphia's historic buildings and, in particular, to
plan open spaces around Independence Hall, Carpenters' Hall, and what the
invitation called other "Shrines of National Importance."

Eighteen people attended the meeting. In addition to Boyd and Lewis, they included important representatives of Philadelphia's cultural, social, and political establishment, among them Lewis's nephew, Rep. (later Senator) Hugh D. Scott, Jr.; Dr. William E. Lingelbach, a distinguished historian and librarian of the American Philosophical Society; H. W. Wills, secretary of the Board of Trade; John P. Hallahan, president of the Carpenters' Company; Frances Wister, president of the Society for the Preservation of Landmarks and a pioneer in Philadelphia preservation efforts; Joseph Jackson, antiquarian and author; Sydney E. Martin, president of the Philadelphia chapter of the AIA, Roy F. Larson, chairman of the organization's Committee on Municipal Improvements; and C. C. Zantzinger, president of the City Parks Association.

This small group discussed plans and prospects and agreed to prepare for a subsequent organizational meeting. On June 30, 1942, fifty-seven persons assembled at the Hall of the American Philosophical Society. The major business of the meeting, the formation of an organization, was accomplished quickly. Debate over a name took longer, and the issue was not fully decided. The group did elect officers and an executive committee: Lewis as president, Larson and Miss Wister as vice-presidents, Joseph F. Stockwell as treasurer, and Boyd as executive secretary.

The executive committee finally settled on a name on August 11, selecting the catchy and comprehensible "Independence Hall Association," even though it did not fully express their aims. Meanwhile, the organization was busy on many fronts. Larson chaired the Committee on Research and Planning, which at its first meeting began to define alternatives and techniques for acquiring various areas to be included in a park. Among its members was George Nitzche, who assumed the task of assembling and analyzing financial data on the properties in the three city blocks north of Independence Hall. By January 1943 Nitzche was able to report on the approximately 200 properties, valued at about $5 million, "which would have to be acquired by the Federal Government to provide a suitable approach to Independence Hall." Joseph M. McCosker, curator of the Atwater Kent Museum, heading up the Committee on Public Relations and Exhibitions, began to plan the Independence Hall Association's first public event, an exhibit dealing with the history of the Independence Hall group and proposals for its future.

From the beginning it was obvious that the founders of the Independence Hall Association had bigger ideas than simply protecting Independence Hall from enemy bombing. Clearly they wanted a national park in Philadelphia. In early August Larson and a new recruit to the board of directors, Sylvester K. Stevens, Pennsylvania state historian, met with the National Park Service's director, Newton Drury, in Washington. Drury and Herbert E. Kahler, acting chief historian, gave them a copy of the abortive 1941 cooperative agreement. Undoubtedly Drury informed them that a cooperative agreement and designation of the Independence Hall group as a national historic site were prerequisites to any National Park Service involvement in the project. Lewis moved quickly. Within a week after the Washington meeting, he had arranged to see Mayor Bernard Samuel to reopen the question of a cooperative agreement. Negotiations with the city government were not easy, but Lewis was persuasive. On December 21, 1942, City Council passed an ordinance "Authorizing the execution and delivery of an agreement between the City of Philadelphia and the United States of America, designating the Independence Hall group of structures as a National Historic Site and providing for its preservation and improvement," and repeating the language of the 1941 draft agreement. On the federal level the way had already been cleared earlier in the month, when President Roosevelt acceded to Secretary Ickes's request to exempt Independence Hall from the wartime ban on designating national historic sites. On January 11, 1943, the mayor delivered the agreement, executed by the city, to Lewis. However, the city had executed a version of the 1941 agreement from which language had been stricken requiring the city to "secure the approval" of the director of the National Park Service— rather than merely to "consult" with him—before making changes to the buildings. Drury advised Lewis that the stricken language was incorporated in the agreement as approved by Roosevelt and suggested impartial arbitration as an alternative. But Stevens pointed out that it had been difficult enough to obtain the city's consent to the milder wording. The National Park Service gave in. With the offending language removed and continuing city control assured, Ickes announced consummation of the agreement on March 30.

This was perfect timing. On April 22, 1943, the Independence Hall Association opened an exhibition in Congress Hall. Arranged by McCosker's committee, it brought together rich material on the history of the buildings on Independence Square. The items on display, some of which had never been exhibited previously, came from both public and private collections. The concluding section of the exhibition introduced the association's basic aim:

A NEW IDEA FOR AN OLD SHRINE

> Independence Hall no longer needs to be saved. An informed public will not permit destruction, nor even slight change without the most exhaustive study and research. But Independence Hall needs care in a larger sense. The Association wants to put it into a proper setting, by removing unsightly buildings that were long out-moded and have ceased to be useful. These plans are here first submitted for the consideration of the public.

Other projects went less smoothly. Boyd continued to pursue one legacy of the Sons of the American Revolution committee: the scheme for lowering the Liberty Bell into a bomb-proof vault. However, there was growing protest about disturbing the Liberty Bell. Eventually the city vetoed the project on the grounds that the excavation might imperil the foundations of Independence Hall.

Progress was also discouragingly slow on the legislative front, although, under the tutelage of Isidor Ostroff, the organization launched an aggressive lobbying campaign. Ostroff, the Democratic district leader who had persuaded Sacks to introduce his bill, wrote to Lewis a few days after reading about the formation of the Independence Hall Association. Lewis suggested a meeting. He quickly persuaded Ostroff to join the organization in promoting their common cause, naming him liaison to Congress. Obviously Ostroff could be useful. The judge was a Republican; the Congress and administration were Democrats.

Money was a persistent problem. There were no major gifts in the early years, and attempts to secure financial assistance from the city were unavailing. Despite its lack of funding, the Independence Hall Association began to push hard for legislation. Repeated appeals to elected officials during the war years failed in the face of opposition from the administration, as expressed through the Bureau of the Budget. Even when the end of the war came in sight in 1944 and the administration relented, impressed by the proposal's strong local support, the legislation did not have high priority.

Nevertheless, the Independence Hall Association moved forward with plans for the project. By the end of 1942, Larson's committee had reviewed four plans. The more extensive schemes contemplated redevelopment of three blocks north of Chestnut Street and the area east of Fifth Street toward Christ Church. More important was the concept of a modest mall east of Independence Square, "exposing and glorifying" the Second Bank, Carpenters' Hall, and the First Bank. Larson's committee, spurred on by one of its members, Fiske Kimball, voted to support the most ambitious alternative. The executive committee concurred, with Lewis noting that he thought Congress would give its approval to a big plan as readily as a small one.

Over the next year Larson proceeded to refine the chosen scheme. On January 25, 1944, he and Lewis addressed a luncheon meeting of the Fairmount Park Art Association. Larson exhibited a plan and rendering. Along Chestnut Street opposite Independence Hall, the plan reverted to Cret's scheme for a semicircular reviewing plaza set off by a colonnade. Beyond a broad grassy mall stretched to Race Street, flanked by tree-shaded walks and gardens, interrupted by the major east-west streets. The mall terminated at Race Street in a semicircular plaza centered on a monument. To the east a modest tree-lined mall led from the center of Independence Square past the rear of the Second Bank to a landscaped square around Carpenters' Hall. A cross-axis opened a vista of the Second Bank from Walnut Street. Buildings, some existing, some new, remained along Walnut and Chestnut Streets.

David Knickerbacker Boyd suffered a fatal stroke at his desk in the office

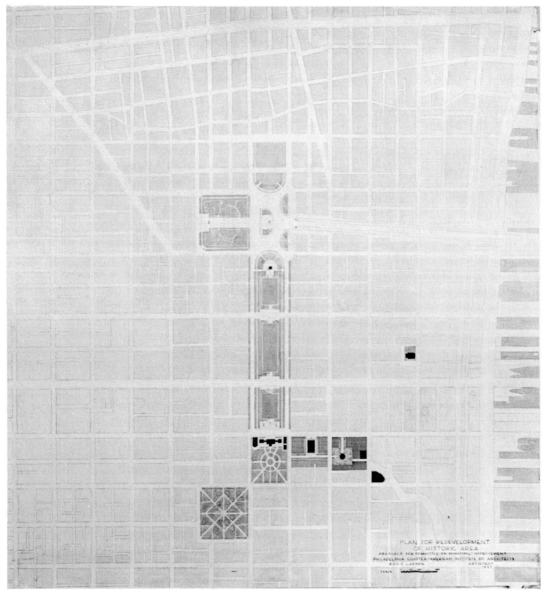

10. *"Plan for Redevelopment of Historic Area," drawn by Roy F. Larson in 1937. This plan was the first to show a mall extending three blocks to the north of Independence Hall, where it linked up with plazas at the approach to the Benjamin Franklin Bridge. In addition, Larson proposed a modest park development to the east, encompassing the First and Second Banks of the United States, Carpenters' Hall, and the Merchants' Exchange, but leaving intact existing development along Walnut Street.*

of the Independence Hall Association on February 21, 1944. Despite failing health, he had been the workhorse of the organization, attending almost every committee meeting, maintaining contact with City Hall, carrying on a voluminous correspondence, drafting speeches and letters for Lewis. With Boyd's death, Lewis began to assume a more active role, gradually dropping his other volunteer posts in order to concentrate on the Independence Hall Association. As he took its reins more firmly into his hands, there were fewer committee meetings, and fewer contacts by others with the press and federal and city officials.

Lewis became increasingly dissatisfied with both the pace of legislative action and Larson's plans. Although he approved of the architect's scheme for the mall north of Independence Hall, he rejected what Larson called a "sword thrust to the east." Lewis was determined that there would be a national park in the three full blocks from Fifth to Second Streets between Walnut and Chestnut. In so doing, he dismissed Larson's concept of retaining and reinforcing the urban fabric around the area's historic buildings. Of course, neither the north mall nor the park to the east was a new idea. What Lewis did was to combine the biggest dreams of the 1920s and 1930s and persevere until he turned them into reality.

One step in that direction was to eschew total dependency on the federal government. In early 1945 Lewis approached Gov. Edward Martin. He presented the case for the north mall and was delighted to find Martin receptive. By October the Pennsylvania legislature had voted to undertake development of the mall and had authorized $4 million for the purpose. Meanwhile, real progress had been made toward creation of a national park. With the surrender of Germany and ultimate victory in sight, Congress was beginning to consider potential peacetime projects. In April, after months of hesitation, members of the House Committee on Public Lands finally visited Philadelphia. In June Rep. Michael J. Bradley, now the local sponsor for the bill, triumphantly telegraphed Lewis that H.R. 2551, establishing a commission to study creation of a park, had been reported out of committee. By this time the bill had the support not only of the committee, but also of the House leadership. The House passed the bill unanimously in September; the Senate followed suit in November. The judge's dual goal seemed within his grasp, with the state prepared to fund the north mall and the federal government taking the first steps toward creating a national park to the east. Once again, however, there were delays. News reports of the state's proposed participation reached Washington and caused confusion about the federal role. Mayor Samuel stepped in as mediator, clarifying that the state's interest was confined to the area north of Independence Hall. Finally, after almost four years of effort, Public Law 711 was enacted on August 9, 1946. It called for creating a seven-member commission, known as the Philadelphia National Shrines Park Commission, to investigate the establishment of a national park "to encompass within its area the buildings of historical significance in the old part of the city of Philadelphia."

Almost as a matter of course, Judge Lewis became the commission's chairman. The other members were the realtor Albert M. Greenfield, serving as vice-chairman; George McAneny, a prominent New York preservationist, president of the American Scenic and Historic Preservation Society and also of the Carl Schurz Memorial Foundation, which still occupied the Second Bank; two members of the Pennsylvania congressional delegation, Rep. Robert N. McGarvey and Sen. Francis J. Myers; Judge Hugh Martin Morris; and the author and biographer of Franklin, Carl Van Doren. The group held its first meeting in Philadelphia on November 15. One of its earliest decisions was to retain an architect to draw plans for the park. Although Larson had served the Independence Hall Association in this capacity from its formation, Lewis wanted an architect more in sympathy with his concept of an expansive thrust to the east. The choice was Grant M. Simon, a talented delineator capable of translating Lewis's ideas into attractive watercolor renderings.

Informed of this decision, Newton Drury demurred. He explained to Lewis that although Congress had authorized $15,000 for the work of the commission, it had not actually appropriated the money. Until the funds were appropriated, the National Park Service could not pay salaries or expenses for the project. Furthermore, the law specified that project personnel must have Civil Service status. Drury suggested that park service architect Charles E. Peterson assume the task of advising the commission, detailing Peterson's qualifications. After joining the park service in 1929, Peterson had quickly become its leading expert on historical architecture. He had played a key role in the development of the major historical areas in which the National Park Service had been involved up to that time: among them Colonial National Historical Park in Jamestown and Yorktown, Virginia, Morristown National Historical Park in New Jersey, and the historic areas inherited from the War Department. In 1946, after four years in the Navy, he had returned to work on the Jefferson National Expansion Memorial project in St. Louis, Missouri. Peterson's accomplishments and expertise were widely recognized outside the Park service as well. In 1933 he had originated the Historic American Buildings Survey. A cooperative project of the National Park Service, the AIA, and the Library of Congress, HABS had offered work to hundreds of architects during the Depression and recorded over six thousand structures. Currently Peterson was serving as vice-chairman of the AIA's Committee on Historic Buildings.

These were impressive credentials, but Lewis was adamant. Drury finally agreed to support Lewis's choice of Simon as the Shrines Commission's architect. Nevertheless, he made it clear that the National Park Service intended to have a voice in the commission's recommendations to Congress. In a letter informing Lewis that Simon could be employed as a consultant without Civil Service status, he concluded:

The National Park Service desires to work closely with the Commission, and particularly so in all technical and planning matters. Later on it will be very desirable, as the National Park Service becomes more closely identified with the program, for Mr. Charles Peterson's exceptional talents in these matters to be utilized in the evolution of plans for the project.

Having won his point, and with Simon's preliminary plans committed to paper, Lewis acceded graciously. "We believe we now need the services of Mr. Peterson," Lewis responded to Drury at the end of February 1947, "and if you can have Mr. Peterson assigned to work with the Commission in Philadelphia to go over suggestions before we become too deeply committed to them, I will be glad."

Perhaps Lewis had been convinced of the wisdom of this course by the chief historian of the National Park Service, Ronald F. Lee. Lee was one of a group of young historians who had joined the National Park Service, fresh from the University of Minnesota, in 1933. He rose rapidly within the ranks, becoming chief of the Branch of Historic Sites and Buildings in 1938. His rather cherubic face tended to mask a keen intellect. He was that rare combination—a first-rate conceptual thinker and a good administrator. At the same time he was a skilled negotiator and a man of considerable charm, adept at dealing not only with people within the National Park Service, but also with outsiders who shared his abiding interest in history and the preservation of historic sites. For over thirty years a succession of National Park Service directors relied on his opinions. Lee had been on leave from the park service from 1942 to 1946, serving in the Air Corps, and thus had not participated in the negotiations that led to the passage of Public Law 711. With his return and the establishment of the Shrines Commission, Lee became a more active presence in the Philadelphia project. On February 22 he represented the park service at a meeting in the office of Pennsylvania's new governor, James Duff. Representatives of the city (including Mayor Samuel), the Independence Hall Association, and the Fairmount Park Art Association were also present. Simon exhibited plans for the north mall, the federal park, and other historic structures. The governor assured the group that the $4 million already appropriated was committed to the mall, but pointed out that $4 million more would be needed. The state Department of Highways, which would be responsible for the development of Fifth and Sixth Streets, was working on an agreement with the city to define their respective roles. Lee confined himself to expressing the National Park Service's interest in the "Shrines Park" and its willingness to aid in expediting the project. Immediately after this meeting Lewis requested that Peterson be sent to Philadelphia.

Peterson was in Philadelphia to attend the next meeting of the Shrines Commission on March 11. Lee came up from Washington, accompanied by Dick Sutton, chief architect of the National Park Service. Once again representatives of various interested groups were present: the City Planning Commission; the Fairmount Park Art Association, including its president, the architect Sydney E. Martin; and the Independence Hall Association, including Roy Larson. A major purpose of the meeting was to hear the views of the Market Street Businessmen's Association, which opposed the proposed size of the north mall. It had retained an architect, Louis Magaziner, who argued that the scale was too large and would reduce Independence to insignificance, making the frame too big for the picture. Morris Passon, spokesman for the businessmen, told the group that he was aware of the probable futility of his mission but expressed hope that some consideration would be given to the problems of relocation. Lewis suggested that demolition might proceed in stages in order to avoid undue disturbance of the business community. On this conciliatory note, the meeting with the merchants' representatives ended. The commission then proceeded to examine once again plans by Simon and the City Planning Commission. Judge Hugh M. Morris proposed that the commission adopt the Simon plan insofar as the inclusion of existing buildings was concerned, and Lewis concurred, although no vote was taken. This issue—which buildings would remain and which would be demolished—would be the subject of debate for twenty-five years.

In April Arthur E. Demaray informed Lewis that arrangements had been made for Peterson and another park service professional, Roy Appleman, to assist the commission. Appleman was one of the trained historians hired by Ronald Lee in 1935 as part of the Civilian Conservation Corps program for work in national and state parks. In 1947 he was regional historian in the old Region I office in Richmond, Virginia. Both Peterson and Appleman were present at a meeting in Philadelphia on April 18. Although this was described in the minutes as a meeting of the Philadelphia National Shrines Park Commission, the only member of that body present was Judge Lewis. As usual Sydney Martin represented the Fairmount Park Art Association, Dr. William E. Lingelbach the Independence Hall Association, and Robert E. Mitchell and Edmund Bacon the City Planning Commission. Simon was also present. The discussion focused on park boundaries. There was general agreement that the national park should extend east to Second Street. Edmund Bacon, on behalf of the City Planning Commission, displayed maps showing not only what was described as the "usual area" for consideration, but also the area south of Walnut Street to Lombard Street. Bacon believed that the latter area, with its concentration of eighteenth- and early nineteenth-century rowhouses, should be developed with "greenways," small parks and landscaped walks. Both of the National Park Service men felt that the southern section, Washington Square East as it was designated on the city's plans, was not suitable for inclusion in the federal project. The areas shown were too narrow and long and were not interconnected. In the proposed national park, Bacon expressed concern for the appearance of the historic buildings as seen from the side. There was agreement, for example, that Strickland had designed the sides of the Second Bank knowing that they would be hidden from view by flanking buildings. Simon's plan took this into account, providing new, low buildings along Chestnut Street on sites where nonhistoric buildings would be demolished. Such buildings, he suggested, might be fitted up as inns and restaurants to serve visitors to the park. Thus, general agreement on the boundaries was combined with a variety of opinions on the treatment of specific sites and on possible additional acquisitions. Peterson called attention to the special interest and restoration potential of the Todd and Bishop White Houses on Walnut Street, and the mid-nineteenth-century Jayne Building on Chestnut Street. The group also discussed the desirability of acquiring the sites of the Franklin House, the Robert Morris House on Market Street, where both Washington and Adams had lived as president, and the Graff House, where Jefferson drafted the Declaration of Independence.

Both Appleman and Peterson spent time in Philadelphia over the next several months. In addition to his visit in April, Appleman was in Philadelphia for the last week of June and the first three weeks in July. Peterson spent about a month there in the spring and another two and a half months during the summer. Although both had been detailed to Philadelphia by the National Park Service, they worked independently, rather than as a team. They conferred on architectural questions, but otherwise saw very little of one another, and neither saw a copy of the other's report. Indeed, they seem to have approached the assignment with very different attitudes. When they arrived, Lewis offered to arrange for both men to stay at the Union League Club. Appleman felt that he could not afford to: the National Park Service *per diem* allowance of the 1940s, pegged to the small towns near which most parks were located, provided six or seven dollars a day. Appleman found that the cheapest respectable hotel he could find took all but a dollar of that. Despite eating most of his meals at Horn and Hardart's, he had spent about ninety dollars out of his own pocket by the end of his Philadelphia assignment. His meetings with Philadelphians were directly related to his assigned tasks. He conferred often with Judge Lewis, with Joseph M. McCosker, who had been retained to write the historical background section of the Shrines Commission's report to Congress, and with Dr. Lingelbach, and he encountered other Philadelphians at various meetings.

Peterson entered more freely into the life of the city, in which he immediately felt very much at home. He accepted Lewis's invitation to stay at the Union League Club and was delighted that Lewis "invited me to everything that was going on and introduced me to everybody." Philadelphia was quick to seek him out as a public speaker. His most important public statement was delivered at the annual dinner of the American Philosophical Society on April 25, 1947, and incorporated into his report to the director of the National Park Service. Asked to comment on Simon's sketches of the Shrines Commission's plans, he expressed some personal opinions. Although he did not directly attack the commission's scheme, he clearly opposed its grandiose malls. Eschewing formal axes, he urged retention of the city's historic street patterns and the sense of enclosure provided by groupings of buildings. To bolster his argument, he quoted letters from distinguished colleagues in architecture and architectural history.

Peterson's written report went much further. After a brief review of the project's history, he touched on some practical considerations that had not been dealt with before. He outlined the need for parking space, public toilets, places to eat and stay overnight, a staging area for guided tours, and a store for the sale of publications and souvenirs. He suggested that these functions might be accommodated in buildings that would help to recreate the historic scene and reinforce the urban character of the neighborhood. Although generally opposed to reconstructions, he reported favorably on a proposal to rebuild the row of three-and-a-half-story houses (Norris's Row) that once fronted Chestnut Street between the Second Bank and Independence Square. The row could be authentic on the outside and modern on the interior to serve as an inn with an eighteenth-century flavor, akin to those at Williamsburg. Peterson forecast that a million people a year might visit Independence, requiring a reception center on a scale previously unknown in the National Park Service. His preferred location was on the north side of Chestnut Street opposite Independence Hall. This would serve two purposes. It would place the major interpretive center close to the park's main attraction, and, if low in height, would allow a good vista of the tower and also provide what he considered a necessary frame, a "north wall for the Square." He thought screened surface parking for 500 cars could be provided on the state's land to the north, and that eventually one or more multi-story garages would also be required.

Peterson's report also cautioned against overzealous demolition around the historic buildings. "If the pulling down is kept up long enough it will leave the historic buildings standing in large open spaces like country churches, a condition which their designers did not plan for." He pointed out that both the Larson plan of 1944 and the City Planning Commission's scheme called for including compatible new construction in the historic area. "What is needed," he wrote, "is not so much open and vacant space as an architectural setting of a sympathetic character." He believed that it would be desirable for the legislation establishing the park to allow the National Park Service to lease land to private developers for erecting compatible infill buildings.

Peterson also drew attention to the City Planning Commission's proposals for rehabilitating the residential area south of Walnut Street. In what may have been the first modern use of the neighborhood's eighteenth-century name, he referred to it as Society Hill. He recommended that the National Park Service give the City Planning Commission as much professional and other assistance as possible. Preservation and restoration in one area would support and enhance efforts in the other.

Without attacking or directly criticizing the Shrines Commission's plan, Peterson was clearly expressing doubts about some of its underlying assumptions. His concept of how the park should be treated was less antiurban and aesthetically more respectful of the historic buildings. The Philadelphia City Planning Commission shared his concern. In July Simon wrote to the vacationing Judge Lewis that Martin and Larson had told him that although they supported the eastern extension in general, they were not prepared to approve the Shrines Commission's design. Furthermore, Robert E. Mitchell, executive secretary of the City Planning Commission, had indicated that the commission would also withhold approval. These differences were largely overcome at a meeting in the City Planning Commission's offices on July 11. Appleman described the planners' attitude at the start of the meeting as "mistrustful." He and Peterson attended the meeting along with Mitchell; Edmund Bacon, the planning commission's senior planner; and the three architects who had long been interested in the project—Simon, Larson, and Martin. The planning commission expressed strong opinions on the retention of street patterns and existing businesses along Walnut and Chestnut Streets. Martin and Larson shared the commission's view that the park should include business buildings along street frontages, although Martin took a less absolute position. Although favoring a screen of buildings along the principal streets, he agreed with Lewis that the area should have a parklike character with extensive expanses of lawn and trees.

Asked by Mitchell to comment on the National Park Service's policy on these questions, Appleman responded that he could not speak for the service. It was his opinion, however, that no fixed policy had been formulated. The Philadelphia project raised new and complex issues. The National Park Service would study these issues and consult with all interested parties. He was sure that the park service would approach planning for the park with "great elasticity of mind in considering and formulating a policy of development on this subject." His comments appeared to reassure Mitchell. It was Martin, in Appleman's opinion, who played the role of conciliator and was instrumental in ensuring that the Philadelphia Planning Commission would not oppose, even if it did not fully support, the Shrines Commission's proposals. He cautioned, however, that other influential Philadelphians might not agree with the views of Lewis and the commission, or, for that matter, with the development the National Park Service might plan in the future. Lewis did not need reminders from Simon or Appleman of the need for widespread public support. Action to whet Philadelphia's appetite for the proposed park had already been taken. In the spring of 1947 the Independence Hall Association had exhibited in Congress Hall a model illustrating its ideas for development. In September the City Planning Commission opened the "Better Philadelphia Exhibition" on the fifth floor of Gimbel's department store. Through a scale model occupying over an acre of floor space, the exhibit showed a five-year plan for civic improvement projected to cost over

$300 million. Over three-quarters of a million people filed past the model, which showed the proposed redevelopment around Independence Square as an integral part of plans for the revitalization of Philadelphia.

In addition to raising planning questions, Peterson's report dealt briefly with the areas and buildings he thought should be included in the federal park. The Walnut to Chestnut, Fifth to Second Street, area had been generally accepted. Peterson also believed that Franklin Court and the site of the Jefferson (Graff) House should be included. He recommended that Christ Church be given national historic site status as "a detached area of federal reservation" and that the National Park Service should secure land across from Independence Square, after it had been acquired by the state, as a site for a visitors' reception center. Appleman's thoughts on federal acquisition were similar. He agreed with Peterson that the National Park Service should control the block north of Independence Square. Although he was not sure that the specific location for a reception center recommended by Peterson was the ideal site, he too believed that such a facility should be somewhere on that block. Furthermore, he thought it important that the National Park Service control the immediate approach to Independence Hall. In addition, one of the key historic sites was within the block. This was a lot on the north side of Market Street, where the Robert Morris House had stood. As the residence of Presidents Washington and Adams, it deserved recognition.

In addition to recommending areas and boundaries for federal acquisition, Appleman devoted considerable attention to the treatment of particular buildings and the handling of these and other issues in the Shrines Commission's report and the bill authorizing the park. He suggested that the insurance companies should be permitted to retain their buildings on the north side of Walnut Street for a decade or two, to avoid disruption of their business. Provisions of the legislation should cover two of the area's historic private institutions. The Carpenters' Company should be allowed to "tenant" its building, and the American Philosophical Society should be given the option of constructing a replica of the old Library building on Fifth Street. During his visits to Philadelphia, Appleman had met several times with Dr. Lingelbach, the society's librarian. Appleman found Lingelbach a sound and helpful source of information on the history of the project area. He was also influential: Lewis, in particular, respected and relied on his judgment. Lingelbach had been one of the strongest proponents of the idea of a federal park. He was motivated, like many of its other adherents, by patriotism and an interest in the past. In addition, he was concerned for the future of his institution. The Philosophical Society had long since outgrown its ancient headquarters on Fifth Street behind Old City Hall. It was currently housing many of its books in rented space in the Drexel Building at the corner of Fifth and Chestnut Streets, but a move to larger quarters elsewhere in the city had been discussed. Lingelbach preferred to remain close to Independence Square. Early in his acquaintance with Appleman he had broached the feasibility of reconstructing the Library Company's building to serve the society's need. Appleman believed that there was sufficient evidence on which to base a good reconstruction and recommended that these matters should be covered in the bill. The legislation should also provide for the preservation of all existing structures erected prior to 1800 and pinpoint those erected after that date that were also to be preserved, such as the Second Bank of the United States and the Merchants' Exchange. Appleman believed that the bill should not go into detail on development plans. The development issues were complicated and required considerable additional research and study. The legislation should ensure that the National Park Service had broad powers in planning development and an interpretive program.

Appleman shared the fruits of his researches into Philadelphia's documentary and pictorial resources with Lewis and McCosker. Although Appleman helped to determine the content and, indeed, provided a detailed outline of the Shrines Commission's report, Lewis felt that the final product should be prepared by someone retained by the commission—working under his supervision and guidance—not by an employee of the National Park Service. "The final body of the report, [the] ideas expressed, however," Appleman remembered, "of course had to be Judge Lewis's and the commission's, but from my early work with Judge Lewis, it would appear to me that his views were accepted by the rest of the commission with very little objection, if any at all, and that he in effect was the commission, and it was his drive and his energy and his leadership at that time that saw the thing through to a successful conclusion."

McCosker appeared to be well qualified for the task of preparing the historical section of the report. As director of the Atwater Kent Museum, he had a broad familiarity with Philadelphia history, and he had been chairman of the committee that put together the Independence Hall Association's 1943 exhibit on the Hall and its neighbors. Over the summer, despite bouts of illness, he proceeded to collect historical data and illustrative material for what he referred to as "the book." True to his conviction that the report should be a Shrines Commission project, Lewis had raised $4,000 from the Insurance Company of North America to pay for the services of McCosker and a staff of three: a research assistant, a secretary-typist, and a photographer. McCosker resented the involvement of the National Park Service specialists. He was particularly at odds with Peterson, who, he believed, was attempting to make him alter the findings to emphasize Christ Church at the expense of the commission's plan for a narrow extension of the park south of Walnut Street. He found Appleman helpful, but became annoyed when he had not received the latter's research notes by the end of the first week of August. "I fear," he wrote to Lewis, who was vacationing in Maine, "that the combined 'help' of the two Federal men has not meant much in concrete aid to the work at hand." A week later, however, he reported to Lewis that Peterson had returned to Philadelphia and had "become cooperative." Perhaps McCosker sensed that the two were not impressed with the quality of his work. Appleman subsequently recommended that the commission's report not be published unless it was carefully edited to remove its many mistakes.

While McCosker worked on the historical background, Lewis was composing the section detailing the Shrines Commission's recommendations for the scope of the park. On October 6, 1947, the commission, which had not met for six months, gathered to consider a draft. The members present, in addition to Lewis, were McAneny, Morris, Van Doren, and McGarvey. Guests included Edward Hopkinson, Jr., representing the City Planning Commission; E. Norris Williams II of the Historical Society of Pennsylvania; Edward M. Biddle, treasurer of the Independence Hall Association; and Sydney Martin. What might be termed the commission's staff was also present: Simon, McCosker, and Lewis's assistant, Dwight Lowell. The commission quickly proceeded to recommend four areas for acquisition by the federal government: the three blocks east of Independence Square, a lateral extension south to Pine Street, Franklin Court, and the site of the Graff House. The idea of extending the federal park to the vicinity of Christ Church won support from McAneny. The other members of the commission, however, decided that Christ Church should be a separate area, with sufficient land cleared around it to constitute a firebreak.

Two other recommendations made by Appleman and Peterson fared badly. The first was a proposed extension to the east side of Second Street, which the commission vetoed because the then-current city plan called for widening the street as a major artery. In a more important vote, the commission rejected the suggestion that the federal government acquire the block north of Independence Hall. Lewis was afraid that such a move might jeopardize the state's project for the mall. As usual, the commission followed the judge's lead. As Appleman had said, Lewis *was* the commission. At times he had been the only member of the commission present at its meetings. It was Lewis who had conferred continuously with Simon, McCosker, Appleman, and Peterson on the content of the report. He would prepare the text of its most important section, the recommendations.

The commission duly submitted its report to Congress on December 29, 1948. Copiously illustrated, it filled seven fat volumes. Most of the bulk consisted of McCosker's "historic appendage," which described buildings and sites within the proposed park and its vicinity and events associated with them. Modern photographs and historical views accompanied each description. Carl Van Doren provided a graceful preface. The heart of the report, however, comprised the commission's recommendations for property acquisition (with cost estimates), expressions of support from the city of Philadelphia, and the draft of a proposed bill establishing the park.

The report called for a park consisting of five areas, each designated by a letter of the alphabet. Although the letters are now virtually forgotten, they were used for handy reference to the park's various sectors for almost two

decades. Project A was, of course, foremost. This was the core area east of
Independence Square, with an estimated acquisition cost of $3,560,000.
Language undoubtedly calculated to conciliate the City Planning Commission
of Philadelphia proposed postponing the removal of existing business struc-
tures on the north side of Walnut Street until, in the judgment of the
secretary of the interior, they should "become reasonably obsolete." Project
B, with an estimated cost of $300,000, was described as a "small mall" from
Walnut to Pine in the middle of the block between Fourth and Fifth Streets.
It linked St. Joseph's and St. Mary's Roman Catholic Churches with the Pine
Street Presbyterian Church, along with such other sites as the Contributionship
Garden behind the offices of one of the oldest of the city's venerable fire
insurance companies, and the Cadwalader and Shippen-Wistar Houses.

The three remaining acquisitions were more modest in scope. Project C,
with a price tag of $175,000, was Franklin Court, a narrow lot with frontage
on Market Street, and an extension on Orianna Street, connecting it to
Chestnut Street in the vicinity of Carpenters' Hall. More remote from the
core area was Project D at the corner of Seventh and Market Streets, the site
of the house where Jefferson wrote the Declaration of Independence. It was
also more expensive. Acquisition was expected to cost $250,000. Finally,
Project E, lands and buildings to provide a firebreak around Christ Church,
would cost $110,000. The total expenditure required came to $4,485,000.
The commission recommended an appropriation of $5 to $5.5 million, which
would allow the National Park Service to construct a building housing offices,
an auditorium, and restrooms. Although Independence Hall was the first
building discussed and illustrated in the historical section, there was no
mention of its future ownership or management in the recommendations.

The report included expressions of support from the mayor and the
director of the City Planning Commission. By this time Philadelphia's government saw the federal park as the linchpin in its plans for rehabilitating the
area to its south and east as a prime residential district.

Grant Simon's large-scale illustrations supplemented the written report.
Several of these were merely pretty pictures, watercolor renderings of how
some of the historic buildings would look after restoration. Others fleshed
out the Shrines Commission's vision of the eventual appearance of the park.
There were, however, some discrepancies among the drawings. An aerial
photograph of Philadelphia, with the park areas skillfully airbrushed in,
showed Project A bisected by a broad grass mall. All of the buildings on
Walnut and Chestnut Streets were gone, with the exception of the main
historic monuments and a few unidentifiable eighteenth-century houses on
Walnut Street. Double rows of trees took the place of the buildings. A site
plan drawing was more specific. The buildings to remain on Walnut Street
were identified as the Moylan (Todd) and Bishop White Houses, plus the
buildings at 339, 341, and 315–321. However, a perspective watercolor
rendering of the same area, dated 1947, showed Walnut and Chestnut Streets

11. One of the plans by Grant M. Simon that accompanied the Philadelphia National Shrines Commission's report to the Congress in 1948. It shows a broad grassy mall running off-center through the block between Walnut and Chestnut from Fifth to Third Street, which Simon referred to as a "commons." On either side of this lawn, axial vistas were open to the few surviving historic buildings. Other areas of the park are shown as rectangular lawns bordered by double rows of trees. Oddly enough, in view of Judge Lewis's opposition to their preservation, the nineteenth-century buildings at the southwest corner of Chestnut and Third Streets are depicted as surviving.

lined with new, low construction, in the "colonial style." The 200-by-850-foot grass plot remained consistent. It was, indeed, integral to Simon's ideas for the east mall. He had developed all his plans on the assumption that the historic buildings were to be given a dignified and impressive setting through the creation of what he termed a "commons," a broad lawn with double rows of trees on all four sides, bordered by the historic buildings and new construction of sympathetic character. The plan of the proposed park also showed development at Franklin Court. It encompassed four buildings on Market Street, the passageway between them, and a reconstruction of Franklin's house. Project B, the southern extension, was also treated as a relatively broad mall, although a discontinuous one. It stopped on the north side of the graveyard of St. Mary's Church and began again to its south.

Despite the inconsistency of the drawings, the members of the Shrines Commission evidently believed that they had not only prepared a report demonstrating the desirability of a national park in Philadelphia, but also worked out the best scheme for its development. Section 3 of the proposed legislation incorporated in the report read, "The park shall be developed in accordance with the report of the Philadelphia National Shrines Park Commission to the Congress of the United States, dated December 29, 1947."

Over a decade had elapsed since George Nitzche first broached the idea of a national park in Philadelphia. Since the seminal meeting in the Architects Building, Judge Lewis, using as his vehicle first the Independence Hall Association and then the Shrines Commission, had conducted a masterly public relations campaign, skillfully coordinated a successful lobbying effort, and supervised research and planning. He had garnered support from federal, state, and local government, from the Philadelphia newspapers, and from a host of civic and patriotic organizations. He had overseen production of a document impressive for both its bulk and its rhetoric. Now, after all the years of effort, the question of whether there would be a national park in Philadelphia rested with the federal government.

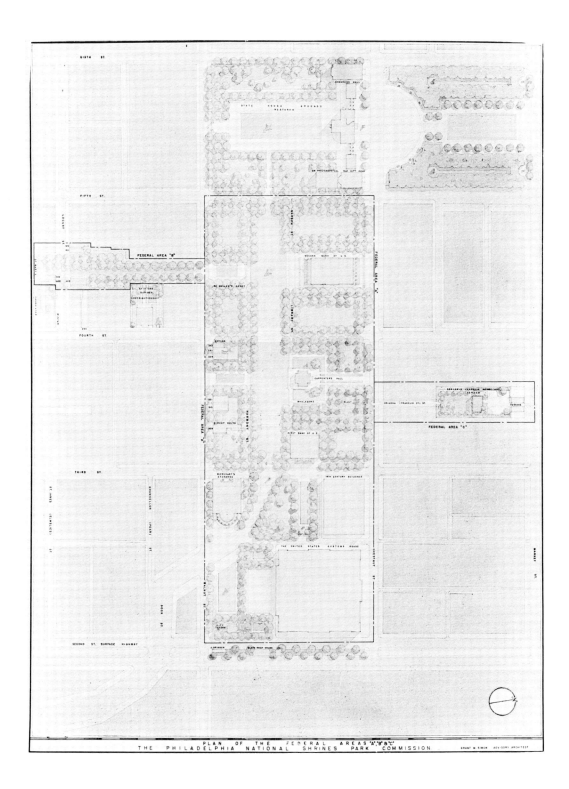

PLAN OF THE FEDERAL AREAS "A","B" & "C"
THE PHILADELPHIA NATIONAL SHRINES PARK COMMISSION

Three
The Beginnings of the Park

Once the Shrines Commission's report had been delivered, congressional action was swift. Rep. Hardie Scott introduced H.R. 5053, authorizing creation of a national park in Philadelphia, on January 20, 1948. Scott, no relation to Lewis's nephew, Hugh Scott, was then the congressman for the district in which Independence Hall is located. Hardie Scott's version of the bill was copied verbatim from the legislation proposed in the report. It authorized the secretary of the interior to accept by donation, or acquire by purchase or condemnation, certain areas to become "Philadelphia National Historical Park."

Although the National Park Service heartily endorsed the creation of the park, the legislation proposed by the Shrines Commission was unsatisfactory in many respects. The park service prepared to submit its own bill in the guise of amendments to the Scott bill. In February Oscar L. Chapman, acting secretary of the interior, commented on the bill to Richard J. Welch, chairman of the House Committee on Public Lands, in a letter drafted by Ronald Lee. It strongly recommended passage of the bill as amended, and enclosed the amendments. So extensive were they that only the first two lines of the original bill remained intact. Even the name was new. In place of the pedestrian Philadelphia National Historical Park, it had become Independence National Historical Park, to express the project's national rather than merely local significance.

Perhaps the most important amendment was a deletion. The National Park Service's draft did not mention developing the proposed park according to the Shrines Commission's plan, or indeed any preconceived plan. On the other hand, the amendments added some requirements. Full establishment of the park would depend on execution of agreements with the city of Philadelphia and the Carpenters' Company for the preservation and interpretation of their buildings. The agreements must ensure that the National Park Service would have access, at all reasonable times, to all public portions of the properties in order to conduct visitors through them. The park service would also have control over interpreting them to the public. The agreements would also provide that no major alterations could be made without mutual consent. Obviously, if such key buildings as Independence Hall and Carpenters' Hall could not be included, there would be little point in establishing a park. The bill did not require that all the land in the recommended areas be acquired before establishment; two-thirds would be adequate. However, this partial acquisition would have to include certain designated buildings: the First Bank of the United States, the Merchants' Exchange, the Bishop White House, the Todd House, and the site of Benjamin Franklin's house. At the same time that it clearly specified those buildings essential to the National Park Service's concept of the park, the amended bill omitted two areas recommended by the Shrines Commission: Project B, the southern extension between Walnut and Pine Streets, and Project E, the lands around Christ Church. Undoubtedly this decision reflected, in part, the park service's long-established reluctance to acquire properties associated with religious buildings, although precedent for a lesser form of involvement with sectarian structures existed in cooperative agreements with Gloria Dei Church in Philadelphia and Touro Synagogue in Newport, Rhode Island. The reason cited for the omission was that the areas were not sufficiently related to the essential nationally significant properties and that it would be more appropriate for the city to include them in its redevelopment plans.

Whether or not he was responsible for their precise language, Ronald Lee had undoubtedly shaped these amendments. Following his return from military service in 1946, Lee had assumed responsibility for the negotiations for Independence, without much communication with his colleagues in the Branch of History. Although no memoranda or other documents record his thinking, Lee's decisions were probably influenced by experiences with other historic areas. In at least three of those developed before Independence, the National Park Service's historians and other professionals had lacked sufficient control. Disagreements, sometimes acrimonious, had arisen with local supporters of the projects, and history had too often been on the losing side. The actions taken to propitiate the local groups had damaged the integrity of the sites and made it difficult, if not impossible, to interpret them in a historically accurate manner.

At Colonial National Historical Park the Lightfoot Stable was reconstructed fifty feet from its original site because the rector and parishioners of neighboring Christ Episcopal Church objected to the proper location. At the George Washington Birthplace National Monument at Wakefield, Virginia, inadequate research and planning, combined with pressure to complete a commemorative building in time for the 1932 bicentennial of Washington's birth, had resulted in reconstruction of the house on the wrong site. Freshest in Lee's mind must have been the philosophical disagreements between the National Park Service and Luther Ely Smith, the chief local proponent of the Jefferson National Expansion Memorial in St. Louis. Smith wanted a "City Beautiful" open park along the Mississippi River, with a major monument on the lines of the Washington Monument or the Lincoln Memorial in Washington, D.C. While the Independence legislation was being discussed, he was promoting an international architectural competition for a memorial. Many professionals in the National Park Service opposed Smith's grandiose concept, which required clearance of the site. They would have preferred to interpret it through retention of the historic commercial buildings along the waterfront, from which the country's western expansion had been supplied, and a relatively modest museum in the old courthouse. It was a losing position. Director Drury supported Smith's proposal.

Lee and his associates wished to ensure that the errors that had been committed at other sites did not recur in Philadelphia. Independence was not merely the most important historic site the National Park Service had dealt with, but the premier historic site in the nation. The attention of the country would be focused on its treatment; whatever was done must meet the highest standards. From the time the Shrines Commission had begun its deliberations, the park service had made it clear that this time it intended to maintain control over the development. As Drury had informed Lewis when recommending that Peterson come to Philadelphia to assist the commission, the National Park Service ultimately would be responsible for the planning. Roy Appleman had indicated at the decisive meeting in the office of the City Planning Commission, in July 1947, that his agency would want to devote considerable time to research and study before drawing up a development plan. His final report on the situation in Philadelphia had recommended that the legislation for the proposed park list by name those buildings that were to be preserved, but not be specific about the plan for development, reserving broad decision-making powers for the National Park Service. These recommendations undoubtedly had a strong influence on the amendments to the bill.

Although the National Park Service was firm about retaining control, it approached Independence with caution. This was an enormous undertaking on many levels, not least of them financial. Most previous parks had been established on land already belonging to the federal government or acquired through donation. For the first time the National Park Service was asking Congress to authorize millions of dollars to purchase property. The provisions in the Department of the Interior's version of the bill establishing priorities for cooperative agreements and certain acquisitions recognized that there would be no point in making these expenditures if key sites could not be included within the park. The proposed omission of Projects B and E probably reflected concerns about costs, not only of acquisition, but of maintenance of discontinuous parcels of property, as well as about the separation of church and state.

The final amendment, the change of name, was the product of a longstanding concern. As early as December 1945, when the bill creating the Shrines Commission had just passed the House and Senate, Herbert E. Kahler, assistant chief historian of the National Park Service, noted that the "name for the proposed area needs careful consideration." Changing the name could thus scarcely be considered an impulse, but it was certainly an inspiration.

The Subcommittee on Public Lands held hearings on the bill as amended by the Interior Department on March 1, 1948. A large contingent from Philadelphia traveled to Washington to testify or to lend support by their presence. Lewis, of course, led the delegation, accompanied by two fellow members of the Shrines Commission and by McCosker. Hopkinson and Mitchell were there for the City Planning Commission, and representatives from several cultural institutions and the business community also attended. Director Newton Drury of the National Park Service was there to testify, accompanied by Assistant Director Hillory Tolson, Lee, Peterson, and Chief Counsel Jackson Price.

Rep. Hardie Scott opened the proceedings by introducing the visitors. Lewis was the first to testify. His testimony was eloquent and well calculated to appeal to the intense patriotism of the postwar period, as well as to the uncertainties of the burgeoning cold war. He linked Independence to the greatest treasures of the American people, the Grand Canyon, Mount Vernon, the majesty of creation seen from a mountain peak:

> When you come to Philadelphia; when any person from California, Nevada, Texas or anywhere comes to Philadelphia and enters Independence Hall and entering it is immediately met with the full view of the Liberty Bell, crack and all, there registers every sentiment of patriotism that runs through the mind—everything taught in the schools to that person as a child relating to American history—is so strong that goose pimples come out upon the body of anyone who is really an American and many who are not Americans. Everybody knows.

Lewis went on to describe each of the buildings and sites in the areas recommended in the Shrines Commission's report. He stressed their associations with the founding fathers. Here Washington, Adams, Jefferson, Franklin, and their fellows had lived, worked, worshiped, and participated in the city's social and intellectual life. He included the two projects eliminated by the National Park Service, Project B, the south mall, and Project E, land around Christ Church. At this juncture the committee interrupted Lewis to ask why the Shrines Commission had recommended the two areas. One congressman pointed out that National Park Service disapproval was not conclusive for members of Congress. Lewis responded that it was his understanding that the park service opposed the two areas because they involved Christ Church, St. Mary's, and other churches, although they did not actually take land belonging to religious institutions. Furthermore, the park service believed that these projects should be undertaken by the city. Encouraged by the subcommittee's response, he launched a spirited defense of the Shrines Commission's decisions, especially in regard to Project B. He concluded by reminding the congressmen of the importance of protecting these national shrines from fire. Only weeks earlier there had been a fire in a building on the north side of Chestnut Street, directly across from Independence Hall. Every piece of fire apparatus in the city had been called out, and it had been necessary to turn on the sprinkler system that protected the Hall. The safety of the historic sites demanded the removal of what Lewis viewed as a collection of deteriorating structures nearby.

The subcommittee accepted Lewis's testimony with enthusiasm. The members had nothing but praise for the inspirational force of the report and its subject. Several asserted that it should be printed and distributed to every school in the country. After this reception, the remainder of the testimony could only be anticlimactic. Others from Philadelphia spoke briefly in favor of the bill. Drury reviewed the National Park Service's proposed amendments, stressing those that were noncontroversial, such as the change of name and the provisions for cooperative agreements. The subcommittee's only question concerned operating costs, about which Drury could not be specific.

A few days after the hearing, Hardie Scott wrote to Lewis, telling him that there was a good chance that the subcommittee would include all five areas in the bill. However, its members would like to hold an additional hearing in Philadelphia. Scott suggested that the Philadelphians entertain them at lunch. Lewis adopted the idea with enthusiasm, and orchestrated, as he had in the past and would in the future, a congressional trip to Philadelphia. On a fine spring morning, members of the subcommittee and their wives, along with several National Park Service representatives, were met at Thirtieth Street Station by a welcoming committee of prominent Philadelphians. After checking in at the Bellevue-Stratford Hotel, the party moved to the Union League Club for a luncheon with the Colonial Society of Philadelphia. (The wives lunched below stairs in the women's dining room.) A tour followed lunch. Each of the congressmen must have had a personal guide, for the group was joined by McAneny, Greenfield, Hopkinson, Martin, Larson, Simon, McCosker, Ostroff, and others. The visitors saw the areas and buildings encompassed in the proposed park, had their pictures taken at the Liberty Bell, and visited Society Hill for a reception at a private house on South Fourth Street. The day ended with a dinner at the Barclay Hotel, where Mayor Samuel and Hopkinson, among others, made brief addresses. Several of the congressmen had never been to Philadelphia before and appeared to be impressed by what they were seeing. Chairman Richard J. Welch of the full House committee was unable to make the trip. Three weeks later, on April 10, Welch and his wife came to Philadelphia at Judge Lewis's invitation. In the course of his visit he told the press that the subcommittee had recommended approval of all the proposed areas with the exception of Project B, the section south of Walnut Street. After his tour, he thought that it too should be included.

On April 21 the full House Committee on Public Lands met to consider the subcommittee's recommendation to approve H.R. 5053, as amended, with elimination of Project B. Chairman Welch immediately reiterated his belief that the area should be included: Although Projects B and E bordered several churches, no federal funds would be spent to acquire property belonging to a sectarian organization. A question was raised on Franklin Court, since it was not certain that anything remained of Franklin's house or print shop. However, the committee agreed that the site should be included because of its importance to Philadelphians. A committee member then brought up Project D, the site of the Graff House, where Jefferson had composed the Declaration of Independence. Despite its illustrious associations, the site was now "nothing but a cheap modern hamburger stand," and there had been no indication of plans to develop it. The committee appeared to be in sympathy with this view. At this juncture Lewis recalled turning to solicit Hopkinson's opinion. In a whispered exchange, the two agreed that it would be wise to settle for 80 percent of what they wanted. In terms of land area they were, in fact, getting more than 90 percent of what they had proposed. Without further debate, the committee proceeded to a unanimous vote recommending passage of the National Park Service's version of the bill, but restoring Projects B and E and dropping Project D, with an authorization of $4,435,000 for property acquisition.

Before the bill went to the full House of Representatives, the National Park Service managed to effect two changes. Project B, south of Walnut Street, was reduced in size so that it ended on Manning Street north of St. Mary's Cemetery, thus eliminating the discontinuous section that ran south to Pine Street. The Jayne Building, probably at Charles Peterson's behest, was added to the list of buildings to be preserved. Although there was every indication that the bill would pass easily, Lewis continued to lobby. He wooed the legislators on their own ground. He entertained congressmen, sometimes over a hundred at a time, at a series of dinners and luncheons at the Congressional Hotel, explaining the proposed park and its importance to the country.

The House passed the bill on June 14, 1948, and the Senate approved a companion bill, S. 2080, on June 18, 1948. President Truman signed it as Public Law 795 on June 28, 1948. The park project now existed on paper, but without funding. The law demanded the acquisition of considerable property before the project could become a park. Any activity toward that end, however, would depend on appropriations made by the next Congress. While the federal government's timetable thus remained uncertain, the Commonwealth of Pennsylvania moved ahead on Independence Mall, north of Independence Hall. Early in 1949, the Public Works Committee of the Philadelphia City Council held hearings on an agreement between the city and the state to establish the mall. The move was opposed once again by Morris Passon, who had represented local businessmen before the Shrines Commission. Passon characterized the plans as "grandiose" and warned that appropriations by the state were uncertain. Another local businessman, Louis

Herbach, suggested that the money might be better spent on cleaning up the city's rivers and slums. He objected on aesthetic grounds as well. In his opinion "Independence Hall would look like a peanut in a two-block vista." The weight of opinion was against the businessmen. Lewis pointed out that every state legislator favored the project, and that Rear Admiral Milo F. Draemel, Pennsylvania secretary of forests and waters, who had been given responsibility for its execution, had assured him that funds were already available. Albert Greenfield assured the committee that the mall would boost the city's tax revenues. Rep. Hardie Scott expressed fears that failure to act would be seen in Washington as bad faith on the part of the city.

Although it was not stated at the hearing, the most persuasive argument for the development was its potential for encouraging large businesses to remain in the city. Three major companies, employing 15,000 people, were contemplating moves to the suburbs because of the continuing deterioration of the area. If the city would commit itself to civic improvement, as represented by the mall, these businesses might be persuaded to participate in redeveloping the neighborhood. (Two of them, Rohm and Haas Company and General Accident Insurance Company of America, did in fact remain.) The committee recommended execution of the pact, and City Council passed an ordinance to that effect on January 18, 1949.

While the state and city were working out the details of their agreement, Congress was wrestling with an appropriation to initiate the federal project. A suggestion for an appropriation of $3 million was quickly whittled down. The Department of the Interior was satisfied with the $500,000 that was finally appropriated. It was all that they expected to be able to use in the next fiscal year. Furthermore, the House and Senate conference committee had worked out a compromise. Although the park service would receive only $500,000 for the fiscal year 1950, the conference recommended that they be authorized to contract for almost $4 million worth of acquisitions.

The bill authorizing the park called for an advisory commission, representing the city, the state, the federal government, and important private organizations interested in the project. The National Park Service, which had worked successfully with such commissions in the past, believed that such a body would "integrate and give effectiveness to the best thought of the city, State and Federal Government in carrying into execution a program." With funding secured, the secretary of the interior moved in June to make appointments to the commission. He chose, as the bill required, eleven members, three selected by himself, three recommended by the governor of Pennsylvania, three by the mayor of Philadelphia, and one each by the Carpenters' Company of Philadelphia and the Independence Hall Association. Among the governor's nominees were Judge Lewis, the banker A. G. B. Steele, and Arthur C. Kaufmann, executive director of Gimbel Brothers department store. The mayoral appointees were Thomas Buckley, Edward Hopkinson, Jr., and Albert Greenfield. John P. Hallahan represented the Carpenters' Company, and Sydney E. Martin the Independence Hall Association. The secretary's own appointments were Sen. Francis J. Myers, Joseph Sill Clark, Jr., then director of the Citizens' Council on City Planning and later reform mayor of Philadelphia and U.S. senator, and Michael J. Bradley, collector of customs, who had, as a representative, introduced one of the bills to study the park.

Meanwhile the state mall moved ahead steadily. In May 1949 Governor Duff and Mayor Samuel signed an agreement laying out the respective roles of city and state. The city would widen Fifth and Sixth Streets; the state would develop the land between them. By November Admiral Draemel announced the beginning of negotiations to purchase thirty-seven properties in the block opposite Independence Hall from Chestnut to Market at an estimated cost of a little under $3 million.

The National Park Service was also preparing to get its land acquisition under way. The project's office opened in Philadelphia on October 1, 1949, with a small staff to handle property transactions, plus two seasoned National Park Service professionals, Charles E. Peterson and Dr. Edward M. Riley. As was customary, the men in charge of property acquisition, Joseph M. O'Brien and Melford O. Anderson, were not long-term park service employees. No matter how good the intentions, land acquisition always was (and is) a potentially controversial practice. Appraisals would be questioned; some owners would be unwilling to sell, and condemnation would be necessary. The National Park Service generally held that the eventual managers of a new park would be more effective if they were free of the taint of involvement in real estate negotiations that were sure to produce some lingering ill-will.

O'Brien, the project manager, had obvious qualifications for the post. He had spent over a quarter of a century in real estate in Philadelphia, specializing in appraisals, management, and sales. He was also well connected politically. A Democrat, he had served for eleven years in the state legislature. The assistant project manager, Anderson, had spent fifteen years in land management for the federal government. During World War II he served with the War Relocation Authority, dealing with housing, employment, and other problems of Americans of Japanese descent who had been involuntarily evacuated to the Rocky Mountains. After the war he transferred to the Public Housing Administration in Chicago, handling the disposal of surplus wartime housing. He had long been a close friend of Undersecretary of the Interior Oscar L. Chapman, who recommended him for the Philadelphia post.

The National Park Service assigned two of its top professionals to Independence. Both had worked at Colonial National Historical Park in Yorktown, Virginia. It was there, in the early 1930s, that Peterson had introduced a methodology for analyzing the fabric of historic buildings and reporting the findings in the form of a historic structures report. Subsequently he had supervised most of the National Park Service's restoration work. He was already quite familiar with Philadelphia and Independence because of his several visits in 1947. Riley, a native of Mississippi brought up in Virginia, had been historian at Colonial both before and after World War II. Accustomed to digging hard for historical evidence in Virginia, he was both awed and delighted by the wealth of documentation available in Philadelphia. "I felt something like a mouse in a cheese factory," he recalled. "I didn't know where to start nibbling."

The new staff, with the exception of Peterson, attended the first meeting of the Independence National Historical Park Advisory Commission on November 29, 1949. In many ways it resembled the meetings of the Shrines Commission. Judge Lewis presided as chairman, and a number of the members were carryovers. Several of the guests had met frequently with the Shrines Commission: the architects Roy Larson and Grant Simon, the city planner Edmund Bacon, and Dr. William Lingelbach. The group gathered not at the project offices, but at the Rittenhouse Club, Lewis's turf. It was a sizable gathering of over forty people. Nine members of the commission attended. Undersecretary Chapman headed a delegation from Washington that included National Park Service Director Drury; Conrad Wirth, then assistant director; Thomas C. Vint, chief of planning; Ronald Lee, the chief historian; and Herbert Kahler, assistant chief historian. Thomas J. Allen, the agency's regional director, was also present, as was Francis J. Ronalds, who, as superintendent of Morristown National Historical Park in New Jersey, had been assigned oversight responsibilities for the new project. There was also a group from the city, led by City Solicitor Frank F. Truscott. Despite the presence of so much high-powered talent, most of the meeting was taken up with a review of the arrangements necessary before the park could be established.

It was only as the meeting drew to a close that a new and important subject was broached. Larson, speaking as the chairman of the city's Art Jury, proposed that the City Planning Commission undertake a study of the areas surrounding the park. He wished to see these "fringes" rezoned to ensure that they would be architecturally compatible with the park's development. It was an idea that immediately appealed to Lee, who not only was one of the strongest proponents of the National Park Service's historic preservation activities, but had recently played a key role in the foundation of a new organization, the National Trust for Historic Preservation. Lee was in close communication with preservation groups around the country. He recommended that Philadelphia study the pioneering preservation ordinances of Charleston, South Carolina, and New Orleans. It would, however, be a number of years before the city took action to preserve areas adjacent to the park.

The meetings of the Advisory Commission were set at six-month intervals. In theory it seemed unlikely that a group that met so infrequently could exercise much power over decision making at Independence. In practice Lewis utilized his position as chairman to wield tremendous influence over

12. An early visitor to the fledgling park project was Horace M. Albright (center in dark suit), former director of the National Park Service. With him are (from left) Francis Ronalds, superintendent at Morristown National Historical Park; Melford O. Anderson, then assistant project manager; Joseph M. O'Brien, project manager; Dr. Edward M. Riley, historian; and Charles E. Peterson, resident architect. Behind the group to the left is the railing at the rear of the Second Bank of the United States. To the right is John's Tailor Shop, one of the disputed early buildings that was demolished to make way for the park.

the park's development. From the beginning the project staff conferred with Lewis about all significant planning activities on a regular and frequent basis.

The project's top priority for its first year was to begin fulfilling the legislative mandate for land acquisition and consummation of cooperative agreements. By the summer of 1950, agreements had been signed with the City of Philadelphia, the Carpenter's Company, and the vestry of Christ Church. Early in 1950 the park project contracted with the Land Title Bank and Trust Company and the Commonwealth Title Company of Philadelphia for title searches on 123 separate properties. By the end of the year, options had been taken on fifteen properties. Two properties—one part of the street leading into Franklin Court from Chestnut Street and the other near Carpenters' Hall—had been offered for donation. The former was being given by the city, the latter by the Fairmount Park Art Association.

While O'Brien and Anderson dealt with property negotiations, Riley and Peterson were laying the groundwork for the necessary research in their respective fields. Riley's first task was to become familiar with the many public and private repositories where documents might be found: the city and state archives, institutions such as the American Philosophical Society, the city's long-established fire insurance companies, and the title insurance companies. He found helpful guides among the park's early supporters. Lewis knew where many of the relevant public records were and used his influence to make them readily accessible. The state historian, S. K. Stevens, with his thorough knowledge of the state's holdings, suggested numerous shortcuts through the maze of the Pennsylvania archives. Riley's chief mentor, however, was Dr. William Lingelbach of the American Philosophical Society. Lingelbach was, in many ways, the *eminence grise* of the early research program at Independence. He was one of the handful of people to whom Lewis assigned a share of credit for the creation of the park. Roy Appleman had depended heavily on his guidance during his 1947 sojourn in Philadelphia. Lingelbach knew not only the holdings of his own institution, but also those of the city's other repositories.

One of the first objects of research at Independence was to establish historic ownership patterns. During his first year in Philadelphia, Riley prepared preliminary chains-of-title for all properties in Project B and determined the boundaries of property owned by Benjamin Franklin in Project C. However, the demands of research for a historical area as large and complex as Independence would obviously go far beyond the background of properties and buildings. It might well be beyond the resources of the National Park Service to carry out the multifaceted research that should be done. Riley saw a possible solution in encouraging graduate students to work on subjects relevant to Independence. His idea appealed to Dr. Roy F. Nichols, an early member of the Independence Hall Association and professor of history and dean at the University of Pennsylvania. They set up a cooperative program to accomplish the purpose.

While Riley was familiarizing himself with Philadelphia's libraries and record centers, and tracing chains-of-title, Peterson was also engaged in research. Since he believed that the understanding of an educated public was essential if important buildings were to be preserved and restored, he hastened to get the preliminary results of his work into print. Peterson seems to have set his own priorities. He first turned his attention to two mid-nineteenth-century buildings that had attracted him during his 1947 visits to Philadelphia. His brief article on the Jayne Building appeared in the October 1950 issue of the *Journal of the Society of Architectural Historians;* an article on the cast-iron Penn Mutual Life Insurance Building was in the December 1950 issue of the same publication. Peterson next dealt with the other buildings enumerated in Public Law 795, publishing an essay identifying them and describing some of the planning problems associated with the park in the July 1950 issue of the *American-German Review.* During the year he explored Philadelphia's pictorial resources and collected reproductions of views, photographs, and measured drawings of historic buildings in the projected park, especially those on Independence Square. By year's end he had also completed research on Library Hall, which the American Philosophical Society remained interested in reconstructing.

Peterson's responsibilities, however, went far beyond research, to include physical planning and architectural design. He made studies of the Second Bank of the United States (Old Custom House), to which the American Philosophical Society had proposed moving its library. Adaptation of the building to this use was impractical, he found; the library simply could not be fitted in. As the time when the National Park Service would assume administrative and interpretive control of Independence Square grew closer, Peterson worked on preliminary plans for adapting the first floor of the United States Fidelity and Guaranty Company's building on Fifth Street as a temporary auditorium and offices, and on designing restrooms for the basement of the west wing of Independence Hall. He also conferred with representatives of the Garden Clubs of America, who had assembled a collection of magnolia trees, one from each of the forty-eight states, for possible donation to the park. This would be the first major gift to Independence from an outside group. But it was at Area B, between Walnut and Manning Streets, that Peterson's ideas of what the park should be were most clearly revealed. He drew up a preliminary site plan showing eleven houses to be rehabilitated for use as staff quarters. Clearly Peterson viewed Independence as incorporating preservation on a scale far greater than specified in the authorizing legislation. His view went beyond the restoration of a handful of historic buildings to preservation of the historic ambience of the entire area and the integration of the National Park Service's project with the existing neighborhood.

At the end of the first full year of operation, major changes in the management of Independence became essential. The land acquisition program was well under way; research had begun. On January 1, 1951, the project staff would assume responsibility for several historic properties: the city's buildings on Independence Square, the Second Bank, and the Deshler-Morris House in Germantown. In 1948 the National Park Service had learned that this last property was being offered as a donation to the federal government by its last private owners, the heirs of Marriott C. Morris. It was a gift that the park service, severely pressed for funds, was reluctant to accept. George Washington had rented the house as a summer residence twice during the 1790s. Fiske Kimball considered it a fine example of a Germantown roadside house. Nevertheless, as Roy Appleman suggested, there was already a superabundance of memorials to Washington. Francis Ronalds, who, although he was at Morristown, also then had administrative responsibility for the National Park Service's holdings in Philadelphia, recommended that it become a part of Independence, provided that a cooperative agreement could be negotiated under which the Germantown Historical Society would maintain and operate the house. When Congress amended the 1949 Interior appropriations bill to include a sum for maintenance of the property, the park service had no choice. It accepted the property and negotiated an agreement along the lines laid out by Ronalds. This enabled the park service to use the appropriated money for needed repairs to the property, which the society would then maintain and operate.

Caring for these properties and interpreting them to the public would require a considerably larger operation in Philadelphia. The added responsibility would also necessitate augmentation of the slender professional staff and reorganization of the project office. It was not practical for the project manager, who had been selected for his skill in real estate negotiation, to supervise the necessary professional and administrative personnel. Independence had reached the stage at which an acting superintendent should be designated. Assistant Project Manager Anderson was named to the post on November 15, 1950. It was a surprising appointment. Just as it was customary that personnel carrying out land acquisition were not National Park Service career people, it was usual, by this period, for superintendents to come up through the ranks. Several candidates within the park service had been considered, including Peterson. Arthur E. Demaray, then associate director, while later discussing a number of appointments and promotions with George A. Palmer, then superintendent at Hyde Park, said that he had appointed Anderson at the request of Secretary of the Interior Chapman.

Although he was not a National Park Service career man and was not always entirely familiar with policies and procedures, Anderson had certain qualifications for the job. With a square-jawed, ruddy face, a shock of prematurely white hair, and the trim, erect bearing of a former athlete, he looked like a leader. Despite an innate reserve, he had a pleasant, appealing voice and low-keyed manner. He was reasonable and willing to listen but firm in upholding decisions. Most importantly, he got along well with Judge Lewis.

On New Year's Eve, at the stroke of midnight, a group of men climbed the tower of Independence Hall and rang the tower bell to welcome the start of 1951 and the 175th year of the Declaration of Independence. The group called themselves the Independence Hall Bell Ringers Association. Among their number were Anderson, Riley, and Warren McCullough, formerly the city's curator of Independence Hall and now, as a park service employee, in charge of maintenance and protection. The Centennial Bell pealing over Independence Square was the first official event under the management of the National Park Service.

On Tuesday, January 2, 1951, at eleven o'clock in the morning, a simple ceremony marked the transfer of custody of Independence Hall from the city of Philadelphia to the National Park Service. About 150 guests, including representatives of local patriotic and civic organizations and the National Park Service, gathered in Congress Hall. With Judge Lewis as master of ceremonies, Mayor Samuel made a presentation speech, which was accepted by Secretary of the Interior Chapman. Morris Duane, a prominent Philadelphia attorney, made an address on behalf of the citizens of the city. The group then adjourned to Independence Hall, where, in front of the Liberty Bell, Samuel turned over a key to the building to Chapman. After a century and a quarter of stewardship, Philadelphia was relinquishing custody of Independence Square and its buildings. Subject to the terms of the cooperative agreement, the National Park Service was now in control.

Four
The First Wars of Independence

Although after January 1951 the National Park Service was in charge on Independence Square, not much difference was perceptible. The same former city employees, now on the federal payroll, opened Independence Hall to visitors. There was little change in the buildings or their grounds, or in the surrounding neighborhood. The major activities—land acquisition, the search for additional funding, and planning—remained invisible to the public. As the acquisition program proceeded, the National Park Service became aware that the legislation authorizing the Independence project provided neither sufficient authority nor sufficient funds. Two bills passed in 1951 and 1952 provided partial remedies. The first permitted the staff to deposit in a special account money derived from rentals of acquired properties. These funds could then be used for operating the properties or for the demolition or removal of buildings. The measure was logical and demanded no expenditure of government funds; it passed easily.

The second bill was more complex and more controversial. As originally introduced, it had three major provisions. First, it allowed the American Philosophical Society to construct a library of approved design, at its own expense, on park land on the site of Library Hall. Second, the bill called for acquisition of a lot on South Fifth Street in Area B; the Irwin Building at the corner of Walnut and Fourth Streets; and the site of the Graff House at Market and Seventh Streets. Finally, the bill almost doubled the previously authorized appropriation to $9,857,000.

The first proposal met with no opposition. The Philosophical Society's reconstruction of Library Hall would be a great asset to the park at no cost to the government. The acquisitions were another matter. Congress had refused two of them before. Eventually a compromise was reached. Congress passed the bill, raising the authorization to $7,700,000, but included only acquisition of the Fourth and Fifth Street properties.

During the legislative maneuvering Judge Lewis once again assumed his role as chief lobbyist. Conrad Wirth, director of the National Park Service from 1952 to 1964, who prided himself on his own skills in dealing with Congress and the administration, was quick to recognize another master of the art. According to Wirth the two soon achieved an unwritten arrangement. Each kept the other informed of his activities and contacts. When testimony before Congress was needed, Lewis would come to Washington. Wirth believed that Lewis "had the stature they liked." Thus, Lewis's standing with Congress translated rapidly into considerable influence with the National Park Service.

Meanwhile Riley was beginning to organize the project's research program. In January 1951 two new historians squeezed into the cramped project offices in the rear of the Second Bank. One of them, Martin I. Yoelson, would remain at Independence until his retirement over thirty years later, becoming the historical conscience of the park, its quality control. He had received a bachelor's degree in social science from the City College of New York during World War II and a master's degree from Temple University after service in the army. His ambition was to be a high school history teacher. But teaching jobs were scarce, and he took a Civil Service examination. Despite his lack of experience in historical research and writing, he was selected from the Civil Service list for appointment at Independence.

A month after Yoelson's arrival, two more professionals joined Riley's staff. Both were experienced National Park Service employees: Dennis Kurjack, a historian from Hopewell Village National Historical Site, and James Mulcahy, a museum specialist from the Washington office. By the end of the year, however, the main energy of the historians was diverted from research to more immediate needs—preparation of a historic handbook and the interpretive section of a master plan.

The master plan concept was one of which the National Park Service was justifiably proud. Since the late 1920s, long before cities and towns in the United States were engaged in comprehensive land use planning, the park service had begun looking at each of its entities in this light. The master plan appears to have been the invention of Thomas C. Vint, then head of the Office of Design and Construction in San Francisco. Although the plans were subject to review by the park superintendent and staff, Vint's design office, the Washington directorate, and, after their establishment, the regional offices, the master plan was the responsibility of the resident landscape architect at major parks.

At Independence, therefore, Charles Peterson was in charge of the process. Peterson, however, was reluctant to commit his ideas to paper. Aware that he and Judge Lewis disagreed fundamentally on what the park should be, he was afraid to give Lewis a target to shoot at. Lewis's views were represented by the drawings submitted with the Shrines Commission's report. Peterson articulated his own design philosophy at the annual meeting of the Fairmount Park Art Association on January 23, 1952. Rather than the stiff axes of the Shrines Commission's plans, Peterson advocated an informal layout, "balanced, but not symmetrical." He hoped to retain the old streets, lanes, and courts and to restore at least a suggestion of the historic contours, especially in the area of Dock Creek. He urged retention of at least fifteen houses a century or more old to reinforce the urban character of the area, while at the same time setting off the more monumental structures. Pointing out that it would be extremely destructive to "freeze" the historic area as it was in any one period, he urged the preservation of important buildings constructed as late as 1850.

Shortly before making his address, at the continued urging of then Director Demaray, Peterson prepared a sketch plan of Area A, the main section of the park, organized on the principle of maintaining the system of city blocks rather than creating a new mall. The pattern of old streets, lanes, and courts would remain or be restored. At least nine old buildings not specifically identified in the legislation would be preserved. These, plus new garages and an office building, would mark the corners where major streets intersected and define street lines. Although the plan thus proposed a considerable amount of new construction as an adjunct to the retained buildings, there would still be ample greenery. All the streets would be planted with trees, as would small courtyards and gardens between and behind many of the buildings. A modest mall on a north-south axis would lead from Walnut Street to the rear of the Second Bank. In the next block a vista would open to the east of Fourth Street, revealing a broad lawn through which the course of Dock Creek would be modeled in the surface of the earth.

Master Planning, 1952–54

By 1952 the lack of concrete proposals for a master plan was becoming disturbing. At a July meeting in Richmond, Acting Regional Director E. M. Lisle stressed to Anderson and Riley the importance of formulating policies on which the master plan would be based. The group agreed that the development had four main objectives: restoration of structures and sites mandated by legislation; reconstruction of certain historic buildings; preservation and rehabilitation of other buildings, including those of the mid-nineteenth century; preservation or construction of other buildings and landscape features to interpret the area's urban character. Because it would not be feasible to operate so many house museums, most of the buildings would have to be used for other purposes.

At this juncture in the master planning process, Peterson's viewpoint, as illustrated by the last two objectives, had prevailed. Furthermore, responsibility for drafting the master plan remained with Peterson as resident architect at Independence. This was more than a paper exercise. What was decided in the process would determine whether numerous individual structures within the park's boundaries would stand or be demolished. By the time a major master plan conference was scheduled in February 1953, much of the discussion centered on the fate of particular buildings.

The largest and most conspicuous of these were two mid-nineteenth-century structures, the Jayne and Penn Mutual Buildings, located in the block bounded by Chestnut, Third, American, and Dock Streets. Peterson had

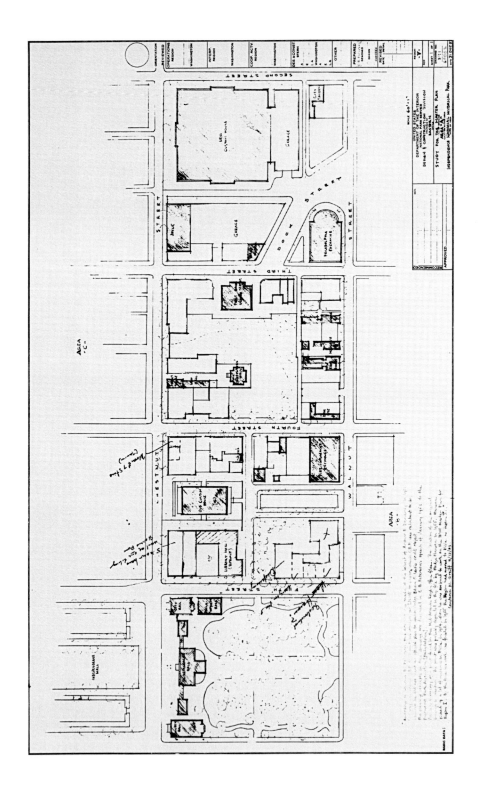

lobbied successfully in the Washington office to have the first of these incorporated in the list of buildings to be preserved in the legislation authorizing the Independence project. Subsequently he published brief articles about the significance of both buildings. At every opportunity he escorted visiting architects and architectural historians to see them. In a report that may have been prepared to accompany the sketch plan for Demaray, he suggested potential architectural treatments and uses for the buildings.

By 1952 several additional eighteenth- and early nineteenth-century buildings had been identified, most through visual observation and title research; others had been brought to the attention of the staff at Independence by Philadelphia antiquarians and the buildings' owners. The fate of most of these buildings was on the table at a major master plan conference held at Independence on February 5 and 6, 1953. Such full-dress debates were a vital component of the master plan process. Every step in the procedure was intended to permit the airing of opposing views and resolution of conflicts. The process was highly democratic, up to a point; once a consensus was reached, the dissenters were expected to maintain silence.

Edward Riley prepared for the February master plan conference by summarizing his thoughts in a long, confidential letter to Herbert Kahler, assistant chief historian. He welcomed the forthcoming conference because it seemed to him that "the planning is being done by individuals working alone, each in his own sphere, without much interchange of ideas." Riley listed four major viewpoints on park development (with the comment that Peterson's unknown ideas might constitute a fifth scheme), categorizing them as "Raze and Reforest," "Dream of the Shrine Commission," "Living Museum of Philadelphia Architecture," and "Tool for Interpretation." The first two were closely akin, calling for extensive demolition and an open landscaped park. The difference was that the Grant Simon plan, which to Riley represented the second view, retained the street lines along Walnut and Chestnut Streets by rebuilding or reconstructing "suitable houses." The third alternative seems to have been an exaggeration of Peterson's position. Riley believed that it was favored by the city as a model demonstrating how attractive a rejuvenated neighborhood could be, and that it would not constitute a national historical park, but rather a city improvement plan.

It was the fourth alternative that Riley favored. He visualized restoration of the historic buildings that were significant in the period from 1774 to 1800 and the reconstruction of selected period buildings to provide a stage setting as a proper ambience for the historic structures. The atmosphere would further be enhanced by landscaping, brick sidewalks, and period street lights,

81

pumps, watch boxes, and other items of street furniture. Above all, he wished to communicate the ideas behind the park, rather than display its buildings as architectural specimens.

The participants in the February planning conference were a who's who of the National Park Service in 1953. A large contingent arrived from Washington, headed by Director Conrad L. Wirth. Wirth, son of a nationally known park planner and administrator, had trained and practiced as a landscape architect. He joined the National Park Service as assistant director in charge of the Branch of Land Planning in 1931. During the 1930s he had supervised Civilian Conservation Corps work in the national and state parks. Although he had made his mark through his administrative talents and his skill in dealing with Congress, he retained an interest in park planning. Among those accompanying Wirth were two men on whose advice he relied: Ronald F. Lee, then holding the title of chief of Interpretation, and Thomas C. Vint, chief of the Office of Design and Construction. Members of the regional staff and the Independence staff were also present, as were three outside architects, including Grant Simon.

The issues were not fully resolved. The group reached a consensus that the general theme of development for Independence would be the conditions that existed and the events that occurred in the period from 1774 to 1800. The statement was so broad, however, that continuing debate on how this was to be achieved was inevitable. Attention then turned to those individual buildings that had come to the fore during the previous year. The Kidd and McIlvaine Houses on Walnut Street were elevated to protected status, although the architectural treatment of the street was reserved for further study. The more thorny question of the Jayne and Penn Mutual Buildings defied a swift resolution. To maintain harmony, Wirth employed a device that had stood the National Park Service in good stead in the past: the appointment of a temporary advisory committee to study the significance of the two buildings. He named Dr. Turpin C. Bannister, a distinguished and respected architect and architectural historian and dean of the School of Architecture at Alabama Polytechnic Institute, as chairman. The committee of three would also include Grant Simon, representing the Independence advisory commission, and, at the recommendation of the AIA, Milton Grigg of Charlottesville, Virginia.

The National Park Service staff was directed to devote further study to the Walnut Street buildings and other buildings on Chestnut and Fourth Streets. The staff would also study the feasibility of reconstructing Norris's Row at the corner of Chestnut and Fifth Streets. Most of the situations too complicated for resolution concerned Area A, the "main park." Proposals for other areas were more easily approved, at least in principle.

The three-man committee studying the Jayne and Penn Mutual Buildings met in Philadelphia on April 19, 1953. A month later Bannister, in his capacity as chairman, submitted the committee's report to Wirth. Prefacing the report by enunciating the premise that American culture did not stop at any fixed point, Bannister told Wirth that the committee had agreed unanimously that the Penn Mutual and Jayne Buildings were very significant, citing the reasons for their finding. Finally, dealing with an issue on which the committee had not been asked to comment, he recommended their preservation. Wirth responded, accepting the recommendation.

It soon became apparent that the device of appointing an outside committee to defuse controversy over the two buildings had not succeeded. Bannister's report proved to be only the opening salvo in a battle that would continue for three years. The first retort came from Grant Simon. Probably speaking for Judge Lewis as well, Simon submitted a minority report differing in almost every respect from the views expressed in Bannister's communication. Simon not only denigrated the importance of the buildings; he also held that if allowed to remain, they would be inharmonious with the park's design and confusing to visitors making a pilgrimage to sacred sites. In addition he claimed that their preservation would be costly.

Although the last official word from the National Park Service was still Wirth's response to Bannister, Wirth then let it be known internally that his final determination in the matter would be contingent on further study. Furthermore, the opponents of preservation had found a strong supporter in Superintendent Anderson. In January 1954 the Society of Architectural Historians would hold its annual national meeting in Philadelphia. In personal meetings and a fairly stiff letter, Anderson forbade Peterson to seek support for the buildings from those attending the meeting. It would be up to Wirth, he told Peterson, to make a decision and then solicit support for it. In the light of subsequent events, it seems unlikely that Anderson's gag order had much effect.

Meanwhile, Peterson was preparing to defend two older buildings within Area A: New Hall and the Front Store, along the west side of Carpenters' Court. Since both had been altered, it would require more intensive documentary research and examination of the physical fabric of the buildings to determine how much original work had survived. Peterson assigned the study to a young architectural student from the University of Pennsylvania, James C. Massey, who was working at the park for the summer.

The Carpenters' Court study was not yet complete when the first draft of the master plan began to take final form in early 1954. The drawings for the plan were prepared not by Peterson's office, but by a team from the office of the park service's Region I in Richmond. By this time Peterson's reluctance to produce drawings had become apparent. To break the logjam, Vint ordered the assistant regional director, Edward Zimmer, to prepare the plans. From this time forward Zimmer would be in charge of master planning for Independence.

Preliminary drawings were reviewed at conferences at Independence on

February 23–25 and March 15–16 and submitted as recommended by the superintendent on March 25, 1954. The most detailed drawing in the set dealt with how the park should be developed for interpretive purposes. Since the main focus of interest, Independence Hall, was located at the western end of the park, the master plan called for a reception center at the eastern end. This would encourage visitors to see other buildings in the park first, reserving Independence Hall as the climax. The drawing thus shows the reception center at a reconstructed City Tavern, where visitors would be provided with background information on Independence, and a museum in the Merchants' Exchange, where an orientation program would be available. From there visitors could choose one of several walking tours leading them past the historic buildings and sites. Fifteen interpretive stations were planned, although it was not clear whether all were to be staffed. It was an ambitious, if not particularly imaginative, scheme. It was also somewhat unrealistic. Operating funds for the entire National Park Service for fiscal year 1955 were under $20 million. It was highly unlikely that Independence could, in the foreseeable future, employ enough ranger-historians to mount and operate so grandiose a program.

In contrast, the plans for physical development were relatively modest. Carpenters' Hall stood in lonely splendor, with no buildings flanking its court. On Walnut Street between Third and Fourth Streets, there were only four houses, with gardens between them. There was ample greenery around the City Tavern, and a parking lot on the oddly shaped site where the Jayne and Penn Mutual Buildings stood. Trees in thick profusion were the chief landscape feature. A great rectangle of lawn was placed at the rear of the Second Bank.

The February and March conferences were by no means the last opportunity for comment on the proposed master plan. Through the spring of 1954, as the drawings circulated through the various offices of the National Park Service, numerous opinions were aired. Peterson reiterated that the Jayne and Penn Mutual Buildings, as well as New Hall and the Front Store, should be preserved. Anderson transmitted Peterson's memo to the regional director, at the same time making his contrary opinion clear. By now he was concurring with Simon's view that the buildings were incompatible with the future park.

Anderson's views found a sympathetic ear in the regional office. They conformed to what had been the prevailing National Park Service attitude toward historic sites since the 1930s. Such sites were worth preserving not, primarily, because of any aesthetic merit, but because of their commemorative and didactic value. The chief purpose in displaying them to the public was to teach a lesson about the events that had taken place at the site, or interpret the broad themes in American history they exemplified. To do this they should be accurately restored. If they were aesthetically pleasing, so much the better, but this was only the icing on the cake of historical significance.

While the internal debates about the master plan went forward, external pressures began to be felt at Independence. As demolition proceeded in the block between Third and Fourth Streets and restoration plans for the surviving buildings matured, a number of proposals for new uses within the park surfaced. Indeed, outside forces would influence the development of Independence more directly in the next few years than would the yet to be completed master plan. One of the first to approach the park was Isidor Ostroff, with a scheme for reconstructing Mikveh Israel Synagogue. The Company of Military Historians expressed interest in establishing a military museum, and the Pennsylvania Horticultural Society also wished to locate within the park. Clearly a policy on tenancy would be required.

Developments within the National Park Service would also have an impact on the planning for Independence. By 1954 Conrad Wirth had been the director of the park service for two years and was beginning to formulate plans to mobilize the agency for a dramatic reversal of the lingering postwar austerity under which it had been operating. One step he took was a reorganization creating additional regional offices. Design and construction activities, then centralized in Washington, would be split between two offices, one in the west and one in the east. The latter, the Eastern Office of Design and Construction (EODC), would be accommodated, along with the new Region V offices, somewhere within the park. EODC was established in Philadelphia by July 1954 and assumed primary responsibility for master planning. Peterson shifted from his position as resident architect at Independence to the new office. He would hold the title of supervising architect, historic structures, with oversight of all park service restoration projects in the east.

In the meantime, although the question of use or participation in construction by outsiders had not been resolved, discussion of the master plan went forward. By mid-May of 1954, the drawings and narrative had been fleshed out with preliminary Project Construction Proposals (PCPs). The architectural data had been prepared under Peterson's direction in his last months on the Independence staff; estimates for the landscaping came from the regional office. The grand total for landscape features and buildings shown on the master plan drawings came to approximately $6.7 million. The modesty of this sum can now only be judged in light of the estimates for rehabilitation of buildings at $.80 per square foot and for full-scale restoration at $2.00 per square foot, figures approximately 1 percent of what they would be today.

With submission of the preliminary PCPs, the master planning process of 1954 was ready for final review. Wirth approved most of the drawings on May 21. He did not, however, approve the introduction, because it appeared to allow for the possibility of too much reconstruction, rehabilitation, and construction. Obviously Wirth now favored the Shrines Commission concept

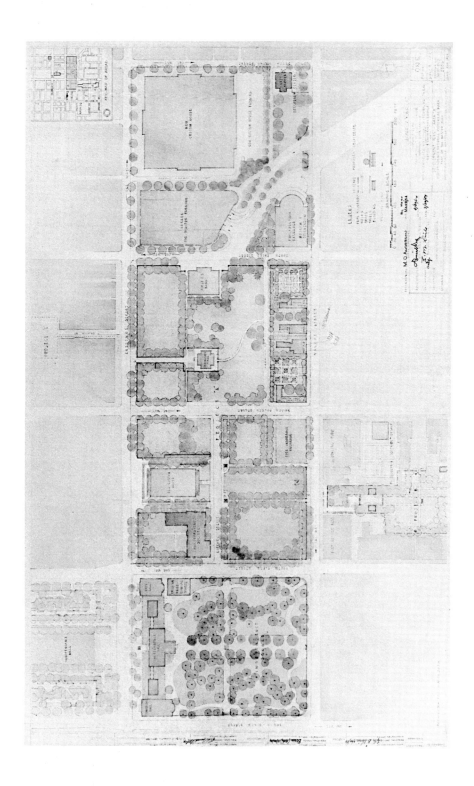

14. This preliminary drawing for the master plan of 1954 (#NHP-IND 2006) adopted the concept of using the internal street pattern, although trees are shown in the middle of Dock Street. Relatively few buildings are depicted, although by this time it had been determined that four houses on Walnut Street would be preserved, with formal gardens between them. Much of the park is still conceived as a series of rectilinear lawns, although the area behind Carpenters' Hall is treated more informally. A parking garage for visitors is proposed at the corner of Chestnut and Third Streets.

of a cleared area with a few historic buildings rather than the retention of an urban fabric advocated by Peterson. Nevertheless, he made it clear that numerous questions remained. Stressing that the plans were still general, he deferred any decision on the Jayne and Penn Mutual Buildings and on Carpenters' Court. The determination of appropriate usage was still troublesome. Noting that space must be found for a headquarters for the park, as well as for the regional office and for EODC, he recommended further study of whether a visitor center should be located in a new parking structure or in the Merchants' Exchange. The frequency of requests from organizations for space at Independence was, in fact, the primary reason he gave for disapproval of the introduction. The language might make it impossible to refuse applications from organizations that applied to reconstruct buildings of the appropriate period, resulting in additions that might compromise the significance of the area. A tenancy policy was needed that would restrict organizations to occupancy of buildings that were being preserved for the proper interpretation of the park.

A revision was proposed quickly. A new introduction set forth a development philosophy considerably more restrictive temporally and interpretively than the original draft. The purpose of the park would be to interpret the story of the struggle for independence and the establishment and development of the United States from 1774 to 1800. Only buildings and landscape features necessary and appropriate for this interpretation, and for the public use and administration of the park, would be included. There was no mention of the preservation of old structures or construction of new ones that would identify Independence as a park in the midst of a city. The identity of the park as one that would commemorate events had been set, although the last argument over the issue had not yet been heard.

Park staff also made an attempt to define the conditions under which outside organizations might occupy park facilities. Anderson submitted a memorandum in July, which started with a list of twenty-two organizations that had already demonstrated interest or might be expected to have some interest in locations within the park. Most of these would be ineligible under the new policy, which would allow occupancy only to those institutions whose history and purposes related directly to the period from 1774 to 1800.

The revised draft of the section stating the general theme of development and the recommended occupancy policy represented a hardening of attitude toward buildings that were not within the strict time frame chosen for   **87** interpretation or that had only a peripheral relationship to events of the revolutionary or federal periods. Had the early nineteenth-century Kidd and McIlvaine Houses not already been approved for preservation, it is uncertain that they would have passed muster under the stated standards. If the policy were to be adopted, any rationale for preserving the Jayne and Penn Mutual Buildings, or even the earlier Front Store at Carpenter's Court, would certainly be discredited. Other buildings beginning to attract the attention of architects and architectural historians would receive even shorter shrift. This was certainly the case with Frank Furness's Guarantee Trust (Tradesmen's Bank), on Chestnut Street along the east side of Carpenters' Court. Its preservation was supported by some of the younger members of the staff, but their opinions were not solicited and would not have been heeded.

Through the fall of 1954, the National Park Service continued to wrestle with the problem of utilization of the buildings at Independence. Assistant Director Thomas Allen wanted to know just what the plans were for fourteen buildings—three in Area A and eleven in Area B—designated as staff quarters. Wirth finally responded to Anderson's July memorandum in October. He too questioned the use of historic buildings, especially in Area A, as employees' quarters. Most of his comments, however, were directed to the use of park properties by outside organizations. The Washington office was far more sympathetic to the concept of such use than the park staff. Funding from outside groups could be extremely helpful in developing and maintaining the park. Wirth was also loath to disturb established relationships, such as that with the Carl Schurz Foundation, which had helped to restore the Second Bank and had maintained it for a number of years. On the other hand, he made it clear that the planning function for the park and for individual projects must remain under park service control and not be delegated to the potential tenants.

These ideas were incorporated in the tenancy policy that was finally approved early in 1955. Organizations occupying buildings within the park would be those specified by law, such as the Carpenters' Company, or those founded before 1800, or those whose primary purpose was to commemorate the events of 1774–1800. No organization could construct a historical or memorial building of its own design; its assistance (presumably financial) in reconstruction could be considered, but only for buildings called for by the master plan and designed by the National Park Service. Further, organizations would have to demonstrate financial stability and competence to exhibit their buildings to the public in a manner to be determined by the park service. Over the years the policy on park service control over planning and design would be maintained; the policy on what organizations might occupy the buildings would be applied more flexibly, as it suited the park administration's needs and wishes.

With the new year the cast of players at Independence was augmented by the arrival of the personnel of the new Region V of the National Park Service, which encompassed the entire northeast. Daniel Tobin, a former assistant regional director in Richmond, came to Philadelphia as director. His assistant was George A. Palmer. Palmer, like Ronald Lee and Herbert Kahler, was one of the young University of Minnesota historians who had joined the National Park Service in the 1930s. He had served as superintendent at the Statue of Liberty and as the first superintendent of Hyde Park, Franklin Roosevelt's home, before assuming his post in Philadelphia. He would remain as the assistant regional director for almost two decades, a participant in and keen observer of planning and development at Independence.

The head of EODC was Edward Zimmer, known to his colleagues as "the Baron." Zimmer, a landscape architect, had entered the park service at Yorktown, Virginia, in 1931, hired by Charles Peterson, whose boss he had now become. Although he usually remained somewhat aloof from the production of drawings, he retained a lively interest in design details. There was always a roll of yellow tracing paper handy in his desk drawer. This would be pulled out whenever Zimmer disagreed with some aspect of a drawing, so that he could communicate his own ideas in the form of rapid sketches, traced over the offending original. According to the table of organization, Peterson, as supervising architect, historic structures, was supposed to report to John "Bill" Cabot, chief architect. It was an arrangement that Peterson never fully accepted. In practice Peterson could always go directly to Zimmer or to Thomas Vint, or even to Director Wirth. Relationships among the "old boys" who had been in the park service since the 1920s and 1930s were close. These men shared a knowledge of one another's strengths and weaknesses. They also had common memories of the idealism and optimism of the era of the New Deal when, as the park service expanded rapidly, their group of relatively young men was given enormous responsibilities. Zimmer never forgot that it was Peterson who had hired him. Vint, who had given Peterson his first park service job, continued to regard him as a protégé. Wirth had also known Peterson since the thirties and respected his opinions, even when he disagreed with them. Thus, although the reorganization technically reduced Peterson's role in the master planning process, his continued advocacy of saving more buildings than were slated for preservation would still receive consideration at the highest level.

Through much of 1955, planning activity centered on revision of proposals for Area A, the "east mall." The revised master plan, issued in draft form in July, showed office facilities at the Second Bank, with proposed offices for the park, region, and EODC at the Merchants' Exchange, where they would share space with a visitor center. The Walnut Street houses were identified as "excellent landscape elements," harmonizing well with the historic buildings. The revised drawing for Area A showed a parking garage on the site occupied by the Jayne and Penn Mutual Buildings. There were fewer trees around the buildings, and a proposed grove in Dock Street had disappeared.

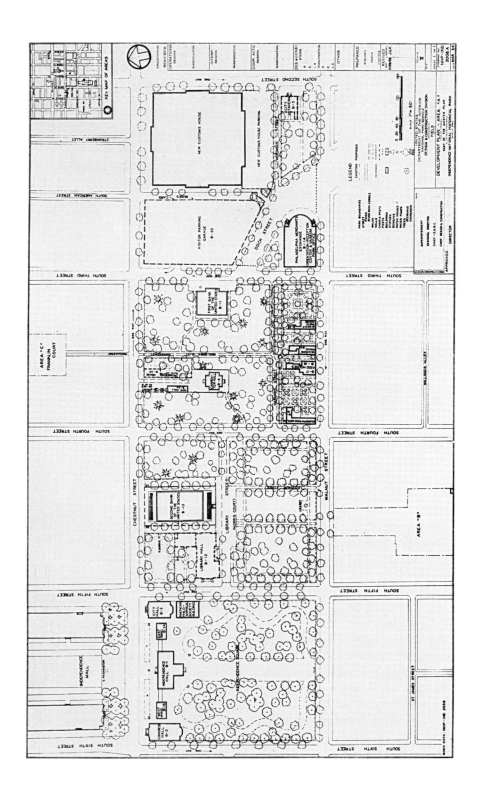

15. As modified after conferences, the master plan of 1954 (#NHP-IND 2006A) went further in recreating the historic street pattern by removing trees from Dock Street and restoring Whalebone Alley. Carpenters' Court was also to be reconstituted by preservation of New Hall and the erection of walls marking the sites of the Fawcitt and Pemberton Houses. The rectilinearity of the entire scheme has been softened by a veritable forest of trees.

Up to this point master planning had been a paper exercise. There was not even enough money to accomplish the demolition that had been universally agreed to, much less restore old buildings or construct new ones. Most of the available funds came from rents from buildings already acquired by the park service, but still occupied by tenants. Although Congress had appropriated money for acquisition and small amounts for operations, it had provided no funds for development. This sorry financial situation was not unique to Independence. The National Park Service as a whole was not receiving enough funding to maintain the park system, much less develop new areas. In 1940 the park service had available annually, including Civilian Conservation Corps funds, $33,577,000. Wartime cutbacks drastically reduced these funds, to a low of $4,740,000 in 1945. Gradually funds were restored, but by 1955, with twenty more areas to administer and trebled visitation, the total annual appropriation for the National Park Service was only $32,525,000. Although this was only $1 million less than in 1940, it was actually a substantial reduction because of wartime and postwar inflation. Furthermore, in 1940, after eight years of intensive activity largely paid for by Depression-era work relief programs, the parks had been in excellent condition. By 1955 they were in a shabby, perhaps even dangerous, state.

Wirth, a planner and a builder, found the situation frustrating. He remembered the accomplishments of the 1930s, when he was in charge of dispensing the emergency relief funds that had fueled the development of the national parks, and many state parks as well, into a first-rate system. Now much of the work had been undone by time and neglect. Early in 1955 Wirth conceived an ambitious remedy, a bold, long-term program to bring the entire park system up to a standard of excellence. In early February Wirth presented his idea to his branch chiefs, who received it with enthusiasm. Special committees were established to plan the program. The title chosen for the effort was intended to both rivet the attention and to summarize the purpose. "Mission 66" referred to the park service's expression of its mission through the program and defined the ten-year span needed to complete it. The National Park Service would celebrate its golden anniversary in 1966, a suitable occasion to mark with completion of a revivified park system. As Wirth had hoped, Mission 66 captured the imagination and support of both the Eisenhower administration and Congress. Over the ten-year period, National Park Service operating funds increased 200 percent, while capital improvement funds increased 136 percent.

91

Planning for Mission 66, 1955–56

In November 1955 Regional Director Tobin explained the Mission 66 program to the park's advisory commission. Judge Lewis was indignant. Philadelphians, he protested, had no intention of waiting ten years for the completion of the Independence project. He also complained about the slow pace of demolition. Lewis suggested, and the commission agreed, that the commissioners should go directly to Congress for special funding outside the normal budgeting process. Lewis and some other members of the commission also took the occasion to condemn proposals to save or reconstruct buildings that were being made in the course of the master planning process. John P. Hallahan, the Carpenters' Company representative, objected to the suggested rebuilding of the Pemberton and Fawcitt Houses on either side of the Chestnut Street entrance to Carpenters' Court. He cited the old fear of fire hazards as a reason for total clearance of the area. Dennis Kurjack supported Hallahan's point of view, saying that the houses had no historical significance. At the end of the meeting, Lewis expressed his concern about the basic concepts for park development. He was perturbed by the efforts of a certain group of architects and "architectural interests" to espouse preservation of the Jayne and Penn Mutual Buildings, the Guarantee Trust, and other structures unrelated to the historical focal period of the park. Lewis maintained that retention of these buildings would be directly contrary to the purposes expressed in the Shrines Commission's report and to the act of Congress authorizing development of the park. The meeting concluded with Lewis requesting Grant Simon, who was acting as an unpaid architectural consultant to the commission, to prepare a report and draft a resolution. The resolution put the commission on record as holding that the park area should include only such existing or reconstructed structures as were present before 1800 and possessed "adequate" historical or political significance connected with the colonial or federal period.

Although the fate of several of the buildings at Independence had been debated for almost eight years, it was simple to defer decisions as long as there were no funds available. Independence would receive only a small share of the money appropriated for Mission 66 in the program's first few years because repair of some of the older parks had a higher priority. Nevertheless, the certainty that funds would soon begin to flow to Independence meant that the issues would have to be resolved. Accordingly, early in 1956 Anderson suggested some solutions based on the adopted tenancy policy and the advisory commission's resolution. Unhesitatingly he first tackled the largest issue, the question of the Penn Mutual and Jayne buildings. For the former he recommended demolition to make way for a parking area or garage. The adjoining buildings were slated for demolition in June, and it would be more economical to clear the entire group at once. On the Jayne Building Anderson's opinion was less definite. Its Chestnut Street location would, he believed, be a good one for regional and EODC offices. These could be obtained either by retaining the building's facade, with sufficient depth to provide the office space, and somehow incorporating this section into a parking garage, or by constructing a new building usable for both purposes. Anderson expressed a preference for the latter course. A new building, he believed, would be more harmonious; in his eyes the Jayne Building would always constitute an intrusion.

Anderson was particularly anxious to commit the regional offices and EODC to the Jayne Building site because he hoped that the Merchants' Exchange would be devoted entirely to use by the park, with a visitor center, museum, and auditorium on the first floor, and offices on the second and part of the third floors. While avoiding the issue of Carpenters' Court, he dealt with potential tenants for the buildings on Walnut Street. Reluctantly he included the Carl Schurz Foundation, although he still maintained that its "tenuous association" with the basic park story raised doubts as to whether it should be housed permanently within the park. He also approved of the Horticultural Society of Pennsylvania, which had joined forces with the Pennsylvania Society for the Promotion of Agriculture in applying for space at Independence. Because the latter group could date its founding to before the magic date of 1800, it passed muster under the tenancy policy and could carry the younger organization as well.

In June 1956 Regional Director Tobin recommended demolition of the Penn Mutual Building to Wirth. After considering the request for almost two months, Wirth approved it. As it became evident that not only the Penn Mutual Building, but also the other significant nineteenth-century buildings in the park would be slated for demolition, well-known architects and architectural historians around the country rallied to their defense with a campaign of letters addressed to Judge Lewis. Lewis answered all the letters punctiliously, but without yielding an inch. A reply to the architect Philip Johnson was typical. Describing the buildings as out of character with the older buildings that were to be preserved, and unassociated with the history of colonial and federal Philadelphia, he also cited costs and lack of potential uses. Lewis's letters were couched in the courteous language of a southern gentleman, but privately he fumed. He permitted his anger to show in a letter to Anderson accompanying copies of his correspondence. The letter also revealed to what extent his opposition to preservation of the buildings was caused not by his feelings about their historicity, but by his personal taste and antipathy to Victorian design:

> Somebody is stirring up letters from uninformed people. It is amazing how easy it is to get people to write letters advocating something, the eventual consequences of which they do not comprehend. If the idea of these art teachers had prevailed many years ago, the City of New York would still be a glorified small town, and even the Frank Furness buildings would never

have been constructed in Philadelphia, the latter of which would have been a great piece of good luck for the City.

Anderson, who had been quick to chide Peterson for expressing opinions to outsiders, found no fault with the judge's actions. He liked and respected Lewis, and probably also somewhat feared him because of his influence with Congress and the National Park Service directorate in Washington. Besides, Anderson shared the judge's opinion about the disposition of the buildings and his belief that the campaign to save them was being orchestrated. There is little doubt that Anderson and Lewis held Peterson responsible.

Anderson also provided Lewis with estimates of the costs for various treatments of the Jayne and Penn Mutual Buildings. These were prepared by Charles Grossman, who had succeeded Peterson as resident architect at Independence. Demolition would cost $132,600; fireproof reconstruction would require $3,543,800, almost half the sum that had been authorized for the entire acquisition and development program at Independence; annual maintenance would be $290,250. With these figures in hand, Anderson wrote to the regional director in late November 1956, requesting a decision on the Jayne Building. The Penn Mutual Building was already down. By January 1, 1957, the remaining leases on spaces in the Jayne Building and the buildings adjacent to it would expire, and the premises would be vacated. Anderson wanted to proceed with the demolition program for the block; again he justified his request for a swift decision by arguing that it would be more economical to issue a single demolition contract. He reiterated his opinion that the site was the most suitable location for offices for the region and EODC and that these could best be accommodated in new construction combining offices with a garage for visitors. Nevertheless, the decision on the Jayne Building was not made in haste. Wirth was not as rigid as Judge Lewis or Anderson in his adherence to an arbitrary cut-off date of 1800. He was willing to consider the importance and quality of later buildings, and was not deaf to their advocates within the National Park Service or to the opinions of respected architects and historians outside it. Nevertheless, he probably shared the view of the majority of park service professionals, backed by the popular opinion of the era, that the buildings were neither historically significant nor aesthetically appealing. For Wirth, however, other factors were perhaps more telling. One was economics. The National Park Service had never before faced the problems of preserving so many structures that would not serve as historic museums. The tenancy policy at Independence had demonstrated Wirth's relatively flexible view of the adaptive use and occupancy of park buildings by outside nonprofit institutions. He was prepared to stretch the instrument of the cooperative agreement to the fullest extent in the interest of obtaining financial assistance for maintenance, and even for restoration or reconstruction. There was no mechanism, however, for selling or leasing buildings such as the Jayne complex to private entrepreneurs in order to ensure their preservation. Even had such an option existed, it is unlikely that Wirth would have exercised it, because the pressure to demolish was so strong.

Certainly Judge Lewis refused to tolerate further delay. In early March 1957 he wrote to Anderson, congratulating him on the progress of demolition, and urging speed in completing the program. His conclusion expressed his impatience to see the Jayne Building down and a not very veiled threat to go to Congress and administration figures if action was not taken soon. Anderson again requested a final determination. Wirth finally approved the demolition in early April.

The decisions on the Jayne and Penn Mutual Buildings were made during a virtual hiatus in formal master planning, while the energies of the park and the regional staffs were devoted to producing the Mission 66 prospectus. This document was, in a sense, an interim substitute for a master plan, containing most of the same elements, but without accompanying drawings. It would serve to guide development until a full-scale master plan could be produced. The introduction noted that the essential purpose of Independence was commemorative, celebrating the events that had occurred between 1774 and 1800, as well as "the economic, political and cultural growth of the new nation." The management and development statement reiterated in slightly different language the substance of the same section of the revised master plan of early 1955, confirming its hardened attitudes toward the design of the park and the retention of buildings.

Nevertheless, the prospectus allowed considerable latitude for new construction. Although overnight accommodations and meals for visitors were expected to be provided by private enterprise in the surrounding city, numerous facilities would be available within the park, including a garage, new offices for EODC and Region V, and a visitors' reception area at the Jayne–Penn Mutual site, closely related to the main visitor center in the Merchants' Exchange. That building would house an auditorium, library, portrait gallery, and museum, as well as the park offices. There would be a special children's reception center and museum in the reconstructed City Tavern. There would also be a subsidiary reception center on Independence Square, as well as auxiliary park offices in the wing buildings of Independence Hall. The first priority for development was continued demolition and landscaping.

Since its initial authorization Independence had received little attention from the national press. By 1956, however, demolition and planning had proceeded far enough that the ultimate shape of the development was beginning to be visible. Between November 1956 and April 1957, a series of articles by the well-known architectural critic Lewis Mumford appeared in the *New Yorker*. The four articles, subtitled "Historic Philadelphia," covered several aspects of the city's redevelopment but concentrated on the area around Independence Square. Concerned almost entirely with design issues,

Mumford scarcely dealt with the interpretive questions that loomed so large for the National Park Service. He found much to criticize and some things to praise. Because he believed that preservation was often an excuse to impede sound new development, he supported the demolition of the Jayne and Penn Mutual Buildings and even of Furness's Guarantee Trust, which he admired somewhat more.

His chief concerns, however, were with the settings for the remaining buildings and with issues of restoration, reconstruction, and new design. The state's project for the north mall struck Mumford as overbearing, its grand Baroque axial scheme at war with the Georgian buildings on Independence Square. What he admired in Georgian architecture was its air of domesticity and intimacy, with which the state's mall was at odds. Mumford could only hope that the National Park Service's part of the project, east of Independence Square, would be carried out with greater sensitivity. He suggested that Carpenters' Hall, which he characterized as "gawky," would look even more awkward at the terminus of another great axis running east from the square.

Mumford also attacked the National Park Service's fundamental planning concept, which had been designed to attract visitors to the eastern end of the federal area. He thought that the projected tours would exhaust visitors, causing them to approach Independence Hall with aching head and tired feet. He opposed the proposed reconstructions of Library Hall, City Tavern, and buildings around Carpenters' Court, which he believed would be counterfeits debasing the genuine old buildings. Instead he recommended construction in a modern idiom.

Mumford's articles caused consternation in Philadelphia. Judge Lewis used them as a springboard for a proposal to raise private funds to employ architects to provide a suggested landscape design for the park. Lewis was motivated less by Mumford's criticism than by a desire to get the planning over with and construction under way. Wirth, whose pride must have been considerably piqued by the suggestion, assured Lewis that the National Park Service staff was entirely capable of producing the park's design. He reminded Lewis that although detailed drawings had not been completed, the basic concept of the master plan, which the advisory commission had already seen, remained unchanged.

Master Planning and Decision Making, 1957–60

By 1957 new master plan drawings were being circulated internally. The key drawing, covering Areas A and B, had been approved by Zimmer on May 31. It was probably just as well that Mumford had not seen this design, which was almost as formal and axial as the state's mall. The most prominent feature was a broad promenade running west to east, terminating in the curve of Dock Street. Other landscape features also tended to be rectilinear, including gardens along Walnut and Chestnut Streets. West of Third Street was a T-shaped water feature, in the approximate historical location of Dock Creek. Some relief from the prevailing angularity was provided by the proposed restoration of an informal treatment of Independence Square, based on reconstruction of its 1787 landscape.

The plan elicited strong objections from the park staff. Dennis Kurjack, the park's chief historian, serving as acting superintendent in Anderson's absence, protested to Tobin that the plan violated historical values. The staff proposed an alternative that eliminated the central walkway and what was described as the "lagoon." Opposition to a revised version of the plan was aired more fully during a park development conference at Jackson Lake Lodge in mid-September. Tobin and Palmer from Region V, and Anderson and Supervising Historian Murray Nelligan from the park, took the opportunity to present their views to the Washington directorate. Consensus was reached on a number of points. The central walkway would not be constructed. In its stead the historic streets in Area A would be preserved and developed. There would be no lagoon; the branches of Dock Creek would be suggested by contouring. Landscape treatment around individual buildings would relate to their historic appearance.

Despite this apparent agreement, the revised drawing submitted for review in mid-October still contained many of the offending features, plus some new ones. In a blistering memorandum to Wirth, Anderson outlined the plan's sins of commission and omission. In the first place, although the lagoon was gone and the rectilinear garden at the corner of Chestnut and Fifth Streets had been replaced by a less formal one reminiscent of the eighteenth-century appearance of Independence Square, the central walkway remained, along with an entrance structure at its east end and perpendicular walks leading to the rear of Carpenters' Hall. A corollary to the removal of the walkway had been the restoration of the historic street pattern as the basic pedestrian circulation system. The streets as shown on the plan were, however, considerably narrower than they had been in the historic period. The memorandum also raised questions about specific details of the design of walls and plantings, especially those adjacent to the historic buildings. By November a new plan had been prepared encompassing most of the changes requested by the park. Although many details of the landscaping remained vague, Wirth was able to exhibit the major drawing to the advisory commission.

Wirth approved the drawings in late November, but they were quickly subject to modification. At a master plan conference in mid-April 1958, Wirth accepted Anderson's recommendation that the Merchants' Exchange, instead of being adapted as a visitor center, be rehabilitated as offices for the region and EODC. The visitor center would be housed in new construction at the eastern end of the park. A revised plan for Walnut Street was also discussed. Architects' reports on the Todd and Bishop White Houses had noted poten-

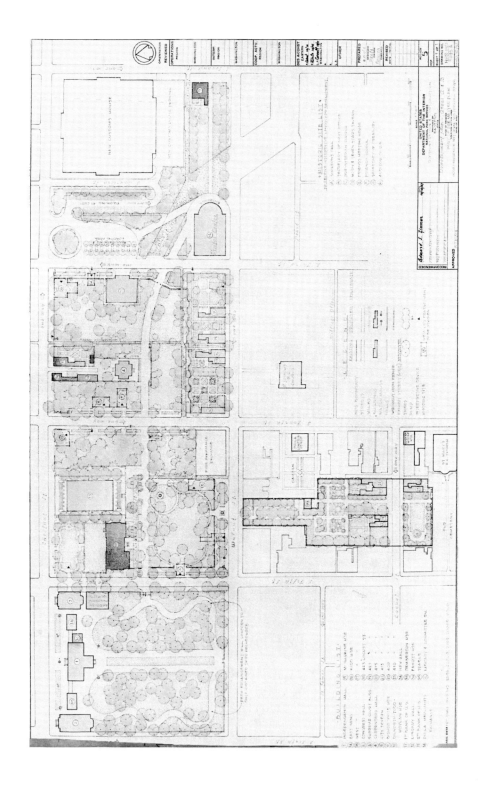

tial structural problems if the houses were restored in isolation. The new proposal was to reconstruct one or two houses east of the Todd House, and to remove the top two stories of the five-story Yoh Building between the Bishop White and McIlvaine Houses; its facade would then be rebuilt on the pattern of the early nineteenth-century buildings that had occupied its site.

While the internal debate on the master plan continued, growing dissatisfaction with the pace of progress at Independence was becoming evident. After almost a decade many buildings had been removed, but some still stood, with parking lots and patches of new grass between them. In the advisory commission's opinion, another decade for completion of the park under Mission 66 was too long to wait; in any case, they had little liking for a program in which other parks had a higher priority than Independence. They had long favored sponsoring a bill that would authorize an additional $7,250,000 appropriation exclusively for Independence. Furthermore, the commission and Mayor Richardson Dilworth were disturbed by indications that the National Park Service had not requested more than $500,000 for development work at Independence in the 1958 fiscal year. As the fiscal year drew to a close in June 1957, the mayor began to exert increasing pressure. He had already wrung a commitment for $1,500,000 for the following fiscal year from the Congress. Before leaving for a vacation, he took Anderson to task for not having expended the $500,000 already available. Anderson hastened to assure him that much of the money had been held in reserve for the first major landscaping project, and that a contract in the sum of $270,000 had just been let.

At the same time, Lewis was adding his importunities to those of the mayor, and in somewhat less diplomatic language. His complaints covered not only the slow pace of the work, but other issues as well. He wanted the demolition completed and renovation under way, parking removed, and Independence Hall floodlit. Lewis now had more time than before to devote to oversight of the park's progress. On his retirement from the bench late in 1957, he had requested and been allocated space within the park. The judge was now ensconced in a pleasant office at the rear of a not-yet-demolished building at 135 South Fifth Street. Here he joined the park's historians, who had been shifted from the overcrowded Second Bank.

Complaints from the mayor and the judge coincided with another major master planning conference at the park from June 4 through 6, 1958. Newly **99**

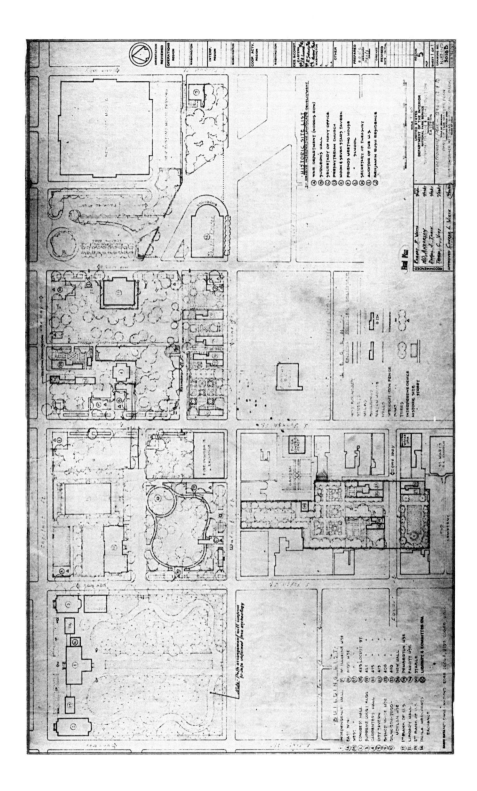

17. The plan (#NHP-IND 3018B, August 26, 1957), as accepted by Director Conrad Wirth on November 24, 1957, removed the center walkway, returning to use of the historic streets at their original width for pedestrian circulation. The dating of the drawing is deceptive. Evidently prepared on an earlier base drawing, this was introduced after, and in response to criticism of, Drawing 3018A (see Figure 16). Although this plan was adopted, changes were made within a few months. The Merchants' Exchange, shown here as a Visitor Center, was chosen as the site for regional offices; a decision was also made to reconstruct additional houses between the four historic houses on Walnut Street.

introduced legislation, plus several issues recently decided by Director Wirth, required reconsideration of the master plan and proposed course of development. Sen. Joseph Clark was sponsoring a bill that would add land to the park for visitor parking east of Second Street. Wirth had now determined that the Merchants' Exchange would be devoted entirely to office use, so that a new location would have to be found for a visitor center. Its site was the subject of a lengthy discussion. Considering that the interpretive program had focused from the beginning on a visitor center at the eastern end of the park, it is surprising that so many participants argued that selection of a location was premature. However, mindful of Wirth's request for swift action, the group eventually settled on a recommendation of the block bounded by Dock, American, Third, and Chestnut Streets, the former site of the Jayne and Penn Mutual buildings. The site had been considered for new construction to house offices for Region V and EODC and a garage when the plan called for rehabilitation of the Merchants' Exchange as the visitor center. In effect, the functions were switched.

The master plan drawings that evolved in 1957 and 1958 would shape the development of Areas A and B through the years of most intensive construction. A basic design philosophy was finally in place. It was a compromise solution that undoubtedly failed to satisfy anyone completely but aroused little opposition on major principles. The opponents of a grand axial scheme had won. The park was organized on a series of broken axes, with open spaces of varying scale setting off the individual monuments. Numerous references to eighteenth-century Philadelphia had been maintained or restored, including the street pattern and a hint of the topography of Dock Creek. Peterson's concept of maintaining or recreating an urban fabric had never received serious consideration from National Park Service management. Yet the historic buildings were not as isolated as they would have been had the advisory commission's wishes been followed. The proposed reconstruction of buildings on either side of Carpenters' Court would partially recreate the sequestered situation of Carpenters' Hall, and the retention or reconstruction, for whatever reason, of the rowhouses on Walnut Street would preserve an urban streetscape on the block between Third and Fourth Streets. Low walls and plantings of ivy would mark the sites of vanished buildings of the historic period. Higher walls and fencing would define the street lines in other areas.

Criticism about the pace of progress at Independence continued. Lack   **101** of funds was no longer an acceptable excuse. With the help of intensive lobbying by the mayor and Lewis, a bill authorizing the expenditure of up to $7,250,000 for development at Independence had been passed in August; the bill also raised the ceiling on acquisition to $7,950,000. The cost of Independence had thus more than trebled since its original authorization. By the fall of 1958, Lewis was once again complaining to Wirth about lagging development and the absence of an approved master plan. Wirth responded that master planning was well advanced and that only details remained to be worked out. He sent an up-to-date set of drawings to Lewis and the mayor.

However, by the end of 1958 objections to park planning began to be heard from other quarters in city government. In contrast to earlier demands for increased speed in the removal of existing buildings, the City Planning Commission protested the demolition of several houses in Marshall's Court to provide a site for a maintenance building. Edmund Bacon wrote to Anderson asking the National Park Service to reconsider its decision, which had been made before the city had formulated its plans for the redevelopment of Society Hill and its newly formed Historical Commission had certified the buildings. Anderson refused to budge. He recited the reasons given previously for the decision to demolish: the park service did not agree that the buildings had historical associations or architectural interest; they were not in a suitable location for staff housing; the site was needed for the maintenance facility. A carbon of Anderson's reply went to Lewis. Although Anderson always held that he maintained close contact with the city administration through the advisory commission, the episode left the impression that to Anderson liaison meant soliciting Lewis's opinion. Officials of the planning commission would be listened to when their views coincided with those of the judge, and could be ignored when they did not.

Lewis agreed with a protest by the City of Philadelphia Art Commission in late October 1958 about the reconstruction of buildings around Carpenters' Court. The commission, chaired by Roy Larson, particularly objected to the reconstruction of New Hall, feeling that it obstructed the view of Carpenters' Hall and that a low wall or some other means of marking the site would have been more appropriate. They also deplored the quality of the work. The modern methods of construction employed would be obvious to anyone familiar with genuine antique buildings. Harking back to Lewis Mumford, and indeed to the National Park Service's longstanding opposition to reconstruction, the commission pointed out that history was not well served by dubious recreations. The Philadelphia ordinance by which Independence Square had been turned over to the National Park Service required mutual consultation on development, the commission observed, requesting the opportunity to view plans as they were developed.

Lewis also disliked New Hall, although for somewhat different reasons. Reconstruction of buildings interfered with his vision of an open park just as much as retention of existing structures. He feared that the precedent of

New Hall would open the way for other reconstructions and, as usual, expressed his views firmly to Wirth. While Wirth was attempting to placate Lewis, Anderson was arranging a conciliatory meeting with the art commission and other representatives of the city. Anderson reviewed the history of the Independence project and pointed out that the National Park Service's decisions were not only the result of extensive internal review, but were undertaken after consultation with the official advisory commission. He also expressed the opinion that the requirement for mutual approval of plans applied only to Independence Square and its city-owned buildings. The commission, however, continued to seek definition of its legal responsibility to review park plans. In rereading the cooperative agreement between the city and the National Park Service, Anderson found that Article III called for the two "to develop a unified long range program of preservation, development, protection, and interpretation for the whole of Independence National Historical Park." This clause could form the basis for participation by the art commission. He asked the regional office for legal advice and policy guidance.

Tobin believed that legal advice would merely give the matter an importance it did not deserve. Nevertheless, he forwarded Anderson's request for assistance to Wirth. Wirth was furious. Anderson, he believed, had virtually invited the participation of the art commission in the development of Independence. This was one of two or three incidents in which Wirth believed Anderson to have acted before proper consultation with the regional office or Washington. Such activity embarrassed the National Park Service which then might be perceived as not presenting a united front. Furthermore, Anderson should have remembered that the advisory commission was the official consultative body and that its members' opinions should be solicited about dealings with the art commission. Now, however, there seemed to be no alternative but to confer with the latter.

Wirth's anger may have been exacerbated by the continuing criticism being directed at him and at the National Park Service as a whole. He had already had to fend off Lewis's suggestion that the advisory commission assume responsibility for planning the park, in addition to unjustified complaints about lack of consultation with that body. He was probably already aware that Lewis and Dilworth had arranged to come to Washington for a meeting with Secretary of the Interior Fred A. Seaton to discuss the park's progress or lack of it. The mayor had already won agreement for an increase in the 1959 appropriation for Independence, from $632,100 to $1,500,000.

The Philadelphians met with Seaton and Wirth on April 8, 1959. Dilworth took the occasion to loose a blast in the press, claiming that after seven years of restoration work by the National Park Service, Independence looked like a blitzed area. He complained that Philadelphia was losing the benefits of tourism because of the condition of the park. Seaton assured him that steps would be taken to expedite the project.

One of the first steps was a meeting later in the month, attended not only by Wirth, but also by Assistant Secretary of the Interior Roger Ernst, National Park Service personnel, members of the advisory commission, and representatives of the city government. Wirth stressed that the two basic reasons for the slow pace of development were lack of funds and the tremendous amount of research needed because of the importance of the sites. Ernst made a number of concessions, promising to establish a mechanism through which the advisory commission and the city could comment on the design and treatment of buildings within the park. Details would await a meeting of the advisory commission scheduled for the following month.

The advisory commission convened on May 25, 1959. Wirth opened the meeting by recommending more frequent meetings for the advisory commission. These should not depend on his presence, since planning had now advanced to the stage where he believed most issues could be resolved among the commission, the regional director, and the park superintendent. The National Park Service had adopted procedures to keep commission members better informed. As a symbol of the new procedures, he presented each member with a copy of the recently completed Independence Hall Historic Structures Report (Part I), which was a preliminary study of the historical background. A proposed reconstruction of the Pemberton House on the east side of Carpenters' Court was also explained. Wirth told the commission that the park service had fully documented the past appearance of the house; its reconstruction would complete restoration of the historic appearance of Carpenters' Court. Besides, based on the commission's previous approval of the concept, Wirth had already begun to raise funds to reconstruct the house as a United States Navy museum. The objections that had already been raised in the case of New Hall were raised again, but since the commission had, in fact, approved the concept there, it would be embarrassing to reject it summarily in this case. The commission appointed a committee to study the matter and eventually approved reconstruction not only of the Pemberton House, but of the neighboring Fawcitt House as well. Although the issues of the Pemberton House were identical to those raised by New Hall, the report of its own committee was accepted by the advisory commission without demurral. Indeed, the fight over New Hall had probably been not so much about design issues or reconstruction philosophy as about the power to make decisions. In agreeing to refer the question to the committee, the National Park Service had soothed the advisory commission, at least for the time being.

Wirth announced another step that would help to stem the growing controversy over the power of the art commission or other city agencies to review design. The art commission had continued to protest against what its members considered Anderson's high-handed attitude, appealing to Pennsylvania's Senators. Since it was Anderson who had tried to conciliate the commission, this was unjustified. However, relationships with local groups probably had suffered because of his personality. Although pleasant and soft-spoken, he remained aloof. He joined no organizations and indulged in minimal consultation with the city, regarding the advisory commission as his official liaison. What defused the situation, without fulfilling the art commission's demands, was appointment of a special seven-man architectural review committee, composed of six architects with experience in historic preservation and one historian. Its establishment appeared to satisfy the demands of the art commission for outside professional review.

In forming the committee, however, the park service was responding less to complaints about its design decisions than to protests against proposed methods of handling the restoration of the buildings on Independence Square. The battles of the mid-1950s had been about whether buildings would remain standing. Those of the end of the decade centered on restoration and reconstruction. National Park Service policy since the 1930s had held that it was better to preserve than to restore, and better to restore than to reconstruct. But there was no firm statement on how this would be accomplished. The art commission's complaint about the quality of the reconstruction at New Hall had been a signal that the park service's handling of these issues could be questioned. A far more serious disagreement arose over the triad of historic shrines on Independence Square: Independence Hall, Congress Hall, and Old City Hall.

As it could be foreseen that large amounts of money would begin to flow to Independence in 1959 and 1960, planning went forward for the long-sought restoration of the key buildings. Almost immediately it became apparent that the structural integrity of all three was doubtful. Considerable reinforcement would undoubtedly be necessary, but to what extent was unknown. Responsibility for determining the need fell to John Cabot, supervising architect in EODC. The choice of Cabot reflected a continuing dichotomy in that office. Thomas Wistar, Jr., who reported to Charles Peterson, was in charge of the restoration work at Congress Hall. Restoration, however, evidently was sometimes interpreted by management, although not by the restoration architects, as a matter of cosmetics. Peterson's crew could see to the replication of accurate detailing where an authentic restoration was called for, but might not even be consulted when, for example, houses on Locust Street were rehabilitated as staff quarters. This was a restoration philosophy that saw only the skin of the building as historic. The bones and muscles beneath were necessary to keep the building standing, but were not valued in their own right.

Cabot retained the George M. Ewing Company, a highly respected structural engineering firm, to study the buildings on Independence Square in the fall of 1958. Their report was submitted in March 1959. On the basis of limited probing, they found that the condition of all three buildings was poor, with Congress Hall in the worst state. Their recommended remedy was tantamount to total reconstruction. The buildings would be supported on new skeletons of steel and reinforced concrete. The interiors would be gutted and then rebuilt with floors of concrete and steel and plaster partitions on steel studs, over which the old ornament and trim would then be fitted. Finally, the buildings would be crowned with tile cast to replicate wood shingles, laid on concrete roof plank supported by steel trusses.

To many this appeared to be a reasonable solution. It was similar to the "restoration" of the White House that had been carried out in 1950–51. Others, however, inside and outside the National Park Service, believed that this was not the way to treat the buildings on Independence Square. In their opinion the fabric of the buildings was itself of historical importance, reflecting the knowledge and attitudes of the eighteenth century. No structure erected on a steel frame would ever have the same appearance, the same patina of age. Besides, the long-range effect of running steel through channels in the old brick walls might itself be damaging, because the steel would react to thermal change in a manner that could crack the walls.

Wistar was among those who disagreed with the recommendations. A member of the Philadelphia Chapter of the AIA, he was well acquainted with prominent members of the Philadelphia architectural community. Quietly he let his doubts be known to some other members of the chapter. Peterson also believed that a less drastic solution could be found, and for considerably less than the $2 million estimated for the Ewing reconstruction. Nevertheless, EODC accepted the Ewing Company's basic recommendations and proceeded to issue bid invitations for emergency stabilization work at Congress Hall. In April 1959 Anderson, following the provisions of the cooperative agreement, of which the art commission had so recently increased his awareness, officially requested Mayor Dilworth's approval for emergency work on Congress Hall, enclosing the drawings and specifications that had gone out to prospective bidders and promising to submit additional plans as the work program progressed. When more than two weeks passed with no reply, Anderson wrote again. This time rather than offering to forward plans for review as they were developed, he requested blanket approval for the National Park Service to plan and execute work on the Independence Square buildings based on the findings of the Ewing report. It was perhaps not a wholly tactful request, considering that the Office of the City Development Coordinator had already asked to review Ewing's report. When Dilworth's reply to Anderson finally arrived, it was not favorable. Although Dilworth had given oral approval to Anderson's earlier request for emergency stabilization measures, he would not agree formally to the park service's recommendations. The proposals had been reviewed by the city architect, George I. Lovatt, Jr., and the chairman of the art commission, Roy Larson. Both reported serious doubts.

Wistar made his views known officially in early May. The Ewing recommendations were aimed, in part, on enabling the second floor of Congress Hall to meet building code requirements for spaces intended for public assembly. Wistar proposed that an alternative solution would be to control access to the second floor. With lighter loads, it would be possible to continue to utilize a wood-framed floor. He objected strenuously to the insertion of steel columns in the brick walls. He had observed no sign of failure in the bearing walls. If, however, the columns were inserted, parts of the walls might collapse in the process. In his view the primary object was to preserve as much of the historic building fabric as humanly possible.

Remedial structural work, with particular reference to Congress Hall, was the sole topic at the first meeting of the special architectural advisory commission in June. Charles Grossman, the park's resident architect, and Grant Simon were the only ones present expressing strong support for the Ewing proposals. Simon believed that only total reconstruction would ensure the building's eternal preservation while making it available to all those who wished to see it. The most eloquent spokesman for exploring other solutions was Edward Brumbaugh, Jr. Brumbaugh, of those present, probably had the most experience with restoration. Congress Hall, he informed the group, was very different in structure and use from the White House and could be preserved with less radical measures. The committee responded by recommending retention of a second structural engineer to review conditions from the viewpoint of minimal interference with the existing fabric. Brumbaugh suggested that the assignment be offered to Sheldon A. Keast.

Keast had been the city of Philadelphia's building inspector for many years. Through this work he had developed unsurpassed familiarity with the construction details of the city's older buildings and considerable experience in evaluating their condition. On his retirement from his city post, he had joined a group of structural engineers, forming the firm of Keast & Hood in 1953. Keast was a pragmatist rather than a theoretician. His approach would be to see what could be done to make the existing structures function, rather than applying mathematical formulae to arrive at some ideal. Not only was Keast generally respected; his opinion would carry considerable weight with city officials, with whom he had a longstanding professional and collegial relationship.

Keast's report was ready by the fall of 1959. He had followed a conservation approach. The purpose was to let the original structure function where it could and to supplement it, or as a last resort supplant it, where it could not. Even where the old structure was supplanted, it would usually remain as historical evidence, and new structural elements would be introduced carefully so that the original fabric would suffer the minimal amount of damage. Keast's conclusions that this could be done at Congress Hall were accepted by both the National Park Service and the city. From this time on Keast & Hood would consult on the structural aspects of work on the buildings on Independence Square.

Although the National Park Service staff spent much of its time in 1959 embroiled in disputes about how the master plan for Area A would be implemented through restoration and reconstruction, work continued to go forward on refinement of the plan itself, including the selection of plant materials and paving appropriate for the historical period. Several questions pertaining to the disposition and use of individual buildings were reaching final resolution, although the ultimate function of the Second Bank was still uncertain. The First Bank was proposed as a temporary visitor center. However, the proposal called for it ultimately to be devoted to the interpretation of banking and economic development in the federal period. The upper stories could become park offices. Several alternatives were suggested for the buildings on Walnut Street. The Bishop White House would become, as had always been intended, a house museum operated by park staff. Now it was proposed that the Todd House be elevated to the same status. Reconstruction of the two houses east of the Todd House had been approved by Wirth during a visit to the park in September. These, according to the findings of the park staff, would be suitable quarters for the Pennsylvania Horticultural Society and the Philadelphia Society for the Promotion of Agriculture. Moving east on Walnut Street, the Kidd Houses at 323–325 had been recommended for demolition in structures reports submitted in May 1958. However, the regional office had reminded Anderson that their retention had been provided for in the master plan, and the office of the Secretary of the Interior had offered them to the Carl Schurz Foundation in March 1958. Demolition was still recommended for the Fling House at 319–321 Walnut Street, although this meant that some method would have to be found for stabilizing the party walls of the Kidd Houses and the McIlvaine House at 315–317. The latter, together with the adjacent Yoh Building at 311–313, could house the park offices. However, if the Second Bank was not available, the portrait gallery might be housed in these two buildings. In the main, the regional office agreed with these proposals.

Within a month Zimmer informed Anderson that EODC recommended retaining the Fling House, claiming that removing it would require extensive bracing of the party walls of the adjacent Kidd and McIlvaine Houses, as well as considerable alteration to the plan of the latter. Furthermore, the architects believed that there were historical and aesthetic arguments for the building's preservation. It had been erected in "the same architectural period" as the Kidd House, and any rationale for keeping that structure applied equally to the Fling House. Its removal would break up the only relatively intact row of early buildings remaining in the park. The gap would be unsightly and would produce maintenance problems.

One by one a series of decisions made in the course of master planning had entirely altered the design concept applied to Walnut Street. The original plan had envisioned a landscaped area in which the restored Bishop White and Todd houses would stand in isolated splendor. Several factors had produced incremental change in the plan: the structural requirements of the buildings for which preservation had been mandated, discoveries about the historical qualities of some of the other Walnut Street buildings, and the necessity of providing office space for the park and for cooperating organizations. Perhaps the most important impetus for change had been growing acceptance within the National Park Service of the concept of preserving a streetscape that would convey some sense of the appearance and feeling of the Philadelphia the founding fathers knew.

The decisions of a decade were summed up at a full-scale master plan conference in Philadelphia on March 9–10, 1960. Presiding was the new regional director, Ronald F. Lee, who had replaced Tobin in January. Lee, long a member of the Washington directorate, was already familiar with decisions and events at Independence. Although most of the discussion was devoted to implementation of earlier decisions, several of the remaining questions in Area A were also resolved. The Second Bank was now slated to house the portrait collection, as well as storage for the museum and offices for its staff. The First Bank would become the interim visitor center, to be converted to a banking museum when a permanent visitor center was constructed. The park's recommendations for the Walnut Street houses were accepted. Planning for the park south of Chestnut Street and west of Second Street was thus virtually complete. But a new look at the master plan was called for. Several issues remained: a location for the visitor center, the possible acquisition of additional land east of Second Street and of the state-owned Independence Mall, and most important, the treatment of Area C, Franklin Court.

The master plan that emerged at Independence after almost a decade was a product of compromise. The plan probably satisfied none of the participants totally but was at least palatable to most. The main part of the park was neither the formal, barren ceremonial landscape visualized by the Shrines Commission nor the architecturally oriented design sketched by Charles Peterson. Neither the buildings defended by Peterson, nor the broad malls of the earliest schemes, punctuated by buildings in shrinelike isolation, survived. The strong axes were replaced by more intimate spaces, their shapes determined in part by the old Philadelphia city plan. If the park was far more open and green, more parklike than the colonial city had ever been, still there were, at every turn, suggestions of what the country's founders had seen: the course of Dock Creek, the cobble-paved streets and alleys, the outlines of vanished buildings. As planning evolved, more elements of the eighteenth-century streetscape were targeted for retention or reconstruction. The motivation was in part practical and was usually cloaked in the language of pragmatism, citing such purposes as providing space to house desirable cooperating organizations or ensuring the structural stability of neighboring buildings. Yet it was obvious that a sense of history also affected the decisions and was felt by all those who dealt with Independence, not only the historians, but architects, landscape architects, and administrators as well.

Indeed, if there were winners or losers in the debate over master planning, the historians may be said to have won the war, if not all of the battles.

18. Area A of the park from the northeast in 1950. The pediment of the First Bank of the United States and the cupola of Carpenters' Hall can be seen left of center. To the right, beyond the parking lot, is Frank Furness's polychrome Guarantee Trust.

The park came closer to the concept described by Edward Riley in 1953 than to any other vision of what it might have been. It became an area that commemorated the events of the period from 1774 to 1800 and also served as an interpretive tool through which the course of those events could be conveyed to the American people. Judge Lewis and his supporters were also satisfied. The plan accomplished the judge's primary purpose, the replacement of a run-down neighborhood with a park, and the preservation of the most famous historic buildings. Despite occasional protest about specific projects, such as New Hall, Lewis showed little concern for the details of planning; his objective was to see the park completed as quickly as possible. It was Peterson, and his fellow advocates among architects and architectural historians, who had lost the most. Most of the buildings for which they had fought had come down and could never be replaced. The historical architects did, however, carry the day, with the assistance of the city of Philadelphia, on the question of how historic buildings should be treated. In finally rejecting

19. *Area A in 1957. Most of the park's Chestnut Street frontage has been cleared, with sod planted where the buildings were. The walls of New Hall and the Front Store still stand adjacent to Carpenters' Court. In the foreground, the Penn Mutual Building is down and the Jayne Building is being demolished.*

recommendations that would have been tantamount to reconstructing rather than conserving the buildings on Independence Square, the National Park Service made a decision that would eventually guide implementation of the policy that it was better to restore than to reconstruct.

The master plan of the late 1950s was never, in fact, a full or formal document, and was never issued as such. Rather it was a series of approved drawings covering specific areas and omitting others, such as Franklin Court, and based on policies hammered out over the course of their preparation. What it provided was a basis for implementation, and as funds from Mission 66 and special appropriations for Independence began to flow in the late 1950s and early 1960s, development proceeded quickly. It was a startling contrast to the early 1950s, when there was so little visible change. By the spring of 1960, three-quarters of the landscaping south of Chestnut Street and east of Fifth Street had been completed. The Philadelphia newspapers published glowing reports rather than complaints about the lack of progress. During the next several years the major effort would be concentrated on carrying the construction program forward. The planning process would continue, but on a less intensive level; attention would shift to the implementation in brick and mortar of broad decisions already made. What the public could welcome next were not only grass and trees, but also restored and rehabilitated buildings.

Five
Restoring the Buildings

From the time the National Park Service began considering acquisition of what would become Independence National Historical Park, it was assumed that its stewardship would include restoration of the most important of the historic buildings. These were specified in the legislation authorizing establishment of the park. The list included not only monumental structures like Independence Hall and the Second Bank of the United States, but at least two buildings of domestic scale, the Todd House, where Dolley Madison had lived with her first husband, and the Bishop White House.

The National Park Service had undertaken some important restoration projects before World War II, most notably at Morristown National Historical Park in New Jersey, and the progress of the restorations at Williamsburg was well publicized. On the basis of this experience, and observation of the efforts of others, the agency had evolved a restoration philosophy that called for conservation of what was original, removal of later accretions, and the accurate recreation of missing elements. How this was to be achieved had not been codified. There was no recognized methodology for the small staff at Independence to follow in investigating and restoring historic buildings. There was little literature on the subject, no written guidelines or manuals. Knowledge of how old buildings had been constructed and of what physical evidence might provide clues to their original appearance was handed down from one practitioner to another, and some architects with experience in restoration were secretive about what they knew. So those responsible for restoration at Independence were forced to develop techniques, learning as they went along from one another, from the craftsmen on the park's staff, and from the buildings. Many of these techniques were developed at the Bishop White House, the first of the restorations to be completed, and at the park's centerpiece, Independence Hall.

The Bishop White House

The Bishop White House was an unusually commodious rowhouse on Walnut Street. It posed, in microcosm, the full range of conditions that might be encountered in a projected restoration project. Comparison with old views and photographs showed that the upper part of the facade was almost intact.

20. *Members of the permanent and summer architectural staffs of the park and the Eastern Office of Design and Construction pose on the steps of the Second Bank. Standing (from left) are Edward Close, Ethel Reid (secretary), William J. Murtagh; seated are Samuel Edgerton, Jr., Frank M. Boeshore, William M. Campbell, David Connor, Charles S. Grossman, Steven Wolf, Penelope Hartshorne (Batcheler), G. Reigler.*

The first floor, however, had been completely transformed—renovated in a heavy Victorian mode when the building passed from residential to commercial use in the third quarter of the nineteenth century, and then "colonialized" in 1946, complete with small-paned picture window. The situation in the interior was similar. The first floor had been gutted, and the back building or kitchen wing had been considerably enlarged and altered. Thus the building would demand various forms of treatment. Some sections, such as the upper stories of the front wall, would require preservation. Other areas would call for the restoration of missing elements. In areas such as the back building or the gutted first floor, nearly total reconstruction might be called for.

Soon after the park service acquired the property, it became apparent that although construction funds were severely limited, some emergency repair work was essential. Removal of the adjacent building had exposed the east party wall, revealing numerous holes where the wall had been cut to accommodate flues and pipe chases. Woodwork in the upper stories—in particular the cornice and original frames and sash in the dormers—was also in poor condition. Work on the east wall and dormers was carried out in 1953; the cornice was repaired in 1954, at which time the front wall was cleaned. The work was accomplished in a conservative manner. Wherever possible original fabric was preserved and reinforced.

By late 1955, with programming for Mission 66 well under way and additional special appropriations for Independence contemplated, it looked as if the funding drought might finally end. Accordingly, background research for the restoration projects began in the fall. The goal was to determine the appearance of the buildings at the time the historic events commemorated at the park had taken place. The investigative team at the Bishop White House worked under the direction of William Campbell. Campbell had become a permanent member of the Independence staff after his retirement from a teaching post at the University of Pennsylvania. In addition to his architectural skills, Campbell had other important qualifications for his assignment. By avocation he was an antiquarian. He understood archaic construction techniques and had a keen eye for detail. Courtly, gentle, and patient, he was a superb teacher.

Although several junior architects also helped investigate buildings, Campbell's chief assistants were Frank Boeshore and Penelope Hartshorne. Boeshore, like Campbell, had joined the park staff in retirement. His strength was practical knowledge of how to put a building together. Hartshorne was of another generation and had an apparently unlikely background for a restoration architect. She had received her architectural degree from the Illinois Institute of Technology in 1953. The presiding genius of that institution was then Ludwig Mies van der Rohe, doyen of the International Style, whose dictum "less is more" expressed his view that much of the architecture of the past was overdecorated and nonfunctional. Hartshorne, however, had been brought up in a family with strong historical interests and had spent two years working at museum villages in Sweden. Of a generation brought up on the fictional adventures of Ellery Queen and Dick Tracy and the real-life exploits of the Federal Bureau of Investigation, Hartshorne found searching for clues and sifting evidence a natural and enjoyable exercise.

Hartshorne's first assignment at Independence was to take photographs in Independence Hall and to assist in the investigation of the Supreme Court Room. It was her introduction to a building with which she would be involved for twenty years. Within a few months, however, she was shifted to the Bishop White House, although she returned to Independence Hall at intervals to make and record observations, as work on repairing and repainting its woodwork went forward. Campbell already had begun his study of the Bishop White House by reviewing the historical data that had been accumulated in the last five years. The historians had assembled a chain-of-title for the property, found insurance surveys made in 1787 (another survey dated 1795 would be found as the investigation proceeded), located numerous furnishings and decorative objects, and put together an iconography, or graphic record, of the building, consisting of nineteenth-century watercolors by B. R. Evans and David J. Kennedy and old photographs. Campbell also reviewed later photographs and building permits, which showed that numerous alterations had been made since 1910.

The documents provided a good deal of information, especially about the facade, but many questions remained to be answered. The precise appearance of the facade's first story, the configuration of the back buildings, and many of the interior details were still a mystery. To solve it would require coaxing the building itself to reveal its secrets. The investigators approached the house like archeologists searching for a buried civilization. Layer by layer they peeled back plaster, seeking the ghosts of vanished structural elements and decorative trim. They knew that contrary to the later practice of applying wooden trim after a room was plastered, the eighteenth-century builder first put the trim in place and then plastered up to it. Therefore, even if the trim was removed subsequently, its dimensions and profiles would be preserved in the adjoining plaster. Even if the gaps left by the trim were filled in with new plaster, faint differences in color would persist. By carefully chasing back the new plaster to recover the precise extent of the old, it was often possible to obtain remarkably sharp profiles of missing elements.

The west party wall was amazingly informative. It revealed the configuration of the original stair, its slope, the position of the landing, and the size and shape of the half-newel that had once been attached to the wall. Not only could the position of the rear wall of the eighteenth-century back building be found by the scars its removal had left on the west wall, but so could the floor levels and the location of the winding rear stair. The location and size of vanished fireplaces and their flues were discernible through the patterns of soot deposited on the bricks.

The exploration also involved other disciplines. Paul J. F. Schumacher, the park's archeologist, began excavating the subcellar in the second week of December 1955, investigating storage pits and foundations. He not only found the foundation walls for the original kitchen, but also one of the building's most remarkable features. From the area adjoining the kitchen at the rear, a concave marble trough ran north at a downward slope to a small vaulted brick tunnel, which continued across the rear yard. This proved to be the drain of a two-story necessary attached to the rear of the house. In this and a subsequent campaign in the summer of 1956, Schumacher pursued the

course of the drain to the Dock Street sewer and found it crammed with
sherds of ceramics and glassware of the late eighteenth and early nineteenth
centuries. The only access to the drain had been from within the Bishop White
House; thus, these artifacts must have been the remains of White family
possessions.

Like most of the early archeological work carried out at Independence,
the program at the Bishop White House was not a systematic investigation of
the full potential of the site to yield information about the past. It concentrated on individual features, which were explored in order to find information that would forward the restoration process. Nevertheless, the excavations
of the mid-1950s at Independence were among the first in a major American
city and thus among the pioneering efforts of urban archeology.

While Schumacher dug in the subcellar, the architects continued their
examination of the upper floors into the new year. Here more original fabric
was intact. The rear room, which had been Bishop White's study, could be
compared with a painting by John Sartain, made shortly after the bishop's
death in 1836. It remained almost entirely undisturbed. Small human touches
vividly evoked the former occupants of the house. There were charred marks
on the chairrail, just where the Sartain painting had shown that the bishop
rested his partly smoked cigars. On a closet shelf, carved in a childish hand,
were the initials "T.W.," undoubtedly the work of the bishop's son, Thomas.
The front room, unfortunately, had been stripped of its trim only a few years
before the National Park Service's acquisition.

The interior examination supplied the investigators with a great deal of
information, but many details were still missing. There was also the more
amorphous question of the feel of the various elements—what someone
dealing with cloth would refer to as its hand. To better understand what the
components of the Bishop White House would have looked like when assembled as a whole, Campbell and Hartshorne began to examine surviving
contemporary rowhouses. Fortunately, Philadelphia provided a wonderful
laboratory on their doorstep. Within a few blocks of the Bishop White House
were some thirty comparable rowhouses.

Another source of data about eighteenth-century design and building
practices was the park's architectural study collection. This gathering of
everything from windows to cornices to mantels, staircases, shutters, hardware, and nails had been started by Peterson almost as soon as he arrived in
Philadelphia. The examples had been collected by many hands from many
sources. Some were purchased or removed with permission from buildings
slated for demolition. Others were retrieved from the rubble on demolition
sites, or from trash piles and garbage cans. Not all the salvage ended up in
the study collection. Glazed bricks from a stable on Orianna Street were used
in the restoration of the Todd House, and marble steps from seven houses in
the Poplar Street East Redevelopment Area were recut for use at the Todd
and Hibbard-Griffiths Houses.

Through 1956 and 1957 Campbell and Hartshorne continued their

21. *Drawing of part of the west wall, from a series of evidence drawings prepared for the Bishop White House (#NHP-IND 2449, 1–12). The drawing shows the location of several features: trim such as baseboards, chair-rails, and handrails; joists revealing former floor levels; walls and partitions that had been removed; and flues, which provided clues to the location and size of former fireplaces.*

investigations, checking what they found in other buildings against what was present in the Bishop White House. Meanwhile, new evidence was being found. In June a new photograph was discovered, the earliest taken of the house, made in 1859. At the same time Hartshorne was recording the evidence they had found by means of photography and drawing. Campbell also began the working drawings for restoration. The photographs and drawings would become part of an official document then known as a "Historic Building Report." The first such report had been prepared by Charles Peterson for the Moore House in Yorktown, Virginia. Although written after the work on the building had been completed, it contained historical documentation and a report on the physical evidence that had justified restoration decisions. During the years before World War II, a number of such reports were completed for other National Park Service properties. It was not, however, until the restoration work at Independence got under way that such documents were required and their format institutionalized. In 1957 Director Wirth issued a memorandum calling for the preparation of such reports and mandating that they contain administrative, historical, and architectural data. A memorandum of 1958 from the associate director gave them the new title, "Historic Structures Report."

The Wirth memorandum stimulated the completion of full reports for the buildings at Independence, including the Bishop White House. In July 1957 William C. Everhart, then supervisory historian at Independence, assigned a newly arrived historian, David H. Wallace, the task of ascertaining the significance of Bishop White's role in the Independence story. At stake was the important question of how the house should be interpreted—whether it should be a memorial to Bishop White or be put to some other use. Wallace's work formed the major part of what was issued as Part I of a historic buildings report in April 1958. The report recommended that the bishop's study be restored, but that the first floor of the building be interpreted as a museum devoted to the idea of religious liberty. By March 1959, when part II of the report was issued, much had changed. For one thing, the document was now a "Historic Structures Report"; for another, the estimated cost had almost quadrupled, from approximately $141,000 to $494,000. In part this probably represented a more realistic appraisal of construction costs; in part it reflected a change in program. The recommendation now was not to use the first floor as a freely designed museum, but to restore and refurnish the entire house, not only as a memorial to White, but also to illustrate the way of life of a prominent citizen of federal Philadelphia. The report must have

118

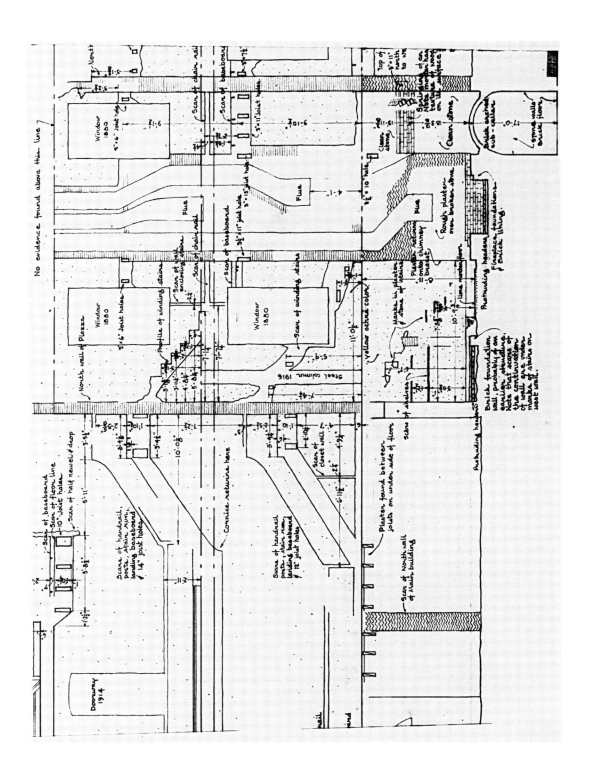

been persuasive. At the master plan conference held in March 1960, it was decided that the Bishop White House would be restored for exclusive use by the park as a furnished house museum.

Higher standards of authenticity were being applied by the time the second report was written. Where the first report had suggested furnishing the house with whatever antiques could be obtained, supplemented by reproductions, the second advocated the use of period pieces exclusively, with the exception of some reproduction seating in the hall for the convenience of visitors. The recommendation for reconstruction of the first floor also represented a change in attitude. The second report contained a longer architectural section. It described the architects' methodology for studying the building and provided a list of precedents on which missing details had been based.

The report on the Bishop White House was among the earliest prepared under the new system established by Wirth's directive. It shows some of the marks of a pioneering effort. The historical section is reasonably detailed but lacks the extensive appendices reproducing key data that would characterize later examples of the genre. Even in the expanded version of the March 1959 report, the architectural data section is notably brief, lacking much narrative explanation of how the house had developed or the reasoning behind many of the decisions on restoration of specific elements, despite the list of precedents for various details. The architects believed that their evidence drawings, which were bound into the report, provided sufficient justification.

By the time the second report was issued, Campbell, assisted by Hartshorne and Boeshore, had produced a set of meticulously detailed working drawings. These were duly forwarded to the regional office and thence to Washington and were accepted, although they had not been submitted to EODC for comment. However, the Bishop White House was never restored in precisely the manner shown by Campbell. In late 1958 responsibility for the restoration of buildings at Independence was transferred from the park staff to EODC's Historic Structures section. At this time Anderson suggested that EODC also assume responsibility for completing reports on historic buildings within the park, except for the Bishop White House, where, in his view, the research data and findings of physical evidence were virtually complete. In fact this did not occur. Historians on the park staff continued to produce the historical sections of the reports, while the EODC staff prepared the architectural sections.

The move was accompanied by a considerable augmentation of the Historic Structures staff. Peterson looked for certain interests and attitudes in selecting personnel. He sought out architects and craftsmen who were so interested in their work that they were willing to spend their free time reading about, visiting, and analyzing the construction of old buildings. The man on whom Peterson depended as his chief assistant and field lieutenant, Henry A. Judd, filled these criteria. Although he held the title of architect in the National Park Service, he had no formal degree. He had learned the practical aspects of construction from his builder father. Before coming to Philadelphia, he had worked for Peterson in Natchez. Two craftsmen who had also worked previously with Peterson, William A. Ernst and Gordon Whittington, came to Philadelphia to join what was informally known as the day labor force. This was something of a misnomer; the day labor force was composed not of common laborers, but of skilled carpenters and masons. These craftsmen were capable not only of carrying out repairs on old buildings, but also of carrying out full-scale restoration work, as they did at the Bishop White House.

Several architects and draftsmen were also hired. Hartshorne was transferred to the EODC roster. Despite her considerable knowledge of the Bishop White House, she was assigned to work on Congress Hall as an assistant to Thomas Wistar, Jr., an experienced architect who joined the National Park Service from private practice.

In September 1960 two EODC architects, Norman M. Souder and George L. Wrenn, began further investigations at the Bishop White House, under the supervision of Peterson and Judd. One of the first results of their labors were new estimates, increasing the projected cost of restoration to $567,000. Their findings, presented at the end of the year, differed in several particulars from those of Campbell's team and reflected reinterpretation of the evidence uncovered by Campbell, as well as a number of fresh discoveries. Some of the proposed changes in the recreation of missing features were more a question of taste or judgment than of demonstrable fact—for example, designs for dormer consoles based on the Carpenters' Company price book issued in 1786. The report also recommended different methods of reinforcing the building's structure and incorporating a modern heating system.

The recommended changes were submitted in the form of new drawings without written justification. They were not well received at Independence because they were unexplained. In January 1961, therefore, EODC submitted a supplement to the historic structures report. It was couched in language that did little to soothe the park staff. Commenting that the earlier reports had not contained written data supporting their conclusions, the report went on to justify the changes made by EODC. Some of these were based on new evidence; others, such as the decision to redesign the front doorway, were actually matters of taste. Obviously the park staff did not enjoy having its conclusions called into question. Superintendent Anderson suggested to Regional Director Ronald F. Lee that in instances where questions persisted, such as the dormer consoles or the necessary, it would be helpful if EODC personnel consulted with members of the park staff who had worked on the earlier reports. Materials studied by the staff were available, if EODC chose to consult them.

The photographs intended to accompany the January 1961 report were not ready until March, and the park historians, of whom Campbell was now one, waited until June before responding to the report with a blistering memorandum. The comment that their report had not contained written justification for restoration conclusions seems to have been particularly galling. The mcmorandum pointed not only to its ten sheets of evidence drawings, but also to its lists of the precedents, either within the house or in similar buildings, for fifty-five missing details. The EODC had declared that no two-story necessaries dating to the eighteenth century had survived; the park staff cited two examples in the city that had been examined from the exterior in the course of their study. The memorandum also attacked several of EODC's conclusions. The latter's prototypes for the frontispiece were all later in date than the Bishop White House. The choice of stone facing for the basement was against the weight of precedent. The dormer consoles based on the Carpenters' Company price book did not resemble those shown (although not very clearly) in early photographs of the Bishop White House; appended was an exceptionally fine photograph of dormers on the building that had served as the first location of the United States Mint, which, indeed, appeared closer in design to those suggested by the photograph of the Bishop White House.

This debate seems to have engendered some bitterness between the historians on the park staff and the architects on the EODC staff, which would flare up repeatedly over the next decade. Restoration is rarely a scientific undertaking, based entirely on documentary or physical data. Because experience, taste, and professional judgment must be applied where factual evidence is lacking, room for disagreement remains. The Bishop White House was only one of several buildings about the details of which the two parties differed. Yet the tension also had positive results. It forced thorough exploration of all possible solutions to disputed issues, and the final results were better because of it. At the Bishop White House, the architects eventually used the photograph produced by the historians as the basis for the dormer consoles, and, having found a molded watertable brick on the site, faced the basement with brick rather than stone. The historians, on the other hand, agreed that the structural solutions proposed in the January 1961 report were preferable to those shown in the original drawings.

As the working drawings were prepared, another facet of restoring and interpreting the Bishop White House began to receive intense consideration—the question of furnishing the building. In June 1960 Charles G. Dorman joined the staff of Independence as a curator. His first assignment was to prepare a furnishings plan for the Bishop White House. Dorman had attended the University of Delaware, where he continued to pursue a lifelong interest in the furniture and decorative arts of the Delaware Valley. For five years afterward he worked as the manager of an antiques shop in Wilmington, before concluding that the life of an antiques dealer was not for him. He was a curator at the Smithsonian Institution before coming to Independence.

As Dorman worked on the furnishings plan, the program became further refined. The building would be furnished not merely with period antiques, but with pieces that had been owned or might have been owned by the bishop. Building on the tracing of White descendants and inherited furnishings begun by Peterson and Campbell, Dorman became so familiar with the White furnishings and their disposition that he could tell his startled hostess in western Massachusetts that the rest of her dining room chairs were in Baltimore. Dorman knew that there would be little or no money available to purchase furniture. Congress appropriates funds to the National Park Service to purchase, restore, reconstruct, and maintain historic properties, but little to furnish them. Furnishing the Bishop White House and other buildings at Independence would depend on the generosity of White's descendants and other patriotic citizens, and Dorman took steps to engage their interest. He wrote to and visited many of the descendants. When the house was finished, he invited all of those in the Philadelphia area to tea in the still-empty rooms.

Thanks to Dorman's persistence and personal charm, his cajolery and persuasion were highly effective. Despite the intrinsic and sentimental value of the furnishings, Bishop White's descendants and the institutions that owned his effects proved to be remarkably generous. Because of their gifts, a large percentage of the furnishings in the Bishop White House are those that were there in the eighteenth and early nineteenth centuries. Only one major item once owned by Bishop White had to be purchased.

There were not, however, enough of White's former possessions available to furnish the house fully. For knowledge of what the missing furnishings might have been, there were two major sources. One was the archeological evidence derived from excavation of the bishop's sewer. The sherds of ceramics and glassware provided clues to the kinds and quantity of the wares used in the Whites' dining room and kitchen. Further information came from contemporary household inventories. Usually prepared after the death of a property owner, these were often very detailed. Unfortunately, no inventory for Bishop White could be found. The park's historians therefore found, and Dorman carefully analyzed, twenty-two inventories of householders whose wealth and social position were comparable to the bishop's and who lived in houses of similar design.

The report embodying the furnishing plan for the Bishop White House was issued in December 1961. It was extremely thorough, providing a furnishing guide that was complete to the smallest detail and illustrated by plans and elevations showing the furnishings in place. Historian David A. Kimball had supplied the historical narrative, piecing together a picture of the bishop's economic and social position, and of his family life. Dorman hoped to furnish the house in a manner that would portray the busy life of the bishop and his extended family. Accordingly he had provided a plan for every interior space in the house from cellar to attic. It was an ambitious scheme, and one that has never been executed fully. Only the first and second floors of the front building and the first floor of the back building, including the kitchen and necessary, have been furnished and opened to public view.

After construction work had been completed, and while Dorman assembled the furnishings, Hartshorne returned to the Bishop White House to determine the original finishes on walls and woodwork. Her task began with an analysis of all painted surfaces. She used techniques that she had learned from Anne F. Clapp, an art conservator who had joined the park staff to oversee the restoration of the portraits of leading figures of the revolutionary and federal periods that had hung in Independence Hall when the National Park Service assumed custody. In addition, she had worked on determining the original paint colors at the Todd House, with Hartshorne as an apprentice. Paint analysis then consisted of two basic procedures. First, with a surgeon's scalpel, the analyst gradually scraped down a "bull-eye" from the top coat to bare wood, exposing seriated layers of paint. Next, an intact sample of all the layers was cut and observed in cross-section under a microscope. Through careful study of the layers, it was possible to determine what color had been applied first to the wood, and whether that color had simply been a primer or a finish coat. The primer would sink into the wood; the finish coat would retain a layer of dirt. Subsequent coats would also exhibit a dirt layer. Through establishing how many layers there were and how thick the dirt was, it was possible to form a relative idea of how often a surface had been painted and how long each color had been exposed to view.

At the Bishop White House, Hartshorne determined that the original trim colors had been predominantly buff or cream. The walls of the first floor and hallway, however, had been papered rather than painted, although the remaining vestiges of paper were too small to reveal its color or pattern. Once again study of neighboring buildings where paper survived was called for. Other interior details also remained to be studied. In 1964, after considerable research, Hartshorne prepared a schedule for doors and hardware.

The Bishop White House was opened to the public in October 1967. Over the previous seven years the exterior and interior had been restored and the back building reconstructed, largely by the day labor force, authentic or appropriate furnishings had been installed, and wallpaper of the period of the house had been copied and hung. The bishop's books were back in the bishop's bookcases in the bishop's study, thanks to the generosity of the Philadelphia Divinity School; much of the bishop's silver was in the dining room, thanks to the generosity of the bishop's descendants; and his brother-in-law's sofa adorned the parlor.

The process of restoring the Bishop White House had covered a span of almost fifteen years. In part this was due to lack of funding; in part to interruption of the work of the historians, archeologists, architects, and craftsmen, who were spread thin. The transfer of responsibility for restoration of the house from the park staff to EODC also occasioned some delay. Besides, there was almost no way that the National Park Service, with its numerous levels of review and comment, could carry out a project with the speed that might be possible in the private sector. On the other hand, the thorough study of a building by several disciplines, and the submission of the fruits of that study to review by peers and superiors in a system of checks and balances, formed the basis for more authentic restoration and more accurate interpretation of the buildings to the public.

The Bishop White House provided a testing ground and laboratory for many of the restoration staff at Independence. It was the project on which they cut their teeth, learning and trying out methods of discovering and analyzing evidence. Because the knowledge they required could not be found in books or manuals, they had to acquire it through experience, from dealing with the buildings themselves. They would profit from that experience and would continue to learn more as they dealt with the park's centerpiece, Independence Hall.

Independence Hall

Preservation of this sacred icon was the ultimate purpose for which Independence National Historical Park had been created. Its custody had been transferred to the federal government, somewhat reluctantly, by the city of Philadelphia so that the National Park Service could lavish on it the attention that the city had not been able to afford. Just what that attention should be was not, however, simple to determine. Independence Hall had been both altered and restored several times in the course of two centuries. It had been depicted in virtually every medium and written about in hundreds, if not thousands, of publications. Yet it was obvious that the available information left many questions unanswered about the appearance of Independence Hall in 1776, and certainly provided no guidance about the methods to be employed in returning it to that appearance. Finding the answers, exploring the options, and carrying out the work would take almost a quarter of a century.

It was evident, however, as soon as the National Park Service took custody of Independence Hall on January 2, 1951, that some immediate steps were required. There were leaks in the roof; sections of the brick exterior walls needed repointing; and parts of the exterior wooden trim had rotted. Repairs were essential, lest these conditions lead to progressive damage to the building. In addition, the staff of the new park project was anxious to demonstrate the care that would be devoted to the relics with which they had been entrusted. To express this in an immediately visible manner, the exterior and most of the interior of the building would be freshly painted. There was some urgency: it was hoped that the entire program could be accomplished by the first week in July, which would inaugurate the celebration of the 175th anniversary of the signing of the Declaration of Independence.

New treads were installed in the great tower stair, the product of an ingenious design by Peterson. Although the existing treads were badly worn and thus presented a hazard to visitors, it was feared that their removal and replacement would require disassembling the staircase, which Peterson had determined was the original. The potential for damage was high if this course was followed. Rather than replacing the treads completely, Peterson devised a system of removing the main walking surface, leaving the tread ends intact. New sections of board were then slipped into place and fastened down, and the entire tread was stained, shellacked, and varnished. The separate boards, he believed, could readily be replaced when the treads once again became worn.

Even as the emergency remedial work went forward, Riley and his staff were beginning to search for historical data on Independence Hall, its contents, and the events that had taken place within its walls and on its grounds. It was a formidable task. Over the next three years, researchers from Independence would examine approximately 2 million manuscripts and published items, and could estimate that 10 million more required investigation. By 1953 they had assembled a selected bibliography of some 8,000 titles. The magnitude of the research effort can be appreciated only if one remembers that it was accomplished before publication of the National Union Catalogue of Manuscript Collections and before the invention, or at least the common use, of copying machines. Each potential repository of manuscripts, rare published materials, and pictures had to be visited and systematically explored. Every relevant item had to be painstakingly copied by hand and then transcribed onto the five-by-eight-inch research cards that were both record of and index to the findings. The staffing was rarely adequate for the task. During six weeks at the end of 1953, when the first written report on Independence Hall was due, the historians logged 495 hours of uncompensated overtime.

The first fruits of the research on Independence Hall and other buildings in or related to the park were published in 1953 as a volume in the *Transactions of the American Philosophical Society,* in a compendium entitled *Historic Philadelphia.* The opening article by Dr. Edward M. Riley covered the Independence Square group. It dealt with acquisition, construction, and alterations to the buildings and the State House Yard. Illustrated with early views gathered by the research staff in the previous two years, it depended heavily on published records of the Congress, the commonwealth of Pennsylvania, and the city of Philadelphia, as well as travelers' accounts and early guidebooks. One of the most valuable sources of information was the Horace Wells Sellers Collection at the Historical Society of Pennsylvania. This represented the fruits of Sellers's research, which was performed after the Philadelphia Chapter of the AIA assumed responsibility for overseeing work on the buildings on the square in the early twentieth century. In addition, a few manuscript collections had been consulted. Although much information had been assembled about the design and construction of Independence Hall and its subsequent alterations, it was obvious that more would be needed. Very little was known about the appearance of the interior of the building or its furnishings at the time that the Declaration of Independence was signed.

Even before Riley's article was published, the National Park Service had received fresh impetus to conduct more detailed research on the interior of Independence Hall in the form of a generous offer from the General Federation of Women's Clubs. In October 1952 representatives of the park project and the federation met informally in Philadelphia. The federation proposed a nationwide campaign to raise funds for the restoration and refurnishing of Independence Hall. In February, even before details of the federation's plans were complete, several members of the historical staff were detached from other duties to concentrate on intensive research on Independence Hall. The campaign was successful. On August 2, 1954, the federation sent Wirth a check for $209,541.82, with the stipulation that priority was to be given to refurnishing. It was the largest single amount that had ever been applied to Independence Hall since its construction was proposed in 1729.

National Park Service management was eager to see the project substantially completed by May 1955, when the General Federation of Women's Clubs was scheduled to hold its annual meeting in Philadelphia. The mass of potential documentation rendered the task formidable, especially since information about the furnishings could be found only by searching the records for minute details. Having already been through the printed documents relating to Independence Hall, the historians now began to concentrate on manuscript sources, first in Philadelphia repositories and then further afield. In September 1954 Dennis Kurjack investigated papers at the William L. Clements Library at the University of Michigan in Ann Arbor, while Marty Yoelson perused the collections of the New-York Historical Society.

In the meantime, the Washington office of the National Park Service had decided that it should be possible to proceed with the acquisition of at least some of the furnishings concurrent with the research program. Preliminary research had already unearthed considerable information on the appearance of the Assembly Room between 1776 and 1787. Riley had located a painting at the Historical Society of Pennsylvania that would prove to be a key document for both the architectural restoration and the refurnishing. This was a canvas entitled "Congress Voting Independence, July 4, 1776," thought to have been begun by Robert Edge Pine in 1784 and completed after his death by Edward Savage. Cruder artistically than the far more famous "Declaration of Independence" by John Trumbull, it was nevertheless, the Independence staff had concluded, on the basis of careful study of the painting and the objects shown in it by Museum Specialist James M. Mulcahy, much more accurate. The Pine-Savage painting shows the members of Congress in various poses, some seated at tables, others standing, still others occupying Windsor chairs. Riley had found partial confirmation for such seating—a bill to the Pennsylvania Assembly from the Philadelphia chairmaker Francis

22. *The so-called Pine-Savage painting of "Congress Voting Independence, July, 4, 1776," and this unfinished copperplate engraving derived from it, were executed early in the nineteenth century by Edward Savage, who was familiar with the Assembly Room before the destruction of its eighteenth-century finishes. It was, National Park Service historians and architects concluded, the most accurate representation of the room at the time of the signing of the Declaration of Independence, and thus an important document guiding its restoration. Many of the furnishings shown—the Windsor chairs, baize-covered tables, and Venetian blinds—could be confirmed by documentary and physical evidence, as could such architectural elements as the cove ceiling and "cockle-shell" frieze in the tabernacle frame.*

Trumble (or, with the varied spelling common in the eighteenth century, Trumbull), dated November 27, 1778. The Assembly had purchased twenty Windsors, probably to replace furnishings destroyed or stolen by the British during the occupation of Philadelphia. A private collector claimed to have knowledge of Trumble account books showing that four different types of Windsors had been sold to the Assembly in 1775. A search for chairs signed by Trumble could provide additional guidance to the forms of chairs that should be acquired.

For advice and assistance in obtaining furnishings, the National Park Service turned, as it often did in that period, to a committee of outside experts: Charles Nagel of the Brooklyn Museum, Charles Montgomery of the Henry Francis du Pont Winterthur Museum, and Mrs. Francis B. Crowninshield, a noted collector. By the time the committee held its first meeting, the park staff had determined that it would be possible to achieve a partial architectural refurbishing and refurnishing by May 1955, but that research and procurement of a number of desired items would take longer. Superintendent Anderson advised that the following could be in place by the target date: the secretary's and speaker's tables; the president's (or "Rising Sun") chair; and the silver inkstand by Philip Syng, all of which had been displayed among the room's contents when the park service had acquired custody from the City of Philadelphia; thirteen delegations' tables (period or reproduction), with green baize cloth coverings; at least sample Windsor chairs from a group of forty to be acquired eventually; a Penn family coat of arms; Charles Willson Peale's portrait of George Washington, either the original owned by the Pennsylvania Academy of Fine Arts or a copy; and miscellaneous minor furnishings such as writing paper and hickory firewood. Future acquisitions would include appropriate inkstands, captured British flags, engravings and maps, books and newspapers, stoves, candles and candlesticks, and Venetian blinds.

Anderson also entered a plea for patience, asking the Washington office to intercede with the General Federation of Women's Clubs, which was pressing for completion of the project and exhibiting a limited understanding of the nature of the research problem, as well as a reluctance to allow use of the funds for research, which the park believed to be a basic requirement. It was not the first time that Anderson issued such a plea, nor was it by any means the last. Repeatedly Anderson defended his staff, reminding outsiders and Park Service management that they had embarked on a project of enormous scope, requiring an unprecedented commitment of time and manpower. Independence Hall had been restored several times before; this time Anderson and his colleagues were determined that it would be done with the highest degree of accuracy possible.

Fortunately the advisory committee was fully supportive of the thesis that the furnishings program should be based on careful research and documentation. In a lengthy and substantive discussion in January 1955, the committee agreed to support retention of the "Rising Sun" chair in the Assembly Room, based on evidence of its presence there during the Constitutional Convention. It also agreed that the speaker's table should remain, provided that expert examination validated its authenticity for the period. For the time being it would be sufficient to equip the room with one or two antique delegates' tables; the others could be reproductions, since they would be hidden under their green baize covers. It was suggested that swatches of this material at Winterthur and Williamsburg be examined so that appropriate cloth could be reproduced. On the important issue of the Windsor chairs, Nagel and Montgomery opined that those shown in the Pine-Savage painting were a few years too late in period; they preferred a branded Trumble chair of which a photograph had been obtained. The group agreed to circulate photographs of the chair to dealers and to inspect examples that were proffered for sale.

By the end of the following month, this approach had proved successful. Two chairs had been offered for sale by the Ziegler family of Lititz, Pennsylvania. According to family tradition the chairs had been in their possession ever since Conrad Ziegler bought them at a sale of State House furnishings at Lancaster in 1800 and hauled them to Lititz on his farm wagon. By late March Murray Nelligan, who had replaced Riley as chief historian after the latter's departure to join the staff at Colonial Williamsburg, was able to report to Anderson that the purchase of the Ziegler chairs had been accomplished. Negotiations were almost complete for acquisition of a large collection of Windsors assembled by David Stockwell, an antiques dealer. Stockwell had offered to donate two of the finest pieces, chairs signed by Francis Trumble. He would probably also be able to provide at least one delegates' table, and possibly two, of suitable size and period.

Progress had also been made on a number of other items. Charles Montgomery had agreed to procure period writing paper; prototypes for inkstands had been found; and the National Park Museum Division had negotiated with the United States Army to obtain copies of the captured British flags at West Point. Although the curator of the museum at West Point informally agreed to permit the copies to be made, he also suggested that their display might be damaging to British-American relations and that the State Department should be consulted. This diplomatic issue seems to have been taken seriously at Independence; the captured colors were never put on display in the Assembly Room.

Although the dedicatory ribbon cutting duly took place in May 1955, the refurnishing of the Assembly Room was by no means complete, and the architectural restoration had not even begun. No architectural study of the restoration requirements had been made before the federation's gift was announced, and it was impossible to complete such an undertaking before the furnishings were installed. A few months after the annual meeting of the General Federation of Women's Clubs, the furnishings were removed to storage so that a more thorough investigation of the room could be undertaken. The investigation was directed by Charles Grossman, who had succeeded Peterson as resident architect at Independence, after the latter's transfer to EODC. At first Grossman and others on the staff accepted Philadelphia architect John Haviland's work of 1831 in the Assembly Room as an authentic restoration. After all, Haviland had declared that he was "reinstating it with its original architectural embellishments" and that "the materials we have are in good taste . . . and constitutes [*sic*] nearly the whole finish." Although the historians were aware that the original paneling had been removed, they interpreted Haviland's statement as meaning that it had been stored and reinstalled.

Grossman had begun his investigations of the first floor of Independence Hall in early November 1954, assisted by two student summer aides. They began with the frontispiece of the tower entrance. Their first procedure was to strip paint in order to distinguish old work from alterations. Soon, because of the federation's gift, they shifted to the Assembly Room, using the same technique of stripping paint on a section of paneling on the east wall. Almost immediately it became evident that the changes wrought by T. Mellon Rogers in 1897–98 were greater than had previously been assumed. Rogers had removed Haviland's carved wooden cornice and pilaster capitals and replaced them with elements made of compo, a form of plaster.

By mid-December Grossman could only report that because of the several past "restorations," it would be exceedingly difficult to determine the original construction and finishes of the Assembly Room. Furthermore, the more intense search for documentation sparked by the federation's gift had uncovered evidence indicating that the Haviland treatment was not an accurate reflection of the appearance of the room in the eighteenth century. James Mulcahy, after careful study of the Pine-Savage painting and the engraving of it by Edward Savage, was certain that this view, showing architectural finishes quite different from the Haviland paneling, was the most authentic representation of the room. Confirming evidence came from a document Yoelson had found in the Pennsylvania Archives showing that the Pennsylvania Assembly had decided on January 25, 1734/35, that the room should be finished with wainscot to a "convenient height" on three sides, with a full wainscot or paneling at the east end. This document coincided with the treatment shown in the Pine-Savage painting. Although figures of the delegates obscured the wainscot on the north side of the room, the plain plaster above, adorned only with wooden window trim and a cornice, agreed with the description, as did the fully paneled east end. The latter included pilasters and cornice of the Ionic order, all in sharp contrast to the Doric pilasters and cornice present in the Assembly Room. With so many questions raised by the documentation and the most minimal architectural investigation, the staff recommended treating the Assembly Room conservatively for the time being. Old paint would be stripped from the woodwork and a fresh coat applied to the walls and the floor. Otherwise the room would be left undisturbed until a more thorough investigation could be undertaken.

During the summer and fall of 1955, the height of the visitation season at Independence, the refurnished Assembly Room remained on display and the architectural investigation of Independence Hall remained in abeyance. By December, however, the park's painters and carpenters had returned to the work of removing paint on the first floor, repairing woodwork, and, at the same time, providing an opportunity for the architects to study the building. Penelope Hartshorne's first assignment was to assist in the examination of the Supreme Court Room. As part of the refurnishing funded by the General Federation of Women's Clubs, the judge's bench was to be restored. Hartshorne crawled under the existing bench to record joist pockets related to former levels of the bench and the steps leading up to it. Unfortunately, there were two sets of holes left by the joists in the masonry, and she could not determine their relative dates at that time. When paneling on the north and south walls was removed, she also found evidence of the position and stepped profile of the former grand jury boxes. Although Hartshorne worked primarily on the Bishop White House through much of 1955 and 1956, she returned periodically to Independence Hall to make observations and to record the architects' findings.

Grossman's approach to investigating Independence Hall—stripping paint—had several purposes. For one thing, the many paint layers—in some cases built up over two hundred years—obscured the details of the architectural trim, hiding the delicate beauty of finely carved wood. For another the paint was masking areas in need of repair. Finally, Grossman believed that the bare wood would reveal where alterations and repairs had been made in the past. Yet the architects eventually learned that the layers of old paint could themselves provide important evidence, evidence that was irretrievably lost when the paint was removed without careful preliminary study.

Paint stripping began with the east wall of the Assembly Room, proceeded to the Supreme Court Room, and had reached the center hall by January 1956. As the work progressed, carpenters removed loose pieces of trim so that they could be reattached more securely. Examining these closely, the architects found the penciled and inscribed initials of various workmen. A boldly penciled "TN." on a hidden rail in the back of the entablature recorded the presence of Thomas Nevell, later a prominent carpenter-builder, who as a young journeyman had helped master carpenter Edmund Woolley install the paneling in the 1750s. These were exciting findings, vivid links with the past. More significant for restoration technology, however, was a discovery Grossman made in examining paneling over the door from the central hall to the Assembly Room. Here, beneath the existing pediment, and outlined by the residue of the original red iron-oxide primer, was the shape of a triangular pediment used at an earlier period.

Up to this point the architects had devoted attention to the woodwork itself, to the manner in which it was formed and attached, but not to the finishes applied after it was installed. Grossman's discovery suggested that close study of paints might reveal information about the building's original detailing that could not be found by other means. The study of the center hall woodwork led Grossman to look again at the accounts of Samuel Harding, a woodcarver who had supplied architectural ornament for Independence Hall in the 1750s. In addition to woodwork for the center hall, Harding had provided Ionic capitals for what he described as the "green room." Could this, the architects speculated, be the Assembly Room? By this time the architects were accepting the Pine-Savage painting as a reliable document, although clearly the perspective was impossible and the architectural details were crudely represented. If it was accurate, Harding's account, with its reference to Ionic capitals, might provide a valuable clue to the original color treatment of the room.

Even though the woodwork had already been stripped, the tabernacle frame at the east end of the Assembly Room, some parts of which were thought to be original, was examined for traces of green paint. Although paint colors could not be established at this time, the examination did reveal the outline of Haviland's pilaster capitals, which had been removed by Rogers in the course of the 1890s restoration. This confirmed what had already been observed in the center hall: that study of the presence or absence of paint layers could indicate the size and outline of missing architectural trim. The architects were also beginning to consider other materials as possible clues to dating. They sent out for analysis mortar samples from joist holes that were possibly associated with the original location of the judge's bench in the Supreme Court Room. They hoped that when these were compared with dated samples from other parts of Independence Hall and Congress Hall, they would reveal when the holes had been filled in. Although the results of these particular tests were inconclusive, mortar sampling would become another standard element in the approach to dating building fabric.

At the same time the architects began to subject paints to more than examination by the naked eye. Experts from the Glidden Paint Company were called in to take samples for analysis from the Assembly and Supreme Court rooms. Almost immediately this procedure called into question the technique of total paint stripping and application of wood preservative. The Glidden experts found that they could not perform tests on the pediment of the tabernacle frame in the Assembly Room because a coat of preservative had been applied to the newly stripped wood. From then on the process was modified. Although paint removal continued in order to recapture the details of the woodwork, samples were taken beforehand and sections were left undisturbed to preserve evidence of original colors and subsequent coats. Thus, in May, when attention shifted to the exterior of the building, chips of paint and two dentils were obtained and brought into the architects' office before paint removal began on the main cornice of the north elevation. The chips were sent to the laboratory of the National Lead Company for analysis. National Lead reported that the cornice, thought to be original, undoubtedly was. It bore approximately 150 to 160 coats of paint. The first fifty coats over the primer were of white lead tinted a "dirty yellow." The next twenty-five to thirty coats were white; the forty above them again yellowish, although lighter than the bottom coats. The top forty or fifty paint layers were once again white. This was a startling revelation. For as long as anyone could remember, the exterior trim on most colonial buildings, including Independence Hall, had been painted a dazzling white. The information sent Hartshorne on a search through the historical literature. Confirmation of the use of a color other than pure white came from the *New England Farmer* of 1827, which recommended the addition of yellow ocher to white paint to slow the decomposition of white lead. On the basis of these findings, the architects chose a warm cream as the exterior trim color for Independence Hall. It was a decision that would revolutionize the appearance of eighteenth-century masonry buildings over the next decade or two. Private owners of buildings undergoing restoration in neighboring Society Hill followed the example of the park service buildings at Independence. Visitors and restoration architects from other parts of the country also noted the color change and, with or without the benefit of paint sampling, began to use cream for exterior trim on colonial buildings. Gradually the cream of Independence Hall became as ubiquitous as bright white had once been.

While most of the workmen were occupied in repairs to the north exterior facade and the center hall, the architects had an opportunity to review their findings. They also spent part of the early summer mounting an exhibit for installation in the Supreme Court Room. Throughout the long investigation of Independence Hall, at least part of the building always remained accessible to the public. Park Service management believed that visitors who had come to see Independence Hall and the Liberty Bell (which still stood in the tower hall) should not miss the experience. The exhibit, which opened on August 1, 1956, helped the public understand the condition of the building by sharing the research problems facing the park staff and observing the process of restoration.

By late October the repairs to the north facade were completed, and attention turned again to the interior. While repairs in the center hall proceeded, scaffolding went up in the tower stair hall so that the woodwork there could be examined and repaired as well. The tower stair hall was added to the original building in the 1750s. Its interior is extraordinarily felicitous in design and detailing. A broad staircase rises against its walls, lit midway by a large Palladian window in the south wall. The space is crowned by an elaborate cornice, with a dentil course and a frieze with acanthus leaf modillions interspersed with carved flowers on the soffit. When the flowers were removed so that the old paint could be stripped, it was immediately obvious that they were part of the original decoration. The wood surface beneath them was clean, and they had been attached with wrought nails. To guide the workmen who had originally installed them, those in the corners had the word "corner" marked on the back, while those along the sides were marked with the orientation of the wall to which they were to be affixed. Over the windows in the east and west walls, the flowers were oval rather than round, in order to preserve the rhythm of the spacing of the modillions in relation to the windows. Here someone, perhaps the master carver Samuel

Harding, had sketched the proper shape in chalk on the underside of the soffit.

Mindful of the potential loss of evidence caused by wholesale paint removal in other parts of the building, Hartshorne scraped paint down in selected areas. It soon became apparent that there were more layers of paint on richly carved elements than on flat surfaces, and that the latter bore torch marks. This suggested that paint had been removed previously by burning. On a dentil removed from the north corner, paint had been stripped from the front face, but not from the sides, which would have been difficult to reach with a torch. The National Lead Company, to which this dentil was sent for analysis, found that the original color was blue. Their report sent Hartshorne back to a soffit panel, a horizontal member that also might have escaped the torch. Scraping down layer by layer revealed that here too the bottom layer was blue. With these tests made, paint removal on the cornice proceeded, with the exception of a section in the southeast corner, where the full layering was preserved as evidence for future study.

As work proceeded in the tower stair hall, further aspects of the building's original appearance came to light. Removal of a wainscot panel on the stair landing revealed the original brickwork of the main building in an almost pristine state because it was covered over only some fifteen years after its construction. The architects ordered a plaster cast made so that the evidence could be used as a guide for future repointing of the exterior. Other important clues were discovered by Carpenter Foreman Joseph Silberholz, who was not only a highly skilled artisan, but also a keen observer. While repairing paneling in the wainscoted dado, he noticed one panel that had been repaired previously. Under an applied wooden strip, the old paint layers had escaped the earlier stripping. These established that the dado, like the cornice, had originally been blue. While working on the doorway leading from the landing to the second floor, Silberholz also found the outline of the original carved floral decoration behind compo flowers that had been applied in the 1890s.

Silberholz was one of the first to indicate that there might be underlying structural problems at Independence Hall. In the summer of 1957, while repairing the wooden arch of the Palladian window, he discovered that the detachment of the wooden trim from the wall was caused by the fact that the arched brickwork behind it had cracked and fallen. Although he and the mason carried out temporary repairs, they told the architects that they believed the cause to be settling of the tower's southeast corner. Grossman warned Anderson immediately about this condition. Similar signs of collapse, caused by deterioration of mortar, had been observed in the center hall walls and in the Supreme Court Building (Old City Hall). These findings suggested that similar conditions might prevail elsewhere in areas that were still concealed. However, he did not recommend a thorough study of the building's structure, although additional areas of weakness began to surface as repairs to the south side of the exterior were undertaken in the fall of 1957. The cornice of the tower was found to need considerable repair because the blocking and outlookers supporting it had rotted. By Christmas the roof was leaking badly. When the carpenters began to attempt to trace the source of the leaks, they reported that the roof trusses should be inspected. Some had shifted as much as three and a half inches out of position.

While repair work was being carried out in the tower stair hall and on the exterior, the architects returned, in October 1957, to their investigation of the Assembly Room. Armed with the skills they had acquired in paint analysis in the center hall and tower stair hall, they began a closer examination of the room's fabric. One of their primary objectives was to establish the original color scheme. They began by having the carpenters remove paneling along the west wall, so that they could search for evidence of earlier paint and plaster. Unfortunately, all the old plaster, save for a few small scraps, had been removed before the 1831 paneling was installed. Grossman began to despair of ever finding the original paint color. With the west wall barren, the architects turned to the east wall, which proved far more rewarding. Looking more closely at the tabernacle frame, the pedimented feature that occupied the center of the wall, they realized that both cut and wrought nails had been used in its construction. The presence of wrought nails suggested the possibility that some elements of the frame might, in fact, be part of the original decoration of the room.

As the tabernacle frame was dismantled, Hartshorne looked with special care at the cockleshell frieze. Such a feature was represented in the Pine-Savage painting, and the carving of the piece, with its deeply scalloped shell and richly entwined foliation, was reminiscent of the finest of Philadelphia eighteenth-century furniture. John Haviland had evidently reused it, but in a frame of somewhat different configuration, exposing more of the center of the board, but covering sections at its ends. Despite the wholesale stripping of paint from the Haviland paneling, traces of the original red primer could be discerned in the wood pores, and on the ends, which had been protected by the Haviland frame, the original green color and all subsequent paint layers were intact.

Repairs to the interior woodwork of the center hall and the tower stair hall continued through 1958. In the meantime, however, the question of the basic condition of the buildings on Independence Square came to a head. Repairs of woodwork at Congress Hall revealed the failure of a major roof truss. Here the problem was not hidden; the failure had caused a highly visible bulge in the building's east wall. In view of the seemingly critical situation at Congress Hall, the park service decided in the fall of 1958 to suspend further work on the buildings until a structural survey was completed.

At the same time, responsibility for architectural research on the buildings at Independence was shifted from the park to EODC, which prepared the contract and specifications for an outside engineering group to conduct the structural survey of the buildings on the square. These documents were written, however, not by Peterson or Thomas Wistar, Jr., to whom Peterson had assigned responsibility for restoration of the buildings on Independence Square, but by the "modern" architectural group under the direction of John Cabot. The contract was awarded to the Ewing Company, which submitted its controversial report, with its radical proposal for reconstruction of the buildings, in March 1959. The debate over this proposal was not resolved until June. By this time it had been decided that restoration work on the square would begin with Congress Hall, the structural system of which appeared to require rehabilitation more urgently than either Old City Hall or Independence Hall. It was also a far smaller building than Independence Hall, and more readily understood, so that its restoration could be completed with more speed, satisfying the demands for progress that had been coming from Judge Lewis, the mayor, and the Philadelphia newspapers. It was to Congress Hall, therefore, that structural engineer Sheldon Keast was first asked to turn his attention in considering alternatives to the Ewing Company's recommendations.

Meanwhile, Independence Hall remained in a state of suspension, its first floor unpainted and its structural problems unattended to. The first situation was partly remedied in the spring and summer of 1960, when the center hall and tower stair hall were painted. The second was left in abeyance, pending further study by EODC. Even without work at Independence Hall, there was enough activity to occupy the architects assigned to Independence and the park's carpenters, mason, and painters. In addition to the structural rehabilitation of Congress Hall, research activity and construction work were in progress in 1959 and 1960 on the exterior of the Merchants' Exchange, the Bishop White House, and the other houses on Walnut and Locust Streets. There was also time to consider what was and was not known about Independence Hall. Indeed, although the historic section of the historic structures report on the building was completed in 1959, and Grossman and Hartshorne had been examining the first floor since 1956, a great deal of concrete information was still lacking. The center hall and tower stair hall had been established as largely original, along with major segments of the Supreme Court Room's paneling. But little was known about the position of such elements of that room as the judges' bench and jury box, and still less about the actual appearance of the Assembly Room in the historic period. Architectural investigation of the interior of the second floor had never been undertaken by the National Park Service, nor had the nature and condition of the building's structure been fully examined.

In June 1961 Regional Director Ronald F. Lee convened a conference on planning and programs for Independence, attended by representatives from the region, the park, and EODC. Lee recommended a five-year moratorium on restoration work at Independence Hall. This would allow for thorough research and investigation before any alterations were made to the building's fabric. Indeed, a new phase of such research was about to get under way. When the Ewing Company's proposal for structural reinforcement of the buildings was rejected, the park service had determined that it would perform further structural studies in house. As a preliminary step, a summer measuring team consisting of an architect and three students was assigned to make measured drawings of the roof framing. The team worked under the supervision of a young park service architect named Lee H. Nelson. For Nelson it was the beginning of an association with Independence Hall that would last for over a decade, until completion of the building's restoration in 1972.

Nelson was another of Peterson's recruits, carefully nurtured through a succession of work and learning experiences. Nelson had been brought up in Oregon and had already produced a book on covered bridges that had brought him to Peterson's attention. His first job with the National Park Service was as supervisor of a HABS summer team at Fort McHenry in 1958, just after he finished graduate school. Peterson watched Nelson carefully and at the end of the summer suggested that he stay on with a draftsman and make more drawings. Whenever Peterson passed through Baltimore, he would have Nelson meet him at the train station so that he could review the younger man's work and suggest new leads and fresh avenues of research. By the time funds for the recording project ran out, Nelson was in trouble at Fort McHenry. In his enthusiasm he had carried his architectural investigations into the realm of archeology, excavating a cellar room. That earned him censure from the archeologists and some official letters of reprimand, but was not enough to preclude further employment with the park service. Anxious to keep him, Peterson next sent Nelson to Yorktown to work on the Archer and Dudley Dix Houses. Nelson came to Philadelphia, somewhat reluctantly, in the summer of 1960 to supervise a student measuring team at Old City Hall. He remained to prepare the building's historic structures report and supervise rehabilitation of its cupola, and then to work on Independence Hall.

The work of Nelson's measuring team in the attic of Independence Hall in the summer of 1961 was arduous and uncomfortable. Their task was to record the trusses that support the building's roof and help to support the ceiling of the second floor as well. In order to examine and record the bottom chords of the trusses, Nelson had had the attic floorboards taken up, adding to the awkwardness of working in a cramped space. The attic was hot and dusty, and the task must have seemed somewhat dull, at least until July 13 at 11:45 a.m., when part of the second-floor ceiling cracked. Blaine Cliver, a student on the measuring team, heard a sound that seemed familiar. Almost instantly he remembered the collapse of a ceiling in his fraternity house at Carnegie-Mellon Institute and called to his fellow draftsmen to vacate the building.

As soon as they could find a telephone, Cliver called Nelson, who was lunching at his desk in the Merchants' Exchange. Nelson and others in the office immediately began a frantic telephone search for the carpenters, who were then headquartered on Market Street. He needed them fast, with a load of shoring timbers. His great fear, like that of the students, was that the trusses, which were obviously overstressed, were now in structural failure that might lead to the collapse of the building. Nelson, accompanied by Judd, Hartshorne, and Wistar, then headed on the run for Independence Hall, where the plaster cracking was extending rapidly and parts of the ceiling were beginning to fall. Concerned for the safety of the public, they asked the guards to clear the first floor of visitors and to remove the most valuable furnishings, such as the Syng inkstand and the Rising Sun chair.

Happily, the incident was not as serious as it had first seemed. No major components of the building were in structural failure. Instead, the activity in the attic had loosened the inadequately nailed furring and metal lath for the plaster ceiling installed in 1922. Over the next few weeks the ceiling, floor, and relatively modern woodwork on the second floor were removed to prevent further incidents and facilitate study of structural conditions. Observation of the Assembly Room ceiling showed that it too was in perilous condition. To prevent its collapse, temporary shoring was installed until the plaster could be taken down, and the furnishings were once again removed.

The condition of the ceilings led National Park Service management to conclude that the urgent need for immediate remedial measures overrode the previous decision to delay disturbance of the fabric of Independence Hall for five years. The park service decided to hasten the structural investigation and to retain Keast & Hood as consulting engineers. Nelson was named project supervisor for the park service, with Gary Dysert as his assistant, and Hartshorne was also assigned to work on the investigation. They would work closely with Keast and his younger associate, Nicholas L. Gianopulos, over the next two years, analyzing the structure of Independence Hall, pinpointing its problems, and devising solutions that would preserve as much of its historic fabric as possible.

By the end of the summer of 1961, the team of engineers and architects had acquired a good understanding of how the structural framing system in Independence Hall functioned. One of the conclusions they came to was that the exterior masonry bearing walls and the foundations of the building were still sound and would need only minor underpinning. The attic trusses had been weakened, in part, by the mid-nineteenth century removal of trussed east-west partition walls on the second floor. These wall trusses had helped to support the ceiling of the first floor. Their replacements had been hung from the roof girders and had overstressed those members. Although new wall trusses were installed by T. Mellon Rogers in the 1890s, they had been poorly designed and had sagged. There was no point in trying to save them. Since the interior of the second floor would be entirely redone in the course of restoration, Nelson and Keast decided to replace the wall trusses with steel plate girders. In the attic, the old trusses would remain but would be supplemented with new steel beams and girders. The attic floor would be supported by hanger rods from the new beams, and additional support for the roof, where needed, would be provided by adjustable steel pipe columns.

The contract for the steel work was let to the A. Raymond Raff Company in June 1962. They had taken on an unconventional job. In order to minimize cutting through the building to install the steel, the design called for relatively small lengths, which required assembly in place. In the attic the steel would have to be threaded through a maze of wooden posts and iron straps that had been installed in previous attempts to reinforce the roof structure. Small holes were cut in the roof to bring in the steel for the attic; the plate girders for the second floor were eased in through a window. In addition to working out technical solutions to these unconventional requirements, the contractor had to coordinate scheduling with the park service staff, who had determined that at least parts of the building would remain open to the public during structural rehabilitation. While this first phase of the work was under way, Nelson and Keast's office designed systems to reinforce and stabilize the building's tower. By late in the summer of 1963, work in the tower had been completed. Most of Independence Hall was now in good structural condition; the restoration of its eighteenth-century appearance still lay ahead.

It was a restoration that Charles Peterson would not supervise, for he left the National Park Service in October 1962. Peterson had sent a long memorandum to Conrad Wirth the previous February, detailing his reasons for considering such a step after thirty-three years of service. Although he expressed a desire to carry on his work, he felt that this would be impossible unless the position of the historic architecture section improved. He complained that good people he had trained were transferred to what he referred to as the "modern department," that his historic structures section was routinely deprived of secretarial and drafting help, and that the "modern department," technically his superiors, had no understanding of his group's work. He hoped that historic structures could be given a position akin to that of the museum function in the National Park Service, closely associated with the history office, but not subordinate to it.

The memorandum was never answered. At an earlier time Wirth might have considered such a request seriously. By 1962, however, Peterson's major supporters in higher management, Vint and Zimmer, had themselves retired. Wirth himself was considering retirement. Although the directorship of the National Park Service had traditionally been a nonpolitical appointment, and Wirth had been named director at the end of the Truman administration, most of his accomplishments were associated with the Eisenhower years. Soon after John F. Kennedy's inauguration, newly appointed officials raised fundamental questions about the philosophy of the National Park Service. What the park service had traditionally viewed as pride in the institution and "family" closeness among personnel was interpreted as elitism and exclusiv-

23. *The east wall of the Assembly Room in Independence Hall before restoration. The tabernacle frame within the niche and the flanking pilasters remain from John Haviland's work in 1831. However, most of what is visible, including the pilaster capitals, the cornice, the doors, and the mantels, as well as the configuration of the fireplaces, was the work of T. Mellon Rogers in 1896. On the dais are two cherished remnants of the room's eighteenth-century furnishings, the Rising Sun chair and, on the desk, the Syng inkstand. Behind them, at the top of the tabernacle frame in the niche, is one of the few surviving fragments of the original woodwork, the elaborately carved cockleshell frieze.*

ity. Wirth did not step down as director until January 1964, but undoubtedly even in February 1962 he was concerned with issues that loomed far larger to him than Peterson's resignation or the position of the unit dealing with historic structures. When no reply was forthcoming from Washington, Peterson carried out his intention. He could leave knowing that at Independence, at least, the restoration program was in good hands. Wistar would also leave when Congress Hall was completed, but Nelson and Hartshorne would remain. They would continue to apply the principles to which Peterson had adhered. Restoration would be based on careful research and observation, attention to detail, and high standards for materials and workmanship.

Further investigation to uncover the original appearance of interior **141**

24. *The east wall of the Assembly Room stripped for investigation. In this 1964 view, restoration has already begun; structural repairs have been completed, and the fireplaces have been returned to their original configuration. To the right is the bricked-up doorway that once led to the committee room. The wooden barriers allowed visitors to observe the process. Mounted boards described the restoration and included a photograph of the Savage engraving, the most important single document in determining the room's original appearance.*

features at Independence Hall began even while the structural survey and rehabilitation were under way. Although the historical section of the historic structures report on Independence Hall had been completed in 1959, by the summer of 1961 new records had been discovered in Harrisburg and in the Philadelphia archives. Penny Hartshorne, Marty Yoelson, and two other historians, Miriam Quinn Blimm and Paul G. Sifton, crowded into Hartshorne's Volkswagen "bug" and drove out to make a concerted attack on the new Harrisburg materials.

Between September and December carpenters Phil Lang and John Pecoraio carefully disassembled the Haviland paneling in the Assembly Room. Architect Gary Dysert keyed each piece to the measured drawings, so that the

142

25. *The east wall of the Assembly Room restored. The completed room has been furnished with part of the park's collection of authenticated Philadelphia Windsor and ladderback chairs. The tables are covered, as they were in the eighteenth century, with green baize, specially woven for the park.*

paneling could be reerected. For the first time the entire interior of the 1730s walls was laid bare for examination. Even the most cursory observation of the walls imparted basic information about the original location and shapes of door and window openings and of fireplaces. The ceiling structure, if not the plaster, was original; although much of the structure of the floor and the floor itself had been replaced, three original joists remained. Thus, the level of the floor and the height of the room could be established. Nailing patterns in the surviving joists also revealed the width of the original floor boards.

Some fragments of the original wooden trim remained in place. The architects determined that many features of the doorway between the Assembly Room and the center hall were undisturbed. Other pieces of the original woodwork, some fifteen of them, including the cockleshell frieze on the east wall, had been reused in the Haviland restoration. One minute but important fragment was detected by the sharp eye of Gary Dysert, wedged between a joist and the brick wall. This was a dentil from the original cornice, evidently lodged there when the room was dismantled in 1816. Although it measured only two inches high by one and five-sixteenths inches wide and one and one- **143** quarter inches deep, it provided the key dimensions from which the internal proportions of the cornice could be extrapolated.

Other aspects of the room could be determined by a careful reading of the walls. Unfortunately, most of the original plaster had been removed, so that the type of clue that had proved so important in the Bishop White House was of little use here. However, in the eighteenth century it was customary not only to install woodwork before plastering, but to prime paint it as well. Because the painters knew that traces left on the masonry walls would be covered by the plaster, they made no effort to maintain neat edges. Thus, the position and outline of much of the woodwork could be traced. The iron anchors with which the woodwork and marble fireplace surrounds had been affixed to the walls remained in place. From these the architects could determine the position and size of the fireplace openings and their surrounds.

Although the location of most elements and some profiles could be established through the evidence of the paint traces and the original paneling of the frame of the west doorway, many details were still missing. For these the architects turned to a variety of sources. Most important of these were the Pine-Savage painting and the Savage engraving, which showed the general arrangement of the east and north walls, and, by inference, the south wall as well. The painting was not, however, correct in an architectural sense. The architects therefore looked at eighteenth-century books for proportions and proper forms for such features as the cornice. They depended particularly on two books by the English architect James Gibbs, published in 1728 and 1732 and known to have been available in Philadelphia. Careful study of Gibbs's plates had already convinced both the historians and the architects that the general form of Independence Hall, as well as much of its decoration, was derived from Gibbs. The building itself provided other prototypes; the paneled window jambs were copied from originals in the Supreme Court Room, the baseboards and chairrails from the tower stair hall. There was one design, however, for which the architects had to look elsewhere. No eighteenth-century fireplace surrounds remained in Independence Hall; the written documentation described the fireplaces in the Assembly Room as embellished with keystones. For these, the architects based their designs on two houses of the same period in the Philadelphia area: Hope Lodge and Whitby Hall.

By the fall of 1962 the architects had solved the riddle of the appearance of three walls of the Assembly Room; the west wall remained a mystery. True, they knew the location of the central door and the appearance of its pedimented surround. Documents suggested that the west wall also had had a paneled dado. But the distribution of the panels and the treatment of the wall above them was unknown. A few days after Peterson retired from the National Park Service, a friend showed him a sketch bearing on its back an inscription in John Trumbull's hand: "Jos. Sansom's Sketch of the Room in which Congress sat at the time of the Declaration of Independence." The owner's grandfather had purchased the sketch, drawn by an ancestor, at a

sale of Trumbull's possessions in 1896. The drawing showed what could only
be the west wall, with a central pedimented door flanked by pilasters, a
paneled dado, coved ceiling, and ornamental plaster panels on the wall above
the dado. On the face of the sketch, in a hand other than Trumbull's was the
inscription "40 ft. sqr. & 15 high to the c[o]ving, 4 or 5 more."

The owner had been unaware of the sketch's potential importance until
he conducted some foreign visitors on a tour of Independence Hall. As was
their custom, the architects had mounted a small exhibit to inform the public
of the progress of the restoration. The exhibit included two alternative
schemes for the west wall, with the frank admission that the architects did not
have sufficient evidence to form a definitive conclusion about the original
appearance of that part of the room. The owner realized that he held what
might prove to be a key document. The architects were elated by the drawing.
It was not to scale, but the dimensions noted on its face agreed with those of
the room. Although sketchy, it revealed more architectural understanding
than the Pine-Savage painting. Such a drawing might well have been made by
someone like Sansom, a Philadelphia merchant who was, according to information produced by the historians, also an author, antiquarian, and self-
proclaimed "admirer of architecture." Nevertheless, the National Park Service
subjected the drawing to the most rigorous tests. Wilman Spawn of the
American Philosophical Society analyzed the paper on which it was drawn.
He was able to confirm not only that the paper was genuine, but also that it
could be dated within the five-year span from 1809 to 1813. A photocopy of
the inscription on the front went to the FBI, along with three signed letters
of Sansom's, for handwriting analysis. The FBI concluded that the inscription
had indeed been written by Sansom. Armed with these assurances, the
architects proceeded to produce drawings for the west wall based on the
Sansom sketch. The sketch also established the shape and placement of the
dado panels on the north and south walls and confirmed that not only was
the west doorway frame authentic, but so was the double-leafed paneled door.

The research on the Assembly Room had been minute and highly productive. It had also been time-consuming. The final report on the restoration
was not submitted to the architectural advisory committee until July 1964. In
the meantime the new city administration, along with Judge Lewis, showed
renewed signs of impatience about the progress of the restoration. Mayor
James H. J. Tate complained to Lewis about his embarrassment over the
condition of Independence Hall when important visitors, such as Rose
Kennedy, came to Philadelphia. Lewis immediately put pressure on Superintendent Anderson, although privately he told Anderson that he was not
"mad" at anybody in Philadelphia, but wanted to make National Park Service
management aware of the need for haste. In response to demands for an
accelerated schedule, Robert E. Smith, Cabot's replacement as chief architect
in EODC, in February 1965 transferred responsibility for construction activities at the Independence Square group from Lee Nelson to Hugh Miller.

26. The west wall of the Assembly Room stripped for investigation. Each of the white rectangles is the key to a detail photograph recording the evidence that enabled the architects to determine the placing of such elements of the trim as baseboards, chairrails, cornice, and door surround.

Nelson retained control over the research and, by inference, the design decisions based on that research. The move appeared to be logical, but the divided authority would itself cause delays through lack of coordination and the resultant poor phasing of aspects of the construction.

In January 1965 Murphy, Quigley & Co. was awarded a contract for restoration of the Assembly Room for the sum of $88,400. By May the new paneling had been installed and the plasterers were working on the walls and ceiling. A few highly specialized tasks were not executed by the contractor. John Pecoraio of the day labor force carved replacements for missing or broken fragments of the cockleshell frieze; Albert Cooper, a woodcarver from Doylestown, Pennsylvania, replicated the pilaster capitals and other ornamental carving of the east wall. For all involved it was a particularly rewarding job. According to William J. O'Connell, president of Murphy, Quigley, everyone working on it considered it the most important job in the United States. Even a wildcat teamsters' strike did not prevent the completion of the room in time for a dedication ceremony at the end of June. The last pieces of

27. *Visitors, standing on a temporary plywood floor, view the Assembly Room, with the Rising Sun chair and Syng inkstand displayed, as workmen position samples of the west wall plaster paneling, cornice, and ceiling cove.*

the woodwork, the mahogany tabernacle frame and its pediment, were brought into the city at night from a Valley Forge farm in a convoy consisting of two station wagons.

With construction complete in the Assembly Room, Nelson moved on to the tower and its steeple. He shared the work with Joseph Petrak, who was assuming Miller's former role in overseeing construction. They noted that the steeple had been reshingled in 1961, and the weathervane repaired and regilded, but that the lower roof deck was in poor condition and that the condition of the cornice was questionable. They also recommended reinforcing the interior stair with steel, so that it could withstand the expected loads of millions of visitors. To strengthen the handrail, they advised replacing a few of the balusters with cast-steel replicas.

28. The west wall of the Assembly Room with restoration almost complete. The woodwork has been prime painted, and painters are beginning to apply the second coat in the north corner.

At the same time, Nelson was examining the paving in the central hall and tower stair hall and the front and rear entrances. This aspect of the investigation demanded both architectural and archeological skills. Because Independence no longer had an archeologist on its staff, Nelson requested and received cooperation from the Mid-Atlantic Region. The chief regional archeologist, John L. Cotter, and a staff archeologist, B. Bruce Powell, supervised excavations inside the building and around both sets of exterior steps. They found that the floor of the center hall had been paved with bricks when the building was first constructed in the 1730s. When the ornamental woodwork was installed in the 1750s, the paneling was erected over the paving. Subsequent repavings were laid up to the paneling, but not under it, so that the original bricks, and the herringbone pattern in which they were laid, survived around the periphery of the hall, establishing its design and its original level. In the tower stair hall the paneling and flooring had been installed at the same time, and none of the original paving survived, but the level of the floor could be determined by the depth of the baseboards and door frames, as well as by the height of the first step of the great staircase. Nelson's report, issued in February 1966, recommended restoration of the floor to its original level and appearance.

Outside the archeologists excavated in an attempt to establish the original configuration of the steps, which had been changed at least once at the tower entrance and more often on the Chestnut Street front. Although both fronts had been shown in old views, and the rear steps had been described in some detail, their dimensions were not known. Besides, the ground level had obviously changed in the course of two hundred years, so that the number of steps would necessarily differ. The excavation uncovered the original foundations for both sets of steps, thus establishing their original extent. Because they were pyramidal—the steps rose on the sides as well as at the front—the excavation also revealed their profiles preserved in the foundation walls of the building. Nelson also determined that although the doorsills had been replaced even more frequently than the steps, fragments were preserved at both the Chestnut Street door and the tower entrance. The original sills had been integral with the construction, wider than the doorways and set into the brick walls on either side. The masons replacing them had cut out the section within the width of the doorways, leaving the ends that were embedded in the walls in place. From these Nelson could determine that the original steps had been made of soapstone, which had also been used for the building's stone trim of quoins and beltcourses. Unfortunately, certain details about the steps, such as the shape of the nosings or curved edges, could not be established. In the restoration these would be based on the profiles of surviving steps at eighteenth-century houses in the Philadelphia area, such as Stenton.

The paved area in front of Independence Hall on Chestnut Street was also excavated. Here the archeologists confirmed that conditions in the third quarter of the eighteenth century had been accurately depicted in the Birch engraving of the area published in 1800. The main paving had been of small stones set in mortar, bounded and crossed by brick walkways. Sections of both the pebblestone and the brick walks remained below later resurfacings. Nelson recommended restoring the front area to its appearance in the Birch print, complete with watchboxes and pumps, especially since the existence of the latter had been confirmed by the archeologists' location of the wells that had supplied them.

By the time the architects began their renewed examination of the remaining major space on the first floor, the Supreme Court Room, they had acquired considerable sophistication in applying a broad range of investigative techniques. Paint research remained one of the most significant tools, but it had developed considerably since the search for original colors had been initiated in the mid-1950s, although this remained an important purpose. By this time Hartshorne had learned to perform the analyses herself, rather than sending the samples to commercial laboratories. In addition to examining scraped layers *in situ,* she now ground up paint from some of the layers so that the color of the pigment could be observed more closely; some of these samples were sent to outside laboratories for analysis of their chemical content. Experience in comparing the scraped layers to freshly exposed paint in microscopic cross-sections had made Hartshorne aware that the exposed paint surfaces had been dimmed or yellowed because of exposure to light, the aging of the oil medium in which the pigments were suspended, and the effect of pollutants in the air. The colors in the centers of the cross-sectioned layers, which had been protected from the atmosphere, were far brighter. The paint analyst would have to compensate for these changes in choosing a color. This was a step that had not been taken, for example, at Williamsburg in the 1920s and 1930s. The result had been a muted palette of "Williamsburg" colors that became enormously popular in interior decorating and gave the American public the false impression that eighteenth-century taste had been subdued in matters of color. Although the colors at Independence Hall were, in fact, rather soft, they were stronger than those that had been used at Williamsburg. The techniques developed at Independence, when applied to such eighteenth-century houses as the Paca House in Annapolis, Maryland, or Stenton on the outskirts of Philadelphia, have revealed the use of colors of a sometimes dazzling vividness. Indeed, at Williamsburg itself refined research in the last two decades has resulted in a far brighter palette than was conceived of in the 1930s. Nevertheless, paint analysis remains an art rather than an exact science. It is still dependent on matching color by eye and on the analyst's judgment of the effects of aging.

In 1960, when Hartshorne chose the colors for the center hall and tower stair hall at Independence, she also selected a new system for designating them. In a preliminary report on the colors, she had used such descriptive phrases as "onion white," "warm cream," and "olive drab." Such designations were open to misinterpretation, with one person's "onion white" being another's "warm cream." By the time she prepared her final report, she was using the Munsell Color Company's system of color notation. This system describes color numerically, in a manner akin to that in which written notes are used to represent sounds in music. It is thus a permanent, objective means of recording the value, hue, and tone components of a particular color.

Hartshorne also made a careful study of the documentation on Independence Hall and concluded that eighteenth-century paints must have been longer-lasting than their modern equivalents. Accounts for the building showed that a great deal of money had been spent on painting between 1754 and 1759, and then, except for some minor expenditures in 1779, not again until 1789. Thus, she concluded, the first color over the primer had been visible on the walls in the key year of 1776. Accordingly, she recommended painting the woodwork in the tower stair hall blue and that in the central hall a sandy beige.

Hartshorne's research led to something perhaps even more important than the determination of the original paint colors. It established paint as an important tool in dating pieces of woodwork. Already in the 1950s Grossman and Hartshorne had observed that the profiles of missing features could often be reconstructed from paint outlines. By 1960, however, the architects had realized that the paint layers on specific pieces of woodwork could be diagnostic. For example, the dentil found in the Assembly Room carried the same sequence of primer and first coats found on the cockleshell frieze, but none of the coats found above the primer on the Haviland paneling. Thus, they could conclude that this small piece had formed part of the original decoration of the room and had been removed before the Haviland paneling was installed. Examination of this type of evidence would prove particularly helpful in the Supreme Court Room, where fragments of the original cornice, which had been used as blocking and furring for the plaster ceiling installed in the 1890s, could be identified by the sequence of paint layers.

In addition to increased sophistication in using and interpreting paint evidence, the architects had developed a considerable body of knowledge about the evolution of nail-manufacturing technology in the late eighteenth and early nineteenth centuries. In the 1950s the architects had been able to distinguish between wrought nails, which they assumed to be of eighteenth-century date, and nineteenth-century cut nails. Nelson refined this technique by making a detailed study of Philadelphia nail manufactories of the period and collecting as many examples as he could from dated buildings. Change and improvement in manufacturing methods had been rapid in the period from about 1785 to 1830. Thus, in the Supreme Court Room it was possible to distinguish between alterations made in 1815–16 and those made later in the nineteenth century by careful study of the nails. The architects attempted to discover the character of nails that had been removed by making molds of the holes. After blowing talcum powder into a hole, they inserted an unbent and barbed paper clip surrounded with latex. After the latex had set, it could be removed by pulling on the paper clip.

Above all, the architects had learned the importance of careful investigation. Clues to the original design might be discovered in the reduction in size of a structural member, a change in coloration on a brick wall, the shape of a nail hole, or the presence of a metal anchor or strap. In 1965, when they began their investigation of the Supreme Court Room, much of the basic information about the space had already been established by Hartshorne's work of a decade earlier. By studying the existing paneling and old photographs, Hartshorne had come to the conclusion that on all but the west wall the woodwork below the entablature and above the dado was original. The entablature and the capitals of pilasters had evidently been removed when the ceiling was lowered nine inches in the 1890s; their appearance could be readily determined, however, from photographs, paint "ghosts," and surviving, reused fragments. The paneled dado had been removed and replaced by plaster at an undetermined time in the nineteenth century. The paneling of the west wall was entirely gone, except for pilasters at each end. The old photographs showed two more pilasters and a tabernacle frame with broken pediment, which Hartshorne believed to have been original. Most frustrating was the lack of clearcut information about two prominent features of the room known to have been present through written documentation: the judge's bench along the west wall, and galleries along the north and south walls. Along the north and south walls under the center windows, Hartshorne had found a number of holes that evidently marked the location of the galleries but offered no clues to their configuration. She had also located two sets of joist holes that related to the judge's bench, but they were at different levels, and she could not establish which might have been in place in 1776.

Finding further information would necessitate careful examination of every inch of the room's fabric. In order to do this, the paneling installed during the late nineteenth-century restoration was removed so that the walls behind it could be studied. Assisting Nelson and Hartshorne were a group of younger architects, some working summers, some on temporary assignment during the year. All observations were recorded in photographs and in a set of fifty evidence drawings. The contribution of one young draftsman, John Milner, stood out. Milner had been working his way through architectural school at the University of Pennsylvania in the early 1960s as a parking attendant at a restaurant. One evening he fell into conversation with a customer who was an architect, who told him that the National Park Service hired architectural students for summer work and suggested that he contact Peterson. Peterson in turn referred him to James C. Massey, then supervising the HABS program, who hired him for a summer measuring project. Although Milner's first assignment was to measure the Dock Street sewer, then exposed, his enthusiasm for historical architecture was not quenched. As had been the case with Nelson, Peterson and Massey found Milner a succession of summer and temporary assignments. He became the most consistent of the assistants at the Supreme Court Room, working year round.

By the summer of 1966, the team had established the original configuration of the north, south, and east walls and recommended proceeding with the reinstallation and restoration of the paneling down to the level of the window sills. However, there was still insufficient evidence for an authentic restoration of the west wall; more research would be needed. This recommendation was accepted, although park service management was again expressing concern about the slow pace of restoration at Independence Hall. In January 1966 Lon Garrison, who had succeeded Ronald F. Lee as director of the mid-Atlantic region, received a briefing on the development program at Independence. One of the points discussed was that work on the Supreme Court Room had not progressed as fast as anticipated, and that additional work would be necessary. In the early spring Superintendent Anderson complained to Garrison about the disruptions to visitation caused by continued investigative and construction activity in the center hall and the tower. He wanted the architects and workmen out of those areas before the start of the summer visitation season. After this time relations between the design office and the park appear to have become more formal, with frequent meetings and status reports. The added formality may also have been caused by a reorganization that put an additional level of administration between the park and the architectural researchers. When Garrison received the first formal status report in May, it came from H. Reese Smith. Smith was now chief of design and construction in a new entity that had been set up to replace EODC, the Philadelphia Planning and Service Center. At the same time, a Washington Service Center had been established, which was responsible for all research. Officially Nelson and Hartshorne were now part of the latter organization, although they remained on assignment in Philadelphia. In practice research went on much as it had. Nevertheless, in seven years ultimate responsibility for architectural research had shifted from the park to EODC in Philadelphia to the Washington Service Center, which made the reporting and review process more complicated and time-consuming.

Smith's status report reviewed the progress of restoration at Independence Hall, reminding Garrison that the Assembly Room had been completed and dedicated less than a year before, in June 1965. Many of the practical aspects of the building's rehabilitation were well advanced. Fire protection and security systems had been completed; ductwork for atmospheric controls had been installed; and plans and specifications for the electrical system were almost ready. Arrangements had been made so that the summer's visitors would not be too much aware of construction activity. The day labor force— that is, the staff carpenters and painters—expected to finish repair work on the exterior of the tower by June and would work on rehabilitation of the interior stair at night. True, the Supreme Court restoration had been delayed because of a lack of personnel and the inability of the historians, curators, and architects to locate a suitable eighteenth-century courtroom that might serve as a prototype. However, some of the replacement moldings had been designed, and the day labor force would install them as time permitted. The memorandum optimistically predicted that restoration of the second floor of Independence Hall would commence in the late fall of 1966.

By August there was some progress to report, but less than anticipated. The stairway was half completed, and it was expected that new brick for the hallways would be laid in the fall. The day labor force was making moldings for the cornice in the Supreme Court Room, but working drawings were still needed for the rest of the woodwork, and for the front and back entrances and steps. Nelson had been unable to spend much time at the drafting board. During the summer he had been working on the section of the historic structures report that covered part of the Supreme Court Room, and, in collaboration with Hartshorne, on the architectural data section for a report on lighting in Independence Hall, for which staff historian Miriam Blimm had supplied the historical data. In late October Anderson requested a review of the situation at Independence Hall because he would be away on leave from mid-November to the end of the year. Progress in several areas had been delayed because it was dependent on historical and architectural research. Atmospheric control remained unfinished in the Supreme Court Room because the location of grilles could not be determined until the research was completed. The installation of the electrical system had also been postponed pending approval of the report on historic lighting. There had been no progress on the working drawings for the two main entrances because of other demands on Nelson's time and the lack of drafting assistance. Partial relief for this chronic problem was in sight, however. Nelson reported that a contract would be let to an outside architectural firm for evidence drawings and additional research on the second floor. The contract was awarded to Price & Dickey; one of its principals, John Dickey, had considerable experience in restoration work.

Although this helped, it provided no solution for other underlying problems. A few months later, in March 1967, Nelson and Petrak, responding to Anderson's request for an explanation of the delays at Independence Hall, cited three basic causes. The first was the complicated review procedure through which all reports passed. Although recognizing the necessity of reviews, they complained that the process had been unnecessarily slow. (This was particularly frustrating because it was desirable to schedule construction for times of off-peak visitation. One reviewer who did not comment promptly could throw the construction off by months.) The second was the chronic shortage of drafting help, which had grown worse after the reorganization that separated Nelson and Hartshorne from the Philadelphia design office. The lack of working drawings not only made it difficult to maintain a schedule for the construction work, but threatened the quality of the restoration work. Pushing some phases of the work, such as atmospheric control, ahead of the research created lost motion and inefficiency, as well as compromising the integrity of the restoration. Finally, they reminded Anderson of the importance, magnitude, and unusual character of the task. The scope of the work was so great, and the emergence of unsuspected problems (such as the discovery of dry rot in the hallway) so frequent, that it was virtually impossible to prepare accurate schedules.

That Nelson found the review process frustrating was not surprising. Not only did it take a long time, but the comments were often contradictory. The review of Nelson's report on paving in the hallways of Independence Hall is typical. Frank Barnes, the regional historian, wrote:

> The usual excellent report, but I am appalled at the thought of still further structural upheaval. Is it *so* necessary to restore the original floor level? Can't

we approximate the "look" of the original (historic period) outside steps, keeping present floor level. We're not restoring the wings: why then such detail. The scene is running away with the story. As a matter of fact, we're not "certain" re the look of the period hallway floor: the bricks found date to 1797. *This report has no Admin. Data Section, either!*

In fact, Barnes had evidently not read the report carefully. Although the bricks had been replaced in 1797, fragments of the paving had been found that predated installation of the paneling in the 1750s. Moreover, restoration of the original level was not a mere whim. It would be necessary if the hall was to conform to the restored level in the Assembly Room as well as the restored front entrance. The comment of John Cotter, who had participated in the paving research, was perhaps unusually vehement but was otherwise typical of the views of the historians, architects, and archeologists, who, whatever their disagreements about specific points, were generally united in their desire for an accurate restoration:

> The best break Independence Hall and the NPS ever had was to benefit from the research and scholarship of its best historical, archeological and architectural investigators. Lee Nelson and Penny Hartshorne are tops in their field. There never was an adequate excuse for "the hell with accuracy—who will ever know" school of economy. There isn't now.

Such disputes required reconciliation by management before a decision could be made. This meant considerable discussion, a time-consuming process that, although it was meant to compose differences and end in consensus, nevertheless often left hard feelings in its wake.

Nelson was determined that Independence Hall would be restored with the highest degree of authenticity, regardless of the pressures to hasten completion. The almost desperate tone of the memorandum he and Petrak sent Anderson in March led the latter to appeal to Garrison for help for the architects. No help was forthcoming, however, although the pressure continued to mount. Henry Judd, who, as chief historic architect in Washington, was technically Nelson's boss, told him that the push to complete the Independence Hall restoration rapidly was coming from the highest levels. The restoration should proceed, even if some of it had to be based on conjecture.

Lee reminded Judd that the historic structures report on three sides of the Supreme Court Room had been presented for review in 1966. It had called for further research on the west wall, which had not been carried out because other requirements had assumed higher priority. Furthermore, the chronic shortage of personnel meant that the architects could not produce drawings or provide proper supervision for the day labor force. The situation had worsened since Milner had left the National Park Service to go to work for John Dickey. Thus, although the architects knew how three walls of the Supreme Court Room should be restored, they had been unable to proceed. Nelson pressed Judd to institute measures that would expedite the work. For one thing, although it had been known for many months that the arrangement of the Supreme Court Room had been considerably altered in 1778–79, Nelson had been unable to procure a decision as to what period it should be restored to—1776 or post-1779. Again he pleaded for drafting help. He hoped to rehire Milner, who had the knowledge and experience to make an immediate contribution. If more drafting help was not available, Nelson suggested dismissing part of the day labor force. There was no use keeping them on the payroll when they could not work because they had no drawings to guide them.

Nelson's previous complaints about the chronic shortage of architectural personnel had brought little or no relief. This time action was swift, consummated within a week at a meeting in Philadelphia. The decisions came directly from Ernest Allen Connally, chief of the Office of Archeology and Historic Preservation. This newly established group was the product of yet another reorganization, the second in approximately a year. The office (quickly reduced by the usual federal alphabetizing to OAHP) had been formed to administer new programs, such as the National Register of Historic Places, established by the National Historic Preservation Act of 1966. It also embraced some existing programs, such as HABS, and responsibility for all historical, archeological, and restoration work within the National Park System. Peterson's wish for a group of historical architects who were not subsidiary to the "moderns" had been realized some five years after he had left the park service. Judd reported to Connally, and Connally reported to the director of the National Park Service without intermediaries.

Judd accompanied Connally to Philadelphia on August 30 for a series of meetings with Nelson, Hartshorne, Petrak, Superintendent Anderson, and representatives of the Mid-Atlantic Region, including Regional Director Lon Garrison, and Assistant Regional Director George A. Palmer. In the course of these meetings, the group quickly resolved the issue of the period to which the Supreme Court Room would be restored, choosing 1776. They then settled on a completion date, the summer of 1968, and took a series of steps to alleviate Nelson's problems. First, they gave him immediate authority to hire Milner on contract to complete the drawings. Next, they affirmed Petrak's position as coordinator of the work. Finally, they agreed to circumvent the normal report procedure. Nelson and Hartshorne would no longer have to prepare and seek approval for historic structures reports before construction could commence. Henceforth they would be answerable only to Judd.

These decisions temporarily palliated the architects' situation, and they moved ahead with research and preparation of working drawings for the west wall. Even the pressure for completion could not diminish the joys of discovery, as small fragments provided answers to questions that had puzzled them for a decade. Careful examination of the base of the pilaster in the northwest corner was particularly rewarding. The base, which was still covered by later paneling in the 1950s and thus was not visible during Hartshorne's previous study, had been altered to allow installation of the higher of the two levels of joists supporting the judges' bench. Thus, it was the lower of the two sets of joist holes that related to the original bench, which had been in place from about 1740 to 1778–79. A more serendipitous find was a board that had been used as a scab to fur down the ceiling in the 1897 restoration. This board had the same paint layers as the lower layers of the original metopes in the entablature. In its center was a substantial, but broken, wrought-iron hook, which had been mounted over the original finish paint layer. The architects concluded that the board was the central strip of the glued-up panel in the tabernacle frame. The hook had undoubtedly held the king's arms, which documents showed had once hung in the frame; the hook perhaps had been broken when the sculpted arms were torn from the wall and burned on the evening of July 8, 1776.

By May 1968 research on the Supreme Court Room was complete, and working drawings had been begun. Nelson now turned to a myriad of other details, including supervision of continuing work in the halls and on the exterior; design of several exterior features and a control center in the closet under the stairway; and summary reports on the work completed to date, with recommendations for maintenance. Once the drawings were completed, the architects moved on to the second floor of Independence Hall. Restoration of this area appeared to pose almost insurmountable problems. Like the Assembly Room it had been stripped of almost all of its original finishes, and here there would be no Pine-Savage painting, no Sansom sketch, to guide the architects. Nevertheless, their accumulated knowledge about the building enabled them to interpret minute clues and form sound judgments about the eighteenth-century appearance of the four major spaces: the lobby, the long room, the Governor's Council Chamber, and the Committee Room. At a relatively early date they informed Judd that the second floor would be less conjectural and more elegant than had previously been assumed. They could establish the size and some profiles for much of the woodwork, as well as the location and dimensions of such features as fireplaces and closets. Although the ban on formal historic structures reports was still in effect, Nelson and Hartshorne kept a record of their rationales for elements of restoration. They derived most of the detailing from other parts of the building, painstakingly scaling moldings to fit the known dimensions of the second floor woodwork. Where Independence Hall itself could not supply prototypes, they turned to other early eighteenth-century buildings in the Philadelphia area.

Among the changes at Independence Hall in 1968, one was personal: Penelope Hartshorne married and became Penelope Batcheler. The other was institutional. At the end of the year, Wirth's successor as director of the National Park Service, George Hartzog, removed Anderson as superintendent. He replaced him with Chester Brooks with the charge to "get things moving." When Brooks arrived in January 1969, he discovered that the construction budget had been overspent by $70,000. One of his first acts was to give notice to the day labor force, who were paid out of construction funds. Recognizing, however, that skilled craftsmen were essential to the restoration, he quietly rehired a few of the best people for the park's maintenance staff. Several months later when Hartzog came to inspect progress at Independence, he observed these men installing woodwork on the second floor. He turned to Brooks and expostulated that Independence had no construction money that year. Brooks, in false innocence, replied that the men were doing maintenance work on the building, and that the administrative manual certainly permitted upkeep in any park. Hartzog protested that what was meant was the maintenance of trees, lawns, and the like, to which Brooks simply answered, "The hell you say, George." Hartzog had given him a mandate, and he intended to carry it out as long as he could remain technically within the rules.

Brooks also took immediate steps to involve everyone in setting schedules and deadlines, and to make sure that all understood where their activities fit into the process. Once the schedules were established, he expected them to be met. Brooks had great respect for Nelson's and Batcheler's professional capabilities and integrity but sometimes became impatient with their perfectionism. He felt that they wanted to "love Independence Hall to death." When it came time to install the chairrail on the second floor, Brooks told them that he would instruct Petrak to make a model, and that they would have a fixed period in which they could review it and either approve it or make changes before the final installation. Once they had done that, however, they could not change their minds.

In at least one instance a disagreement between Brooks and Nelson over the treatment of the second floor required resolution at the highest levels. Nelson frequently had raised the issue of split responsibility for the restoration—the decision that gave others authority to design and install mechanical and other systems. Sometimes elements of these systems interfered with the accuracy of the restoration. This had been the case in the Supreme Court Room, where previously installed ductwork required some adjustment of the entablature along the north and south walls. An even more extreme situation involved the west end of the second floor. Here the presence of ductwork for the atmospheric control system would require that the paneling covering the entire wall be placed a few inches forward of its original position. Nelson's recommended solution was removal of the ductwork and its replacement with a newly designed system that would permit installation of the paneling in its proper location. Brooks balked, and Nelson appealed to his superiors, Judd and Connally. Connally came up from Washington and somewhat reluctantly supported Brooks. Although agreeing with Nelson that professional standards of accuracy demanded the change, he feared the delays and extra costs that would be incurred. Brooks suggested that inaccuracies in the restoration could be recorded in structures and completion reports. Connally, however, had already suspended preparation of such reports in order to expedite the progress of construction at Independence. With Nelson's transfer to the Washington office after completion of the second floor, the reports remained unwritten.

Although the last degree of perfectionism was not encouraged, extraordinary care and pride in the quality of design and workmanship were. Howard LaRue, the administrative officer at Independence, was impressed by the dedication and skill of the craftsmen, and especially that of Edmund Whitlock, who installed the chairrail in the long room, hand-fitting it where necessary to compensate for the anomalies found in all old buildings. Although most of the interior of the second floor had been stripped in the course of nineteenth-century alterations, the architects had determined that the window sills were original. These sills had once been integral with the chairrail; that is, the same molding profile had carried across the plaster walls between and under the windows. Nelson and Batcheler decided to leave the sills in place, protected from wear by a covering made of a modern laminated material. Similar protective coverings had been installed in other parts of the building to preserve original material. In the Supreme Court Room, for example, the architects had placed stainless steel plates over some of the metopes, on the backs of which was inscribed:

> These plates are installed to protect the accumulated paint layers dating between 1740's–1890's on the original metope areas. Between the 1890's–1960's no additional paint layers were added because the 1898 entablature covered these areas.

Do Not Damage this Evidence!

> National Park Service Restoration of the Original Entablature, October 1966 Architects Lee H. Nelson and Penelope Hartshorne.

Mindful of the problems their restoration had faced because of the lack of records and destruction of evidence by previous alterations, the architects were determined to leave adequate information for their successors.

Preserving the window sills and creating a smooth transition between the old wood, covered by laminate, and new millwork posed difficulties for which Whitlock, by this time the foreman of the craft crew, found the solutions. In their years of working together at Independence, the architects developed a strong respect for the craftsmen's abilities to solve such problems. Nicholas Gianopulos, who, as Sheldon Keast's assistant and successor on the structural rehabilitation, also worked closely with the craft crew, compared Whitlock and his assistants to the master-builders of eighteenth-century Philadelphia. Without formal architectural education, they had an ingrained perception, based on long experience, of how a building was put together. These skills sometimes enabled them to devise the means to make the architects' and engineers' ideas work without elaborate written instructions or drawings.

They were especially important on the second floor of Independence Hall, where pressure to complete the work was keenly felt. Most of the millwork was fabricated in the park carpentry shop in Franklin Court, run by Gordie Whittington, and installed by the craft crew. This procedure reduced the necessity for detailed working drawings. Often the craftsmen could work on the basis of verbal instructions, looking for detailed guidance to examples in the park's architectural study collection. When the time came to raise the end-wall paneling, it was done as it had been in the eighteenth century—by manpower, not machine. Fittingly, in light of their close working relationship, Nelson, the designer, joined the craft crew in putting the paneling into place.

In 1972, after two decades of effort, the fully restored interior of Independence Hall was open to the public. The restoration of Independence Hall was in itself a tremendous accomplishment. In the process, something even more far-reaching had been achieved. The architects who worked on it had, through trial and error and learning from past mistakes, developed techniques and procedures that became standard for building restoration in the United States.

29. *The Long Room on the second floor of Independence Hall. Paneling of the east wall is being raised, as it was in the eighteenth century, by manpower. Helping to steady the paneling is Lee Nelson (at left), while Joseph Petrak (far right) observes. New steelwork is visible in the partition at right.*

Six

Telling the Park's Story: The First Twenty Years

R esearch and interpretation are the twin foundations of Independence
National Historical Park. All activity—research, restoration, planning,
construction—is ultimately directed to conveying to the public the
events that occurred in Philadelphia in the years between 1774 and 1800.
When Frank Barnes, commenting on Lee Nelson's plans for the center hall
of Independence Hall, complained that the "scene was running away with
the story," he was voicing a sense of priorities shared by many in and out of
the National Park Service. Independence had been acquired and was being
developed not in order to restore historic buildings, rehabilitate a neighborhood, or create an urban park, but to commemorate and interpret the events
associated with the founding of the Republic. Thus, decisions about how the
park would be planned, whether buildings would stand or fall, and how and
to what period those that remained would be restored and furnished depended
on perceptions of how these actions would help tell the "story."

The major events that the park was intended to commemorate were, in a
general way, familiar to all Americans. Yet even the most thoroughgoing
histories of the revolutionary and federal periods had not dealt with the
myriad of questions that would be raised by the National Park Service in the
course of attempting to convey the story of those years in a reasonably
authentic setting. Where did the events occur? What did the buildings in
which they took place look like? How were they furnished? Where and how
did the delegates to the Continental Congresses and the Constitutional
Convention and the members of the new government live? Where and how
did they spend their leisure time? Who was actually present at various events?
What did they think of one another, and how did they interact? It was a long
list; finding the answers would require meticulous research of a nature wholly
different from that used in conventional political history.

When Dr. Edward M. Riley arrived from Yorktown in December 1949,
he was faced with the formidable task of organizing a wide-ranging and
innovative research program. For the first year Riley was the sole historian at
Independence; much of the research effort would have to await augmentation
of the historical staff. Meanwhile he familiarized himself with the holdings of
Philadelphia institutions, with one foray to the Library of Congress in Washington to obtain copies of twenty-four maps of Philadelphia dating between

1683 and 1850. At the same time he introduced himself to the historical community in Philadelphia and formed an association with Dean Roy F. Nichols of the University of Pennsylvania's Graduate School of Arts and Sciences. With the counsel of Dr. William E. Lingelbach of the American Philosophical Society, Riley and Nichols set up a cooperative research program through which graduate students at the University of Pennsylvania and other Philadelphia-area schools would work, for credit, on projects related to the research program at Independence. By the summer of 1950 two doctoral candidates were participating in the program; by fall the number had reached thirteen.

Riley also began to assemble the basic materials that the historical staff at Independence would consult. The books with which he augmented the city's collection became the foundation of the park's library. He surveyed the records of two eighteenth-century insurance companies and the maps and prints of the city and its buildings held by Philadelphia institutions and compiled a bibliography of city directories and guides. He began to assemble an iconography of views of Philadelphia and individual buildings in the historic period. Riley also began a title search for the National Park Service's authorized real estate purchases, and, on the basis of these findings, prepared a report on Franklin Court.

In early 1951 the historical staff at Independence quadrupled, with the hiring of Martin I. Yoelson and Harry Lehman, and the transfer of Dennis Kurjack from Hopewell Village and James Mulcahy, a museum specialist, from Washington. Later in the year a sixth historian, R. W. Shoemaker, joined the group. The historians now formed, as they would through the 1950s, the largest single component of the Independence staff. Riley could begin to put his plan for an organized research effort into effect. Research projects were ranked by priority and assigned to particular staff members. Yoelson and Shoemaker were assigned to projects carrying the highest priority: establishment of chains-of-title and perusal of the insurance company records. Riley, assisted by the entire staff, worked on the physical history of the Independence Square group and also retained personal responsibility for Franklin Court and manuscript collections. Kurjack assumed the iconography project and shared with Riley examination of diaries and journals. Altogether, seventeen research projects had been established by the end of the year. Several of these, however, existed only on paper.

The scope and richness of the historic resources were both exciting and intimidating. Riley felt that he and his staff were like mice in a cheese factory, able only to "bite off very minute portions of the program." The work proceeded slowly because aids to research were still primitive. Many of the needed records were uncatalogued, as indeed were the full holdings of some of the institutions in which they were located. Copying was difficult. The historians laboriously transcribed their notes, including verbatim copies of long documents, by hand and entered them on five-by-eight-inch index cards,

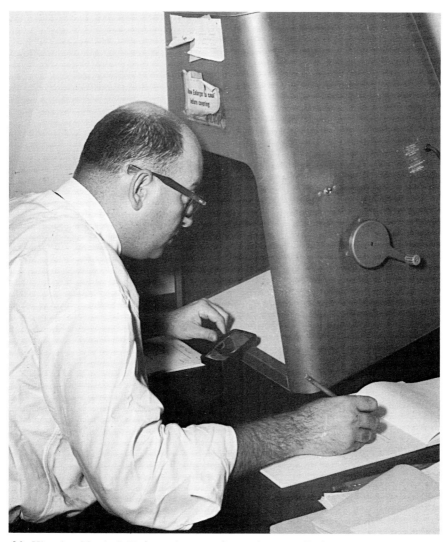

30. *Historian Martin I. Yoelson takes notes from a document displayed on the park's second-hand microfilm reader.*

which were organized into the "Historical Research Master File." Riley took advantage of whatever technology was available. He had acquired a second-hand microfilm reader, and in 1951 important sets of documents were microfilmed, including the early insurance surveys, records from the Pennsylvania Archives, and records from the Federal Direct Tax of 1798 from the National Archives. The last, found by Riley, was one of the most exciting discoveries of the early research program. The Direct Tax was a national tax on real estate, withdrawn, because of its general unpopularity, after only two years. It contained brief descriptions of the property, including buildings, to which the tax was applied. Although not as detailed as the Philadelphia insurance companies' surveys, it was more comprehensive. Information derived from the Direct Tax reinforced the iconography in identifying buildings that had stood within the park boundaries in the historic period but were no longer extant.

There were other obstacles. Although the city had transferred custody of its buildings and their contents to the National Park Service in January, it was not until July 1951 that, following the intercession of Judge Lewis, it permitted access to the city archives. Once the barrier was breached, however, relations became cordial. The city was quick to report the discovery of early records of the Bureau of City Property that shed considerable light on the details of the restoration of Independence Hall carried out between 1896 and 1898. After cleaning and packing these, the city transferred them to the Second Bank, where they would be readily available to the park historians.

In addition to difficulties and delays in gaining access to some groups of records, the historians' research activities were continually subject to interruption. Riley had sought publicity for the research activity at Independence. This helped to ensure cooperation from outside groups that might contribute information and support, but, at the same time, it produced numerous requests for information. To maintain good public relations, the Independence staff would drop work on its own projects in order to carry out the research necessary to answer the queries. Furthermore, while ordinary visitors to Independence were ushered through the Independence Square buildings (all that could then be seen) by the former city guards, groups that had made appointments and visiting dignitaries were conducted around the park by one of the historians. On such occasions the historians, who usually worked in ordinary business suits, would don National Park Service uniforms and assume their other persona as rangers.

A more serious, even if necessary, brake on the research program was the historians' preparation of various interpretive materials and their participation in master planning. During late 1951 and throughout 1952, they spent major portions of their time producing printed material, including a historical handbook, the texts of small exhibits, and memoranda related to the master plan. These tasks created dramatic shifts in the priorities assigned to various aspects of the research program. By the summer of 1952, chains-of-title had dropped from first place to sixth and the physical history and interior furnishing of Independence Hall to tenth and eleventh out of a list of sixteen topics. At least one new subject had been added, City Tavern. This addition probably reflected the historians' developing concept of the interpretive section of the master plan, in which they recommended beginning tours of the park at its eastern end. The top three priorities for fiscal year 1953 were preparation of interpretive sections for the master plan outline, the historical handbook, and a guide manual.

Priorities for the research program could thus shift rapidly and dramatically, depending on management decisions and other events beyond the historians' control. By mid-1953, with the announcement of the proposed gift by the General Federation of Women's Clubs for restoring and refurnishing Independence Hall, the buildings on Independence Square and their furnishings were moved back to the top of the list. While Riley, Kurjack, and Mulcahy concentrated on the interpretive programs and aids that had acquired high priority, the basic research program went forward, but at a much slower pace than had been expected. Yoelson, Lehman, and Shoemaker worked only sporadically on chains-of-title, insurance surveys, and public records because of other demands on their time. Riley's monthly reports regularly expressed frustration at these interruptions in the research program. In his view the sole compensation was the amount of material produced by the cooperative research program he and Nichols had established. This had expanded from the University of Pennsylvania to Bryn Mawr College. By early 1953 it had resulted in five seminar papers, two senior honors papers, two master's theses, and five dissertations on Philadelphia topics. Further fruit of the cooperative program was the production in 1954 of a filmstrip entitled "The Birth of Independence." The filmstrip, along with a tape recording and teachers' guide, was aimed at schoolchildren. It was prepared jointly by staff from Independence and the University of Pennsylvania.

By early 1954 the historians had completed the report on Independence Hall that would be used as the basis for the refurnishing program spurred by the gift of the General Federation of Women's Clubs. Almost immediately they turned their attention to completion of the interpretive section of the 1954 master plan. Shortly after this had been accomplished, Riley left Independence to assume a post at Colonial Williamsburg. By this time the historical program at Independence had undergone a fundamental change. The underlying purpose, providing the background for the restoration and interpretation of the park, remained the same. Riley, however, had viewed this purpose in the broadest possible sense, envisioning a research program that would deal with eighteenth-century Philadelphia in a wide-ranging manner, establishing the context for the physical development of Independence and the events that had taken place there. Circumstances such as the federation's gift and the necessity of drafting a master plan had already skewed research from the general to the specific. This trend would continue. From 1954 onward the highest priority would be assigned to site-specific research, aimed at providing information for whatever restoration was targeted to get under way next. One of the first victims of this change in emphasis was the cooperative research program. To some extent the program had lapsed even before Riley's departure because the University of Pennsylvania's American Civilization curriculum had not been offered in the 1953–54 academic year and because the new chairman of the university's history department and Riley's successor, Dr. Murray Nelligan, did not share their predecessors' enthusiasm for the project. It was the support of Riley and Nichols that had fueled the program. Without them the cooperative research program was not so much killed as allowed to die a slow death.

The mid-1950s were peak years for the research program. In 1955 Nelligan transferred to the regional office, with Kurjack assuming the position of branch chief. William C. Everhart arrived to become supervising historian. One historian left, but two new ones joined the staff in this period: Sydney Bradford and David A. Kimball. There was not only more staff, but also money for travel, first as part of the General Federation of Women's Clubs' gift and from the Eastern National Parks and Monuments Association, and, after 1956, from Mission 66 funds. Until 1955, most of the research had, of necessity, been conducted in Philadelphia. With the infusion of funds, the researchers began to fan out to more distant repositories, Yoelson to the New-York Historical Society, New York Public Library, and Princeton University, Everhart to the Huntington Library in Pasadena, California, Kurjack to the Clements Library in Ann Arbor, Michigan. Even foreign travel was possible. Bradford went to England to examine manuscripts at the British Museum and the Public Records Office. He spent approximately five months abroad, with just over three months devoted to archival work. It was all the budget would allow, and he returned to report that it was insufficient. Considering the intricacy of the British archives and the amount of material relevant to Independence, he thought that an additional year of research in England would be necessary.

Through 1956 most of this research was targeted toward accumulating information about the Supreme Court Room, which was the next space slated for restoration and refurnishing with the funds from the General Federation of Women's Clubs. Neither the documentary evidence collected earlier nor Penelope Hartshorne's architectural investigation had been able to resolve all the questions about its accoutrements. Part of Bradford's purpose in going to England had been to look at British courtrooms of the period. It soon became apparent, however, that it was not efficient to research a single topic in distant libraries. Although reports submitted by Independence continued to list priorities by topic, with the Supreme Court Room and the buildings on the square heading the list, in fact the research was being conducted on the basis of repositories. In 1957 the park requested that the historians be permitted to plan priorities according to collections to be examined, rather than the subject to be researched.

In January 1958 John D. R. Platt came to Independence from the Air Force Historical Program to assume Everhart's position as supervising park historian, following the latter's transfer to San Francisco. Kurjack now held the title of chief of the Division of Interpretation. Museum exhibits and curatorial functions, visitors' services, and archeology were under his supervision, as well as the research program. He also served as de facto assistant superintendent, acting for Anderson in the latter's absence. Platt found a pleasant informality and warmth among the National Park Service staff that contrasted favorably with the Air Force's hierarchical attitudes. When he arrived at his new office, he found the wall adorned with a crayon portrait by Joseph Sharples of Jeremiah Wadsworth, the subject of Platt's doctoral dissertation. It was one of the pictures from the Peale collection that had been removed from Independence Hall and were temporarily being stored in the building the historians then occupied at 135 South Fifth Street. Kimball, who knew that Wadsworth had been Platt's subject, had arranged for its "temporary storage" in his office. On a table beneath the portrait was a worn ranger's hat with a note under its brim. The note, from Everhart, advised Platt that people would tell him about how Everhart did things while he was at Independence, and suggested that Platt tell them to go to hell.

In contrast to Platt's experiences with the military, most decisions in the National Park Service were made on the basis of a consensus formed after discussion among the staff. Collegiality was an important factor in the research program at Independence. The nature of the research demanded minute and painstaking study of millions of documents in search of single nuggets of information. Riley recalled the process as resembling a jigsaw puzzle. Finding a missing piece that fitted the rest of the puzzle was exhilarating. With so many hands seeking evidence in so many sources and through diverse disciplines, the pieces might never have fitted together had it not been for the free exchange of information among the staff. This took place not only in meetings, but in chance encounters at the water cooler, or over lunch, or at the frequent social gatherings among the staff, where, despite the presence of spouses, the tendency was to talk shop.

The knowledge acquired through these informal exchanges was vital to the restoration and refurnishing process, where small clues from varying sources could be highly significant. The appearance of the Assembly Room, for example, was pieced together largely from Yoelson's discovery of the original order for its finishes, Mulcahy's analysis of the Pine-Savage painting, and the serendipitous appearance of the Joseph Sansom sketch, taken in conjunction with the physical analysis of the surviving fabric. All of the pieces were required to complete the jigsaw puzzle.

With Platt's arrival the production of reports assumed new importance. At this time historic structures reports were being required before restoration or reconstruction could begin. In preparation for the master plan, several historic grounds reports dealing with such issues as appropriate planting, paving, and fencing were also undertaken. Platt insisted on high professional standards for the reports, with conclusions backed by solid research. The reports were not only the fruits of the work already accomplished; their preparation also revealed how much remained to be done.

In the meantime, pressures for completion of the park began to mount. Judge Lewis, Mayor Tate, and others in Philadelphia were anxious to see concrete progress in the construction program. Some money would come to the park through Mission 66, and in August 1958 Lewis succeeded in shepherding through Congress authorization for the expenditure of an additional $7 million. Lack of funding was no longer an acceptable excuse; the research program could not be allowed to impede park development. In response to these pressures, National Park Service management took an extraordinary step at a master plan meeting in June 1958, agreeing to authorize the expenditure of construction funds for a two-year crash program of research, leaving the details of what was to be accomplished for later determination. In response to this decision, the historians assembled a proposal embodying their appraisal of the scope of the work and the staff requirements. It called for four teams, each consisting of three historians. Each team would be responsible for specific subject areas and would also be assigned particular repositories or record groups. In addition there would be a supervising historian, two senior historians to evaluate the product and write the reports, a librarian for records management, and a historian to do the research for exhibits, signs, and other interpretive devices. The teams would examine over two million items in thirty-seven institutions scattered up and down the eastern seaboard, as well as in England and France. They would also peruse over two million pages of newsprint, including full runs of thirty-three early Philadelphia newspapers, seven additional Pennsylvania imprints, thirty-four from other states, and selected later papers. The price tag came to just under a quarter of a million dollars. When the park added its estimates for architectural, museum, and archeological research, the sum grew to over a million dollars.

This was far higher than management in the regional and Washington offices had envisioned. Assistant Regional Director Palmer recommended slashing the budget to $100,000, and, since the program was to be paid for with construction funds, suggested that it should deal only with items relevant to proposed construction, not with the general ideas and purposes of the park. Thus, he called for confining the immediate research to the physical history of the Independence Square buildings and their contents. The regional office also questioned the size of the architectural staff requested by Charles Grossman and recommended transferring responsibility for architectural research to EODC. At an August meeting in Washington, park service management decided that the research program would have to be financed from available funds and would be centered on the Independence Square group, and that historical reports on the buildings and their furnishings should be completed by mid-1959.

The meeting had obviously been a call for restraint. It was therefore with considerable consternation that the regional office reviewed the park's revised proposal, submitted in September, for its development program for 1960–63. Although the research program had been stretched out over four years rather than compressed into two, the proposal now called for an even higher expenditure, by some $100,000, than had been requested in July. Over half of the proposed funds were for architectural research. Palmer, as acting regional director, proposed Draconian measures. He first recommended restricting the research to be paid for with construction funds to the $60,000 already authorized for the reports on the Independence Square buildings. Those were scheduled for completion by June 30, 1959, at which time the research program could be reassessed. The more radical recommendation, already suggested earlier, was transfer of the architectural research program from the park staff to EODC.

Palmer's views prevailed, and by late October Anderson was describing how projects for the coming year would be rearranged to accommodate the reduced research program within the established funding limits. He proposed hiring two new historians and one new clerk-typist to assist with report preparation. With the approved increases there were in 1959 nine historians at Independence. Kurjack and Yoelson had been at Independence almost since its inception; Kimball had been on board for several years, and Platt for at least a year. In addition, William Campbell, who had worked on the park's architectural staff for several years, had transferred to the historians' office when responsibility for architectural research was shifted to EODC. In the preceding year not only had two new positions been created, but there had once again been turnover in the staff. New faces among the historians included Mary Anne Hagan, James Mullaly, James R. Sullivan, and Paul G. Sifton.

Some reports were prepared by a single historian. When the reports would be complex, as was certainly the case for Independence Hall and Congress Hall, they became a team effort. Bradford and Mullaly, who had been on assignment at Fort McHenry in Baltimore Harbor, prepared the first draft of the Independence Hall Part I report. (Part I reports were preliminary, providing historical and architectural information sufficient to form the basis for decision making about the disposition or treatment of a building. If the building was to be restored, additional research was done and a more detailed Part II report prepared.) So that the drafters could have the materials at hand, the research cards were microfilmed. The cards went to Baltimore, with the microfilm remaining in Philadelphia for use by the rest of the historians. The final version of the report was written in Philadelphia by Platt and Kimball. Platt based this assignment, as well as others, on his assessment of the interests, abilities, and expertise of the historical staff. He was also insistent that the reports be concise and well-written. It was in this period, Yoelson believed, that the staff at Independence, spurred on by Platt's reviews and comments, "really became professional historians."

Under this system the 1959 fiscal year was extremely fruitful. The basic research program Riley had formulated nine years before began to return its dividends. Most of the information needed for the reports was already available in the park's research files; where it was lacking, potential sources had usually been identified, if not yet studied. The iconography especially was proving to be of great value, at least for evidence of the original appearance of the buildings' exteriors. The staff could also be more productive because the use of construction funds for the reports on the Independence Square group freed other monies to fund additional aspects of the historical program. In addition to the four required reports on Independence Hall, Congress Hall, Old City Hall, and Independence Square (also known by its original name, the State House Yard), the staff had prepared preliminary or final reports on fourteen other topics. Three were at least partial furnishings plans for the buildings on the square. One report, on horticulture, was intended to form the basis for the selection of trees, shrubs, vines, ground cover, and flowers to be planted in the sections of the park that were then being landscaped. This general guide to historically appropriate plant materials was supplemented by more specific reports on the historic appearance of the grounds around the Merchants' Exchange, Carpenters' Hall, and the Second Bank.

Six of the reports were prepared to form the basis of decisions about the use or retention of buildings and sites. The remainder, providing the background for restoration decisions, included the first report on the Bishop White House and reports on the exterior of four houses on Locust Street owned by the National Park Service. Of the reports intended to provide information for administrative decision making, only one had any real effect. The decisions to reconstruct the Pemberton House and demolish the Contributionship Stable and the Marshall's Court Houses were made for political, aesthetic, or logistical reasons rather than historical ones. Only the historical associations of the Market Street Houses, which had been built by Benjamin Franklin as income-producing properties, would ultimately have an effect on shaping the park.

For the time being, however, virtually all the efforts of the historians continued to be concentrated on the Independence Square group. No sooner were the Part I reports completed than the staff began to refine and expand their findings in order to produce the historical sections of the definitive Part II reports. While work continued on other buildings, especially Independence Hall, Congress Hall was the first of the group slated for restoration: not only was it thought to be more in need of immediate structural repair than other components of the Independence Square group, but it required relatively little intervention to return it to a condition of historical accuracy because of the AIA's previous careful restoration.

A few details would require further research, and, there was also the question of the arrangement of the first floor during the period when it served as the chamber of the United States House of Representatives. Physical evidence had long since been obliterated by alterations and restorations. When the first version of the historic structures report was submitted in March 1959, this was one of the pieces of the jigsaw puzzle for which there was no ready reference in the card file. Fortunately, however, a vital piece of evidence was found rather quickly. In November 1959 Fred Hanson joined the museum staff. One of his first assignments was to assemble materials for an exhibit on Congress Hall. The first resource was the park's iconographic file, which included views not only of early Philadelphia and its buildings, but also of events. Among the latter were copies of early political cartoons, which, because of their vivid style and comedic overtones, made particularly good exhibit material. He selected one that showed a fight, with fists and canes as weapons, between Reps. Matthew Lyon of Vermont and Roger Griswold of Connecticut on the House floor. As the potential exhibit materials circulated, the historians, looking at the cartoon with fresh eyes, saw that its background revealed a good deal about the arrangement of the room. Hagan was quickly put to work checking newspapers of the appropriate date for information about the fight and was able to find some further description. The cartoon was thus as key a document for the restoration of the interior of Congress Hall as the Pine-Savage painting would prove to be for the Assembly Room in Independence Hall.

The interiors of Congress Hall posed some interesting research problems, but there was never any doubt that the major spaces would be restored to their appearance in the last decade of the eighteenth century—historians, architects, museum staff, and management agreed on that goal without lengthy discussion or written directives. There was no such consensus, however, for other aspects of the restoration. In the course of preparing the first version of the historic structures report, architectural investigations showed that the rostrum for the Speaker of the House had been located not, as might have been assumed, at the south end of the House chamber, but along its west wall. The members of Congress had therefore usually entered the House through a door opposite the rostrum located approximately midway along the building's east facade, the side adjacent to Independence Hall, rather than through the front door on Chestnut Street. Late eighteenth-century views of the Independence complex showed an arched and balustraded portico in the approximate location of this doorway, although its precise relation to the west arcade and wing of Independence Hall was unclear. Subsequent changes to the wing buildings west of Independence Hall had obliterated any trace of the portico above ground. In 1959, therefore, the historians recommended archeological investigation of its site. This investigation was carried out by Jackson W. Moore, Jr., in June 1959. He found portions of the portico's north and south foundation walls. The east wall had been destroyed during construction of new wings for Independence Hall in 1811, and, indeed, a corner of the extant west wing reconstructed in 1896 had been built over the site of the portico. Nevertheless, when read in conjunction with a recently discovered 1783 ground plan of the complex, the remains below ground were sufficient to establish the dimensions of the portico. The historians believed that the archeological and pictorial evidence was a sufficient guide to an accurate reconstruction.

The second version of the historic structures report for Congress Hall was not completed until April 1960, when the architectural data section was added. By that time the historical data had been available for over a month, and opposition to reconstruction of the portico, on both philosophical and economic grounds, began to surface. Edward Zimmer, chief of EODC, summed up his opinion in a memorandum to the new regional director, Ronald F. Lee. Reconstruction of the portico would require extensive changes to the west wing and delay letting the contract for construction work on Congress Hall; moreover, there was insufficient evidence for an accurate reconstruction. Charles Peterson took a more extreme position, arguing that neither the portico nor the door under it should be reconstructed. The door was not original to the building, having existed only between 1794 and ca. 1812. Without the portico he believed that the door would be meaningless, and there was insufficient evidence of the details of the portico to justify its reconstruction. Penelope Hartshorne voiced an intermediate point of view. Although she agreed that there was insufficient evidence for a reconstruction of the portico, she thought that the side entrance was an important aid to "recreating the aspect" of Congress Hall at the end of the eighteenth century. She suggested reconstructing the doorway, for which there was considerable evidence, while representing the portico through construction of a platform with low walls. The discussions over the doorway and portico went on for over two years. Platt fought hard for full reconstruction. In the end, the decision hinged more on costs than on the philosophy of restoration, satisfying neither Platt nor Peterson. The doorway was reconstructed because of its interpretive value and relation to the building's restored interior; however, it was approached by a simple flight of steps with no suggestion of the portico.

Platt, and some of the other historians, believed that historical accuracy demanded that Independence Hall and its ancillary buildings be totally rebuilt to their appearance in 1776–1800. This would involve an accurate reconstruction not only of the arcades and wings on either side of Independence Hall, but also of the State House Yard and the committee room at the southeast corner of the Assembly Room, to which Congress had withdrawn for some of its most important sessions. National Park Service management, however, took a more pragmatic view, approaching the buildings and grounds at Independence with considerable flexibility, and with one eye on the budget. At the August 1958 meeting that established the limited scope of the immediate research program, the directorate had also decided that the current approach to the buildings would be rehabilitation and stabilization, without precluding eventual full restoration. Thus, the debate about the portico began in an environment in which no ultimate limits had been set. By March 1961, however, Director Conrad L. Wirth had determined that full restoration of the buildings on Independence Square should not be contemplated. The question of historical accuracy did not arise; Wirth's concern was carrying out the work needed to put the buildings in good shape and restore them to an extent sufficient for interpretive purposes within the authorized budget. Because Wirth did not define what would constitute an acceptable partial restoration, there was still considerable room for debate over whether particular features would or would not be restored. In some cases, such as the reconstruction of the doorway and portico of Congress Hall, varying points of view were aired in formal discussions and memoranda. At other times, unspoken underlying assumptions prevailed. The reconstruction of the portico could not have been undertaken unless the 1896 wings and arcades of Independence Hall were demolished and replaced with more accurate reconstructions, because the existing West Wing impinged on the space the portico had occupied. Once Wirth's opinion had been heard, such a reconstruction was never discussed, much less included in the restoration program, nor was reconstruction of the committee room. On the other hand, full and accurate restoration of the exterior envelope of Independence Hall and its interiors was pursued without question, with two exceptions. There was early, if unwritten, agreement that the Strickland steeple of 1828 would remain. The other decision, not made until the 1970s, captured the spirit of Wirth's policy. Originally, there had been two tall-case or "grandfather's" clocks on the east and west walls of Independence Hall. That on the west wall was rebuilt because it provided a needed shaft for the mechanical system ductwork; its balancing companion, an important component of the building's symmetrical composition, was not.

Restoration of the State House Yard was a victim of both Wirth's decision and local political pressures. Master plan drawings through the 1950s portrayed the plot of open ground behind Independence Hall as reconstructed with serpentine walks and informal plantings. Its restoration was recommended in the historic grounds report of June 1959. But, like reconstruction of the portico, an accurate restoration of the State House Yard would have depended on reconstruction of the wings and arcades, which would have been closed rather than open. Furthermore, restoration of the State House Yard would have required a high wall around its perimeter and a massive gate on Walnut Street. The insurance companies on Walnut Street, whose employees were accustomed to cutting through the yard on their way to and from work, objected to reconstruction of the enclosure. City officials supported the companies. These local objections and financial restrictions combined to preclude serious consideration of the area's restoration.

In the years following 1959, the historians at Independence continued their research program and production of reports, although never at the frantic pace of that one remarkable twelve-month period. As time and the budget permitted, they visited the Massachusetts and Virginia Historical Societies, Yale and Princeton Universities, and other repositories on the east coast, as well as the Pennsylvania Archives at Harrisburg, to look at newly found material. In 1964 Sifton went to France to examine material at the Bibliothèque Nationale and in other archives. The historians pursued inquiries in the papers of members of Congress and in the correspondence and diaries of visitors to its sessions. They continued to search for additional material to supply answers to questions about the interior finishes and furnishings of the Independence Square group. Reports were prepared on buildings not yet covered, including lengthy documents on City Tavern, Benjamin Franklin's house, and Franklin's tenant houses on Market Street. There were also reports on the Christian Street houses near Gloria Dei Church, and on several early churches in the vicinity of the park. Another group of reports supported completion of landscaping features in the area bounded by Walnut and Chestnut, Third and Sixth Streets.

In late 1965 George Hartzog, who had replaced Conrad Wirth as director of the National Park Service in 1964, announced one of several periodic reorganizations carried out during his tenure. This established a Washington Service Center, which would bring together in one place historians and architectural historians to carry out major research programs for the entire park service. Only those historians whose functions were largely interpretive would remain at the parks to carry out minor research studies providing background for explaining the park to the public. Under this directive the history staff at Independence gradually began to dissolve, with its members transferring to the interpretive staff, to regional offices, or to Washington. Only Yoelson, Campbell, and Blimm remained to answer the myriad questions of those carrying out the park's restoration and development and its interpretive program, and the inquiries of outsiders. Yet Independence was too big a research project, and the materials were too concentrated in Philadelphia, for such a system to work efficiently. Thus, the architects chiefly responsible for architectural research, Nelson and Hartshorne, while administratively part of the Washington staff, remained assigned to Philadelphia. Platt, after a brief transfer to Washington, returned to Philadelphia to work on the research and reports needed for the development and restoration projects of the late 1960s and early 1970s.

The division between research and interpretation implicit in Hartzog's directive had not always been the case at Independence. Through the 1950s responsibility for interpreting Independence to the public rested with the same group that carried out research and prepared reports: those who were most familiar with the historical background also told the park's story. But because the historical staff was so small, each of these activities could only be carried out as an interruption of the other. Both suffered as a result. Interpretive planning in the early years was carried on only sporadically, and implementation in the form of signs, exhibits, or written materials was meager. In the last months of 1950, Riley put together a three-fold leaflet so that when the National Park Service assumed administration of Independence Hall in January, there would be a piece of literature to replace the somewhat dubious information sheet the city had been using. During the first year that the historians' office was in full operation, Kurjack worked briefly on a manual for the public, and Mulcahy mounted a small exhibit for the first information center, which was in the West Wing of Independence Hall. The emphasis within the office, however, was almost entirely on research.

In the following year the situation was reversed, as basic research was almost laid aside while the staff concentrated on preparation of a historical handbook and the interpretive statement for the first master plan. Although visitors to Independence could then see the interior of only Independence Hall, the master plan, of course, envisioned the visitor's experience as it would be when the park was complete. In order to encourage visitors to view the entire park, not just Independence Hall and the Liberty Bell (then in the hall), the historians recommended a plan focused on entry to the park from the east. This would not only lead visitors through other sections of the park, with Independence Hall as the climax, but would also respect the historical chronology: many of the delegates to the first Continental Congress had initially met informally at the City Tavern before the sessions in Carpenters' Hall in 1774. So the progression from a reconstructed City Tavern to Carpenters' Hall and thence to Independence Hall would, in a sense, retrace their footsteps.

The growing number of visitors also strained the staff's time. In addition to research, they were expected to provide personal interpretive services as tour leaders for organized groups. The task of conducting visitors around the park was not a particularly congenial one for the historians, most of whom preferred research to personal interpretation. Riley's frustration surfaced frequently in his monthly reports on the group's activities. He described preparation of the layout of the historical handbook as tedious and noted that heavy visitation in the spring, especially by school groups, had an adverse effect on the research program. This situation was somewhat alleviated by hiring seasonal ranger-historians to provide tours not only for groups with advance appointments, but for the general public during peak visitation periods. Six seasonals served in 1951; by the following year, the demand was so great that the number was increased to ten. By the mid-1950s two seasonals were also on duty during April and May, when visitation by school groups was at its height. Gradually other devices were designed to ease the burden of conducting tours. In 1953 Yoelson prepared a self-guided tour leaflet, which was made available to groups that could not be accommodated with conducted tours, and the historical handbook went on sale in 1954.

As the number of visitors increased, the West Wing of Independence Hall was no longer adequate as the sole orientation center and exhibit area. In 1955 the orientation center was shifted to the East Wing so that the West Wing could be fitted up as an exhibit gallery. The first exhibit, installed early in 1956, was on Franklin. In addition, two small exhibits explained work that was being done at the park, one at the site of archeological investigations in Independence Square, the other in the Supreme Court Room. Similar exhibits were mounted regularly as restoration and development went forward, explaining not only the historic importance of the park, but also the ongoing work.

In the early 1950s only the most rudimentary printed interpretive aids were available to visitors. In the second half of the decade emphasis shifted to audiovisual aids. These were largely the province of William C. Everhart, who came to Independence in the fall of 1955. Everhart, who would subsequently become an associate director of the National Park Service for interpretation, had considerable interest in the potential of sight and sound for interpretive purposes. By 1956, in cooperation with the Philadelphia affiliate of the Columbia Broadcasting System, WCAU-TV, he had arranged for production of a slide-tape program, narrated by John Facenda, which was shown to visitors in the refitted East Wing. Two years later an audio device was installed at the Liberty Bell, and visitors could hear a three-minute recording of the story of the bell; in 1960 the tape became available in five foreign languages—Spanish, French, German, Italian, and Russian—through the cooperation of the State Department and the Voice of America.

These devices were attempts to compensate the average visitor for the lack of any form of personal interpretation at Independence. Organized groups were fairly well served through conducted tours, which were frequently sparked by the historians' enthusiasm about their fresh discoveries about the park and its buildings. For visitors who came on their own, however, the experience could be far from satisfactory. Independence Hall was still staffed by the guards who had served there during the city's tenure. They were indeed guards, not historians or trained interpreters, although the National Park Service made frequent attempts to train them and to upgrade the information they offered. Visitors sometimes complained about their brusqueness.

This attitude did not go unnoticed within the National Park Service, although it seemed to feel no great urgency about alleviating the situation. George Palmer had been shocked, while touring the park with his family a few years before coming to Philadelphia as assistant regional director in 1955, at the manner in which visitors were elbowed through the buildings. The situation had not improved by the time he took up his post in Philadelphia, and he discussed it with Murray Nelligan, then chief of interpretation in the regional office. Nelligan, however, was not particularly concerned. He believed that one first completed a park, then opened it, and then installed an interpretive program. John Platt also, when he arrived at Independence in 1958, felt that the interpretive program was lagging and urged Kurjack several times to authorize him to take some action, but Kurjack was determined that nothing would interfere with the production of reports.

Palmer did not abandon hope of seeing the situation improved. In the spring of 1959, a historian with considerable experience in interpretation, James R. Sullivan, was assigned to the Philadelphia regional office and was temporarily without a project. Sullivan had worked as a historian-interpreter at Colonial National Historical Park and at Chickamauga-Chattanooga, the Civil War battlefield in Tennessee. More recently, he had served on teams studying the recreational and interpretive potential of proposed National Park Service acquisitions at Delaware Water Gap–Tocks Island and the Great Lakes. Palmer urged the regional director to name Sullivan to a team to study Independence. Serving with Sullivan would be Robert H. Rose, a naturalist and interpretive planner in the regional office, and Albert Manucy from St. Augustine, who had a service-wide reputation as an interpreter. The study was supported at the highest level: Conrad Wirth wanted the park developed, but, always conscious of public opinion, he also wanted the visitor's experience improved and would not allow construction to delay this goal.

The study group presented its report in June 1959. It did not prove to be a panacea for interpretation at Independence. The most radical proposal—that the interpretive master plan be changed to reflect the approach of most visitors from the mall to the north, rather than from the east—was never implemented. Beyond that the report recommended several remedies: preparation of a new self-guided tour leaflet; a warm-weather orientation station at the entrance to Independence Hall, preferably in the form of a reconstructed watch box, manned by uniformed personnel; exhibits in the Supreme Court Building; and use of a restored Congress Hall as an orientation auditorium. The report also suggested a somewhat different route for guided tours and means of controlling traffic flow through Independence Hall. Concluding that the building could accommodate only two hundred people, the team suggested controlling traffic flow through appropriately placed velvet cords and allowing access only through the Chestnut Street doors, which could be closed when that capacity was reached. Finally, they advocated training and direction for the guards, whom they had found friendly and pleasant, but who could be taught something about "the fine art of making the visitor feel welcome."

Recommendations about routing through Independence Hall were put into effect immediately. Another outcome of the report was the appointment of Sullivan to the Independence staff, at first as a historian. Within a few months, the interpretive function was removed from Platt's purview and assigned to Sullivan. This was accomplished through an administrative reorganization that established two subbranches within the Branch of History: the Branch of Research and Planning, reporting to Platt, and the Branch of Visitors Services, reporting to Sullivan. Platt was so angered by the change that he considered resigning. He felt that criticism of his handling of the interpretive function was unjustified and that the reorganization created an unfortunate division between those who studied the materials of history and those who used those materials to educate the public.

In fact, interpretive problems were not unique to Independence, although difficulties were more apparent there because of the park's high visibility and popularity. The guards at Independence and many of the rangers at other parks were there primarily to protect the visitors and the resources rather than to dispense information. Interpretation had largely been the province of the professional staff: historians at the historical parks, naturalists at the others. They had been hired for qualifications relating to their disciplines, not for their ability to deal with people. Sometimes the two skills did not coincide. To determine how other areas with large numbers of visitors handled the situation, the division of interpretation in the Washington office established a study committee. In September 1960 one of the committee members, Roy E. Appleman, called on Maria Lombard, director of the guide service at Rockefeller Center.

Appleman was deeply impressed by his tour of Rockefeller Center, as well as by a visit to the United Nations, where Lombard had also established the guide service. He reported her criteria for selecting guides in great detail and with considerable approval. Although Lombard had at first hired young men as guides, she came to the conclusion that they were unsuited to the work. One of their number was Gregory Peck, whom she described as "irritable" and an unsatisfactory guide. Men, she believed, were difficult to control and acted in too independent a manner, departing from the approved interpretive program. The only ones who made good guides were, in Lombard's opinion, homosexual or had homosexual tendencies, which she found intolerable. Accordingly, Lombard had switched to hiring "young girls" and professed herself pleased with the results. Young women were fitted for the role of guide because they were "natural hostesses," liked being the "center of the show," and were not bored by repetitive tasks. Besides, they were "more susceptible to instruction, more obedient, and they constitute less of a management problem than do men."

Lombard cautioned, however, that not just any young women would do. Those selected should be neat and attractive, but not too good-looking. Too pretty a girl would distract the visitors from the subject of the tour. A warm personality was also required. Age was another criterion: after twenty-five a "girl's" legs would "play out." The employment period was two years, after which she believed that the guides' efficiency and enthusiasm declined markedly. Applicants should have at least two years of college, and a training program in poise, voice, and projection was essential.

Appleman concurred with Lombard: his experiences at National Park Service facilities had convinced him that men were not effective as guides. The park service's uniform made them look like guards, and they tended to act like guards as well. They lacked warmth and did not initiate conversation with the visitors. Not only Rockefeller Center and the United Nations, but also Colonial Williamsburg and many other historic sites, employed women as guides. He forcefully recommended that the park service cease employing men to conduct tours and substitute young women wherever conditions would permit. A quarter of a century later, Lombard's recommendations and Appleman's ready acceptance seem blatantly, even ludicrously, sexist. In the

31. Three of the first "young ladies" hired as interpreters at Independence in 1961 display their uniforms, patterned on those of airline hostesses. From left, Ruth Friday, Judith Rhodes, and Margaret Ciborowski.

early 1960s, however, such views were unremarkable. Questions of equal opportunity had not really been addressed within the federal government, and although the National Park Service employed a few women in a professional capacity, its management and indeed its personnel, except for clerks and secretaries, were overwhelmingly male.

Nowhere was Appleman's proposal received with more enthusiasm than at Independence. By 1960 the ranger-historians at the park were conducting over a thousand tours annually. Even though the regular staff was supplemented by seasonal employees during the summer, and in some years in April as well, the demands on the historians conducting research for the restoration program were still immoderate. The guards, if improved, were still considered inadequate for most contact with the public. Accordingly, Independence immediately began to formulate plans for hiring young women as "hostesses." Their criteria for selection were clearly based on Appleman's findings.   **181**

Letters were sent to local colleges and universities and to placement and employment agencies, seeking young women "possessing a high degree of such personal attributes as a warm personality, cheerful disposition, bearing, poise and good grooming."

By June 1961 five "personable, attractive, and intelligent young ladies" had joined the staff. Because Sullivan was responsible for their training and supervision, the group quickly became known as "Sullivan's Harem." Six to eight weeks of training consisted of lectures, reading, voice and speech instruction, and critiques of recordings of their talks. They also went out into the field, touring Philadelphia and visiting the National Park Service's chosen prototypes: Williamsburg, Rockefeller Center, and the United Nations.

By the end of the summer, the new guides were in place on Independence Square, looking very much like airline hostesses in trim uniforms with perky caps. This was no accident. Discussions of appropriate dress for the women had been part of the planning almost from the first. The suggestion that they might appear in clothing reminiscent of the eighteenth century, although not strictly period costume, was quickly abandoned, but the idea of a distinctive costume was not. Evidently, dressing women in a version of the National Park Service uniform was never considered. Some other prototype would have to be found, and Sullivan targeted the airlines as providing the best example. He wrote to and received advice on uniform designs and suppliers from American Airlines and Trans-World Airlines. Park visitors in the early 1960s were thus greeted by smiling young women who, in place of coffee or tea, dispensed snippets of historical information.

There is no doubt that the new form of personal interpretation provided at Independence was a huge success, although the initial premises were soon modified. Within a few years the two-year limitation on employment, impossible to maintain under Civil Service regulations, had disappeared, and the program had been opened to men. Still, young women remained the backbone. The female presence on Independence Square was augmented in 1963 when the Junior League offered to conduct tours during the peak school visitation period in the spring. The volunteers went through a training program similar to that established for the staff interpreters and were then assigned regular weekly tours of duty. The program lasted for about a decade, and many of the participants were later instrumental in forming the Friends of Independence National Historical Park.

As personal interpretation became more organized in the early 1960s, other forms of telling the park's story also became more sophisticated. There were now two slide programs for visitors to the interpretive center in the East Wing of Independence Hall, and, as noted above, the explanatory tape at the Liberty Bell was available in five foreign languages. Such devices became increasingly necessary as visitation to the park rose to close to 2 million people in 1961, including visitors from over forty foreign countries. The most ambitious program for instructing and entertaining this increasing stream was installation of a sound and light program in Independence Square. The impetus for the program had come not from the park service, but from Mayor Richardson Dilworth. Impressed by such programs then operating at a number of historic sites in Europe, he had appointed a committee to explore the feasibility of sound and light in Philadelphia, and specifically at Independence.

The prospect of such an evening activity was of great interest to the National Park Service because it corresponded with existing practices at other parks. The agency's planners thought of visits to the national parks as total experiences. At many of the larger western parks, visitors stayed within the park, often for several days, at campgrounds or hotels run by concessioners. The day's activities therefore generally extended into the evening: campfire programs, featuring lectures or sing-alongs, were intended to entertain and inform the visitor. Because master planning decisions had precluded accommodation for overnight visitors within the boundaries of Independence, a relatively informal gathering analogous to a campfire would not be feasible. Sound and light, however, could provide a dramatic and appropriate evening program.

Indeed, the park service had already explored the possibilities of sound and light at major historic areas and had concluded that Independence would be the ideal location for a pilot project. Conrad Wirth therefore responded favorably to a proposal that the Old Philadelphia Redevelopment Corporation undertake to provide such a program, although he imposed many conditions. The corporation could charge an admission fee, but it would be entirely responsible for all the expenses of the production, including any liability claims. Any profit would go to a public purpose, such as the National Park Trust Fund. Nothing in the installation would violate the historic integrity of the buildings or Independence Square. In fact, the equipment would have to be so unobtrusive that daytime visitors would not be unduly aware of its presence. Finally, the production and publicity would have to be consistent with the dignity and significance of Independence Hall and would be subject to review and approval by the National Park Service.

The park service sent Anderson abroad to visit European productions. He returned convinced that such a program at Independence would be not only feasible but desirable. With a donation from the Avalon Foundation, in late 1961 the Old Philadelphia Development Corporation retained Lumadrama, Inc., of New York City to produce the program. Lumadrama contracted with Archibald MacLeish, the Pulitzer Prize–winning poet and former librarian of the Library of Congress, to prepare the script. The sound and light presentation was launched in the summer of 1962 and eventually became a permanent element of the park's program, although never enjoying the success of its European prototypes. Its beginnings, however, were not propitious. Attendance was lower than expected, and the program, which was meant to be self-supporting, did not generate enough income to repay the investment. By the next summer the electrical conduits and floodlights on Independence Hall had to be removed so that structural work on the roof and tower could be carried out. After only one season, the program was effectively suspended for a period of three years. The city fathers lost patience with what was, at least temporarily, a useless attraction and agreed to purchase the equipment from Lumadrama and give it to the park service. In the summer of 1966, with the structural rehabilitation complete, sound and light was revived at Independence. Thereafter the presentation, entitled "The American Bell," was shown regularly in the summer months, despite frequent technical difficulties. No fee was charged once the National Park Service had acquired the rights and the equipment; nevertheless, attendance never met the high expectations with which the program had been launched.

Although increasingly the park service arranged events, these also occurred because outside groups chose the park as the site for observances and ceremonies. As a result of publicity about park development, a variety of organizations included Independence in the itinerary of national conventions held in or near Philadelphia. Other events were more parochial. Philadelphians from all walks of life and all backgrounds had long considered Independence Hall a rallying point; several patriotic groups had been accustomed to holding meetings in the historic buildings. Independence Hall was also the traditional climax for Philadelphia parades. By far the most important of the annual celebrations was, of course, the Fourth of July. The celebration in 1951 not only was the first held since the National Park Service had taken custody of Independence, but also marked the 175th anniversary of the Declaration of Independence. Ceremonies were planned on a nationwide scale and with worldwide publicity, with the main focus on Independence. The celebration there went on for four days, highlighted by two events. The more public was a pageant in Independence Square, performed by a group of a hundred costumed actors from New York City and narrated by John Carradine and Oliver Thorndike to the accompaniment of music. Somewhat more sober was a reenactment of the adoption of the Declaration of Independence, carried out in the Assembly Room by costumed members of the Philadelphia Bar Association. Although few spectators could be accommodated, the program, narrated by John Daly, was televised.

Succeeding Fourth of July programs could only be somewhat anticlimactic, although Vice-President Richard M. Nixon delivered the annual address in 1953. By 1955, with some restoration accomplished on the first floor of Independence Hall, Superintendent Anderson began to feel that the Fourth of July celebration at Independence should be of national rather than local importance, with a speaker of outstanding stature, preferably the president of the United States. The advisory commission warned him that such an event

32. *President John F. Kennedy addressed the Fourth of July gathering at Independence in 1962. Like most visitors, he came into Independence Hall to see and touch the Liberty Bell. Looking on is a smiling Mayor James H. J. Tate.*

would require as much as two or three years of advance planning. In fact, it would be seven years before a presidential speech would be delivered from the rostrum in front of Independence Hall. The speaker was President John F. Kennedy, who addressed a large crowd on July 4, 1962. Speakers at subsequent Fourth of July celebrations continued to be prominent representatives of the national government: Vice-President Lyndon B. Johnson in 1963, Attorney General Nicholas de B. Katzenbach in 1965, Secretary of State Dean Rusk in 1966, and Vice-President Hubert Humphrey in 1968. In

1962, the 175th anniversary of the drafting of the Constitution, former President Harry S. Truman delivered the major address on Constitution Day; in 1963 Attorney General Robert F. Kennedy spoke. For Truman it was the third major event at Independence in which he had participated. In 1954 he came to Philadelphia to present to the National Park Service, for display at Independence, Joseph S. Duplessis's portrait of Benjamin Franklin, which had been given to him by the French government. It was among the earliest, and also among the most important, of the additions to the park's portrait collection. In 1958 he participated, along with Chief Justice Earl Warren and Ambassador Abba Eban, at ceremonies marking the tenth anniversary of Israel's independence. The significance of the events that had taken place at Independence was not lost on those nations that had undergone their own struggles for freedom. Greek Independence Day was regularly celebrated at the park. For Israel the associations with the park created so soon after it had achieved nationhood appeared to be particularly strong. Prime Minister David Ben-Gurion had been one of the first foreign heads of state to visit the park, coming initially in the spring of 1951 and returning to give the annual Israel Day address in 1961.

Starting in the late 1950s and with increasing frequency in the turbulent 1960s, the symbolic meaning of Independence, as interpreted by groups of various persuasions, led to its choice as the setting for demonstrations supporting or protesting current political movements. One of the earliest of such events was a ceremony held at the Liberty Bell by members of the 26th of July Movement, supporters of Fidel Castro, on Pan-American Day in April 1958. In those relatively calm times, it did not attract much attention. Nor did the Philadelphia Walk for Peace in May of the same year. By the mid-1960s, however, the protests centered on Independence had become more controversial. In March 1965 a group of students supporting the civil rights movement staged a three-day sit-in at the Liberty Bell. Although public reaction to the event was adverse, the demonstration was peaceful, and it brought the protestors the attention they sought. Their example probably sparked demonstrations by others, such as the one in support of homosexual rights a few months later.

Meanwhile, the possibility of violence had become an ever-present threat. In February 1965 New York City police uncovered a plot to blow up the Statue of Liberty, the Washington Monument, and the Liberty Bell. Police apprehended a small group calling themselves the Black Liberation Front as they were transferring explosives from a Bronx parking lot to an automobile. The episode prompted closer monitoring of future demonstrations. Thus, when about a hundred students marched from City Hall to Independence Mall in April to protest against the war in Vietnam, about two dozen Philadelphia police accompanied them. Inside Independence Hall members of Young Americans for Freedom, a pro-war group, circled the Liberty Bell to "protect" it. Minor demonstrations continued through the summer, and in the fall, as the war impinged more deeply on the consciousness of the American people, the crowds became larger and the occasions more turbulent. In October 1965 three thousand people gathered in Independence Square in support of the war. Demonstrations continued on a smaller scale through the winter and spring, and on July 4, 1966, at another rally against the war, thirty-one people were arrested. Mass demonstrations and rallies continued through the late 1960s and early 1970s on the mall, which was still state property, and in Independence Square. Most were relatively calm and, although they kept the park's protection forces on the alert, required little action. Occasionally, however, there were incidents that, if they did not escalate into violence, could be said to disrupt the peace. Demonstrators chained themselves to the tower stair, placed rice from Vietnam around the Liberty Bell, and spilled animal blood on the front steps of Independence Hall. These gestures were countered by students and disciples of the Reverend Carl McIntire, a right-wing fundamentalist preacher, who requested and received permission to carry out ritual cleansings. Throughout these episodes the National Park Service upheld the constitutional right of free assembly with a steadfast calm that appeared to engender respect in demonstrators of all persuasions. Although some of the situations were potentially explosive, and some resulted in arrests, Independence never suffered from the violence and charges of police brutality that characterized demonstrations in Washington or Chicago.

Dealing with visitors, whether heads of state, schoolchildren, or potentially unruly demonstrators, was a major responsibility for the historians and interpreters at Independence during the first two decades of the park's existence. It was not, however, the lasting accomplishment of the men and women who worked there. That lay rather in the successful completion of a massive research project and the establishment of a system of personal interpretation through the use of well-trained specialists. Yet for all the success of the research program at Independence, it failed to achieve the outside recognition that was accorded the architectural restoration. In part this was due to the conditions set by the National Park Service, in part to personalities, and in part to the attitudes of academic historians.

National Park Service management set two goals for the research program: supplying historical information for the development of the park as a whole and, more particularly, for the restoration and refurnishing of the buildings, and providing the background for an interpretive program. The former task, because it fulfilled an immediate need, always received priority. The latter was limited to generating material for specific products, such as leaflets, tour guides, films, and the like. The pressure to produce materials for the restoration work, combined with the dissolution of the park historians' office when research was centralized in Washington in the mid-1960s, precluded intensive and contemplative efforts.

In addition to the information generated for the park's purposes, the historians' research resulted in the assembly of a body of organized material that could illuminate the urban and social history of eighteenth-century Philadelphia, a collection far larger in scope than had been assembled for any other American city at that time. Yet neither park service management nor the academic historical community appeared to recognize its value. The work at Independence was carried out shortly before such topics began to engage the interest of academic historians, although members of the park staff attempted to arouse such an interest. Riley's cooperative research program, an early effort to involve young scholars in collateral projects based on the park's resources, failed from lack of continued nurturing. Platt attempted to awaken his peers to the potential rewards of interpreting the resources at Independence in a speech delivered at the annual meeting of the American Historical Association in the fall of 1963. He pointed out that the surviving physical fabric of colonial Philadelphia, and the information collected about it, could illuminate such topics as the social organization of American cities in the revolutionary era and the development of municipal services, as well as both the ideals and practical concerns of the men who built the nation.

The historians never promoted and publicized their methods and findings as the architects, under Charles Peterson's impetus, did. Thus, the work at Independence remained relatively unknown to the broader scholarly community, although individual historians turned to the park's staff for the answers to specific questions. It remains a virtually untapped resource for future scholars of the development of urban America.

Seven
The Second Wars of Independence

Until 1968 the leadership at Independence was remarkably stable. Judge Edwin O. Lewis had been promoting and guiding the development of the park for over twenty years, first as president of the Independence Hall Association, then as chairman of the Philadelphia National Shrines Commission, and finally as chairman of the park's advisory commission. Superintendent Melford O. Anderson had been at Independence since 1950; Assistant Superintendent Dennis Kurjack only a year less. Now, however, changes in management would be marked and relatively swift. The first sign of this transition was Judge Lewis's announcement that he intended to step down as chairman of the advisory commission at the end of 1967. Although he would continue as a member of the commission, he could no longer devote the time and energy that its leadership required. He also appointed as vice-chairman his chosen successor for the top post, Arthur C. Kaufmann.

Kaufmann was not only considerably younger than Lewis, but also a man of very different temperament. Lewis had been an effective, indeed forceful, leader, with a remarkable record of achieving his ends through courtliness and persuasion. Kaufmann was more direct, stating his views firmly and expecting quick implementation of the commission's mandates. Lewis was a lawyer, politician, and judge; Kaufmann was a business executive, accustomed to making decisions and having his subordinates carry them out. His accession to chairmanship of the advisory commission was marked by renewed activism, an aggressive stance demanding completion of the park in time for the Bicentennial.

George Hartzog's reorganization and centralization of such professional activities as research, planning, and design also influenced the course of events. Planning, for example, would be carried out by special teams from the Washington Service Center, rather than planners and landscape architects working from the park or the regional office. Design and construction activities were centralized at a new Denver Service Center. Hartzog also created a Division of Planning and Interpretive Services at Harper's Ferry, West Virginia, to plan programs for the parks and implement them through the design and production of exhibits, films, and other audiovisual devices. Further organizational change followed passage of the National Historic

33. Arthur C. Kaufmann. Having worked closely with Judge Lewis in both the Independence Hall Association and the Independence National Historical Park Advisory Commission, Kaufmann succeeded the judge as president of the former and chairman of the latter.

Preservation Act of 1966, which gave the National Park Service responsibility for establishing, in cooperation with the states, a broad-based National Register to identify and give a measure of protection to sites and districts of national, state, and local significance. This was a major expansion of the park service's role in preservation. To coordinate these new "external" affairs with activities within the National Park System, Hartzog established the Office of Archeology and Historic Preservation, generally referred to as OAHP. It would have full responsibility for all historical, archeological, and preservation efforts in the parks, as well as implementing the park service's preservation role outside the National Park System.

Many of those in leadership positions in these new entities were well acquainted with Independence. Dr. Ernest Allen Connally, initially appointed chief of OAHP and later associate director for professional services of the National Park Service, had first worked for the park service as supervisor of a HABS team at Independence. Connally appointed as the first keeper of the National Register Dr. William J. Murtagh, who, after experience on a HABS team, had worked on studies for the restoration of the Merchants' Exchange. These men, both trained as architects and as architectural historians, would be instrumental in shifting preservation policy within the National Park Service away from a concern with associative and commemorative values toward aesthetic and environmental considerations. Along with Henry Judd,

190

who was transferred from Philadelphia to Washington as chief of the Division of Historic Architecture in OAHP, they would support a high standard of authenticity for restoration. The new Division of Planning and Interpretive Services was also headed by an Independence alumnus, William C. Everhart.

Despite these management changes, a degree of continuity was maintained at Independence. John Platt, although briefly transferred to Washington and continued on the OAHP personnel roster, returned to Philadelphia on special assignment. Lee Nelson and Penelope Hartshorne Batcheler were placed on Judd's staff but remained at Independence. Others who would have a voice in developments at Independence, such as Martin Yoelson and Charles Dorman, continued on the park's staff.

In 1968, as the advisory commission under Kaufmann's leadership was intensifying demands for swift completion of the park, a team from the Washington Service Center was studying a revised master plan for Independence to guide the next phase of development. Among the unresolved questions were the treatment of Franklin Court and the area east of Third Street, chosen as the general location for a visitor center, and the relocation of the Liberty Bell from the interior of Independence Hall to a separate structure. Other remaining issues included uses for the First Bank of the United States and a reconstructed City Tavern. There was also the question of what should be done about the Irwin Building, the one large commercial structure that remained within the park boundaries. New ideas on the table included construction of a major educational and research center north of the Merchants' Exchange and a branch office for OAHP.

A major meeting to review a draft of the master plan took place in the office of Director George Hartzog on October 3, 1968. He agreed to support the recommendation of a consultant hired by Anderson to locate a visitor center at the site of the Custom House if a park service review committee concurred. There were many aspects of the proposed plan, however, of which Hartzog disapproved. He did not wish to see Franklin's house reconstructed, nor did he want a secondary interpretive center built at Franklin Court. He also opposed demolishing the Irwin Building and restoring Independence Square to its eighteenth-century appearance. On several of these points Kaufmann and the advisory commission disagreed. They supported reconstruction of the Franklin House and Independence Square and thought that a visitor center should be built on the lot at the southeast corner of Chestnut and Third Streets. Once the site of the Jayne and Penn Mutual Buildings, it was then being used for parking. These were fundamental differences. Because conflicting opinions continued to be voiced, there would not be a final master plan for Independence for another three years, long after the debate over most of the questions had been resolved on an individual basis.

Kaufmann and the advisory commission were undoubtedly impatient with the master plan process, with its thorough airing of all points of view before consensus was reached. They wanted expeditious action. Kaufmann became increasingly displeased with the lack of progress as 1968 wore on. His dissatisfaction focused on the performance of M. O. Anderson, and he did not hesitate to make his feelings known in Washington. It was certainly not the first time that pressure from Philadelphia had been exerted to speed development at Independence, but when Judge Lewis and Mayor Dilworth had protested against the slow pace in the late 1950s, Anderson had not been the target of their wrath. Indeed, he seems to have enjoyed Judge Lewis's full confidence. Ten years later the situation had changed. Lewis, having turned the reins over to Kaufmann, was accepting the younger man's judgment that Anderson could not supervise completion of the park in a timely manner. Furthermore, Anderson had lost his primary protector in the National Park Service's corridors of power, Conrad L. Wirth, who had resigned as director in 1964. Gradually George Hartzog was replacing with his own associates many of the men who had been appointed to top management posts by his predecessor. By the end of the year, Anderson was gone, transferred to Washington, where he briefly held a desk job before retiring.

In his eighteen years at Independence, Anderson had presided over the transformation of a densely built, deteriorating urban area into planted parkland dotted with restored buildings. The philosophy of widespread demolition had evoked some criticism in the planning stage, and planners and preservationists would continue to raise questions about the validity of removing so much of the fabric of an urban area. Nevertheless, the open, mall-like character of the park, with the historic buildings set off as carefully landscaped relics, was the conception set forth in the Shrines Commission's report, accepted by the National Park Service, and reinforced in the early versions of the master plan. Anderson had supported the basic premises of these plans fully and carried them out to the best of his ability. Phlegmatic, patient, and persistent, he had hewn to the program through changing administrations in the city and in the park service's regional office. Neither a historian nor a restorationist, he had overseen the creation of a competent staff and fought to allow them the time to accomplish the research they believed to be vital to the project's success. By 1968, however, although aware that the development was lagging, he appeared to have expended the energy that had enabled him to carry the program so far from its beginnings.

His replacement, Chester Brooks, knew clearly what his role was to be. Hartzog gave him only one mandate—to get the program at Independence moving. On his arrival in January 1969, Brooks immediately began to carry out that directive in his own manner. There could hardly have been a greater contrast with his predecessor. Part of the difference was symbolic, a fresh expression of the National Park Service's presence. Anderson, who had not worked for the Park Service before coming to Independence, rarely wore a uniform, appearing on most occasions in well-tailored business suits. Brooks, who had come up through the ranks, wore full uniform for many public appearances. There were also differences of personality and style. Where

34. *Superintendent Chester L. Brooks (second from right) in 1970 explains proposed park development to Arthur C. Kaufmann (at left) and Secretary of the Interior Walter Hickel (second from left). At right is Assistant Superintendent James Sullivan.*

Anderson was reserved, Brooks was outgoing. Anderson spoke deliberately, in measured cadences. Brooks's speech tumbled out, hardly able to keep up with the pace of his thoughts.

Brooks believed that he could succeed only with the full support of his staff and the community. His way to achieve that was through communication, informing everyone of what the total program was and reminding them of the importance of their individual contributions to its success. He began to participate in the life of the community, instituting what he jokingly referred to as "management by cocktail parties." He also held regular staff meetings with his department heads and urged them to discuss with their staffs what they had learned about plans and activities.

So eager was Brooks to share his thinking with others that he often repeated instructions and information to his staff. A few found it annoying to be told the same thing two or three times, but most appreciated the contrast with Anderson's reticence. Sullivan, for example, found the repetition preferable to an incomplete understanding of how his assignments and responsibilities fitted into the development and operation of the park. One key staff member who found it hard to adjust to the new regime was Dennis Kurjack. Anderson had expected Kurjack to wait for information and for specific assignments before acting; Brooks, on the other hand, expected his assistant superintendent to grasp the initiative. Brooks also felt that Kurjack resisted his attempt to establish strict completion schedules at Independence. Less than a year after Brooks's arrival, Kurjack resigned. Brooks then named Sullivan to the post of assistant superintendent.

Franklin Court, 1950–72

Despite Brooks's attempt to keep everyone informed and moving together toward a common goal, it was often difficult to achieve consensus. Nowhere was this more evident than in the controversy over the treatment of the Franklin House site, a thorny issue that had remained unresolved since the early 1950s. Benjamin Franklin's house had stood on a lot of land that ran from Market Street back toward Chestnut Street between Third and Fourth Streets. Like the Carpenters' Company on its property south of Chestnut, Franklin, when he erected a building for his own occupancy in 1764–65, built in an inner courtyard, reserving the more valuable Market Street frontage for rental properties. After his return from Europe in 1785, he built tenant houses on Market Street on either side of an arched passageway leading back to his house. Franklin's descendants demolished his house in 1812; the passageway from Market Street became the public Orianna Street, running through to Chestnut Street. By the time the National Park Service acquired the property, there were buildings on all of the site but the street itself.

Edward M. Riley prepared the first report on Franklin Court early in 1950. He had found that a good deal of information was available in the public record and in Franklin's correspondence at the American Philosophical Society, but believed that there was insufficient evidence to justify reconstruction of the house. He did recommend, however, that archeological investigation be undertaken to determine whether remains of the foundations of the house could be discovered. If so, he recommended outlining them as one of the central features of a landscaped memorial park.

After this initial effort, interest in Franklin Court subsided. It revived in 1953, under the dual impetus of the master planning process and the American Philosophical Society's intention to celebrate the 250th anniversary of Franklin's birth in 1956. With the assistance of that institution, the first excavations in Franklin Court were carried out from May to September 1953. The society provided the funds for the labor, while the National Park Service contributed the tools and a trained archeologist to supervise.

The archeologist was Paul J. F. Schumacher, who had come to Philadelphia for a two- to three-week stay in February 1953 and remained for over three years to institute the archeological program at Independence. Schumacher had been assigned to the historians' office at Independence to monitor the excavation of the steam-line trench between the Custom House on Second Street and Independence Hall. One of Charles Peterson's first acts as resident architect was to remove the ancient coal-fired boilers from the cellars of Independence Hall and supply heat from an outside source in order to minimize the danger of fire. This required a trench running virtually the entire length of the park and offered an opportunity to locate the foundations of eighteenth-century buildings. Schumacher monitored the steam-line trench in March 1953, but by May he had transferred his attention to Franklin Court.

The premises of the Franklin Court project were very different from those that governed Schumacher's work on the steam-line trench and much of the other archeological work at Independence. In most cases the archeologist's role was confined to monitoring and noting observations at excavations performed for development projects. Franklin Court, on the other hand, was excavated at this time solely for the purpose of confirming and expanding, through archeology, information about the location and configuration of Franklin's house that had been established through documentary research. Because buildings still occupied much of Franklin Court, Schumacher could operate only in a very limited space under Orianna Street and the sidewalks. Nevertheless, he found fragments of the foundation walls, the basement floor, and a privy. In 1955, after the acquisition and demolition of some of the buildings within the court, he was able to extend his excavations.

While Schumacher was undertaking his first excavation at Franklin Court, the site's eventual appearance was under discussion as part of the master planning process. At a meeting on February 5–6, 1953, the participants had accepted Riley's recommendation that the court be developed as a memorial garden. A schematic drawing showing a simple but formal scheme was approved in principle. Shortly after the meeting, M. O. Anderson retained Grant Simon, the architectural consultant to the Independence advisory commission, to prepare alternative designs for the proposed garden. Meanwhile, several questions of principle and policy had arisen about the design, interpretation, and use of the site. These were on the table at a master plan conference on April 17. Some questions were readily disposed of. The participants, including representatives of the Washington and Philadelphia offices of the National Park Service, as well as members of the Independence staff and Simon, agreed that the court should include restrooms and a small museum facility to aid in interpretation. Design issues engendered considerable discussion. The final decisions called for delineating the foundations of Franklin's house as the central feature and surrounding them with plantings that reflected, as far as possible, the landscaping arrangement of the property in Franklin's day. The Market Street frontage, with its row of buildings then thought to date to the mid-nineteenth century, would be demolished; two three-and-a-half-story buildings spanning an arched passageway would be rebuilt on the site of Franklin's tenant houses.

Charles Peterson hoped for maintenance of the site's urban character. After reviewing Simon's next sketches for the project, he suggested that the entire frontage along Market Street be built up, as it had been for two centuries, but this view did not prevail. Instead, when Simon reported that the cost of reconstructing the Market Street buildings would exceed $400,000, they were eliminated entirely.

The plan that Conrad Wirth finally approved in the spring of 1954 might well have been characterized as Fort Franklin. A ten-foot paneled brick wall girdled the property, with a sort of sallyport on Market Street. Within, low walls marked the assumed location of the foundations of the tenant houses and Franklin's House. A memorial tablet relieved the east wall. Along the west wall were small pavilions to house an exhibit, a guard station, and a storage area. A formal garden occupied the space within the house foundations, with large trees and less formal plantings in the remaining area.

During the remainder of the 1950s, Franklin Court was largely ignored as the National Park Service concentrated its efforts on planning and development for the areas of the park south of Chestnut Street. Even the master planning effort of 1957–59 dealt minimally with Franklin Court. It was not until the accelerated research program of 1959–60 got under way that attention turned again to the approximately four thousand square feet of property that had been the center of Franklin's world, starting with renewed interest in its archeological potential.

Paul Schumacher left Philadelphia in October 1956, and for over a year there was a hiatus in archeological work at Independence. The arrival of B. Bruce Powell in January 1958 marked the beginning of a new campaign of exploration of the park's underground resources. Powell was joined in March 1959 by Jackson W. Moore, Jr. Although these men were assigned to the regional office rather than to the park, the bulk of their work was at Independence, then the most important project in the region. Better trained and more experienced than Schumacher, the two worked under the close supervision of John L. Cotter, who had been named chief of the regional archeological office in 1957. Cotter had twenty-five years of field experience when he came to Philadelphia. Trained as a prehistorian in the Southwest, he had also worked at historic sites, notably on a major investigation of Jamestown, Virginia, just before coming to Philadelphia. Cotter also had strong ties to the academic community, serving on the faculty of the University of Pennsylvania as well as on the staff of the National Park Service. With the advent of this team, archeological work at Independence achieved higher standards. Planning improved, records were better kept, and the staff began experimenting with new, more sophisticated techniques, such as electrolytic and ultrasonic cleaning of artifacts. Powell's first work at Independence was in Carpenters' Court in 1958. Moore excavated the Contributionship Stable and the Portico site at Congress Hall in 1959. The archeologists also monitored excavations for extensions of the steam-line trench along Walnut and Fifth Streets.

Indeed, much of the archeologists' work continued to take the form of ad hoc monitoring, often with little advance warning, of excavations undertaken as part of the development program. At Franklin Court, however, a major archeological campaign would be carried out. The largest undertaken in any American city up to that time, it would proceed in spurts for over a decade. Powell began planning such a campaign late in 1959, first reviewing what had already been accomplished and then projecting the level of effort and funding required to complete the program over a period of four years.

Powell carried out his first excavation at Franklin Court between July and September 1960. He again located the features found by Schumacher, plus additional lengths of the north foundation wall, and other walls and wall traces. The park administration was pleased. Anderson told the advisory commission that the results of the excavation, combined with additional research carried out by Marty Yoelson, provided sufficient justification for the reconstruction of Franklin's house. Powell returned to the site the next season, assisted by Moore, this time keeping the excavation open from April to September and extending their exploration to the cellars of the houses on Market Street. By this time the project had produced results that were sufficiently comprehensible to the general public for visits to the site to be included in conducted tours. By the time the second phase of Powell's campaign was completed, he was able to conclude that the cellar of Franklin's house had had at least four, and probably five, rooms, and that one entry was from a brick-paved areaway along the south side. There had also been a necessary with some form of flushing device, and an ice pit. Powell reported finding numerous examples of building materials, including bricks, floor tiles, stone, marble, slate, mortar, plaster with paint, wood, Delft fireplace tiles, window glass, and nails. The campaign uncovered other features of the court as well. The archeologists had found the foundations of walls that bounded the site along the property lines, as well as foundations they believed could relate to the print shop Franklin had erected in 1786–87. So pleased was Powell with the findings that he believed that no further excavation would be necessary.

In the meantime, as part of the expanded work on historic structures reports, Marty Yoelson headed a team that was reviewing the research that had already been accomplished on the Franklin site and searching for fresh documentation. In October 1961, while perusing materials in the Franklin papers at the American Philosophical Society, Yoelson came across a 1765 ground plan, drawn by Franklin's brother-in-law John Read, showing the north wall and gate. Interestingly, a sketch plan had been found by Edward

Riley a decade before on the back of a receipt dated May 17, 1764. Riley suggested that the sketch might be a contemporary plan for the house but was unable to identify it specifically. If there were two sketches, might there be more? Quickly Yoelson recruited a larger team from the historians' office to look at the Franklin papers again. The historians began examining every page of the approximately 250 boxes of material. Their painstaking efforts were rewarded. Miriam Quinn Blimm found, on the back of a letter, a plan in Franklin's hand of the first floor, revealing structural features and the direction in which the house faced; William Campbell found a possible framing plan.

With these documents in hand, and with the knowledge garnered from the most recent excavations, Yoelson could assess the importance of Riley's previous discovery, which was the plan for the second floor. The historians believed that they could now establish the location of the front and rear doors of the house, the windows, and the fireplaces. The voluminous correspondence between Franklin and his common-law wife, Deborah, had long been available and provided information about room usage and furnishings. These accounts, fleshed out by insurance surveys, were almost sufficient to convince the historians that an authentic reconstruction of the house was possible.

One important piece of evidence remained elusive. In the course of their research, the historians had become aware of a rumor that an exterior view of the house existed, a drawing signed with the initials "J.T.," probably for the engraver John Thackara. This, if it could be found, would be a key document. Although a great deal of information about the building could be extrapolated from the documentation and the archeological evidence, many details of its exterior appearance would remain unknown without such a view. Accordingly, the park began to query historical agencies and antiquarians. Their inquiries bore fruit. In November 1961 Dennis Kurjack received a letter from Carl Williams, an antiquarian and dealer headquartered in New York City. Williams claimed that the sketch had passed through his hands and been sold to a Philadelphia dealer, now dead. The present whereabouts of the sketch was unknown, and although Williams thought that he had retained a photograph of the original, his papers were in storage and he could not retrieve it until he had paid the warehouse's bill. In the interim, he thought that his wife, who was an artist, could reproduce the drawing from a description he had prepared while the original was in his possession.

The park service made no immediate response to Williams. By the time this letter was received, Wirth had stricken funding for the reconstruction of the Franklin House from the budget for the following fiscal year. Wirth was not yet persuaded that any treatment other than landscaping was appropriate for the Franklin site. Regional Director Ronald F. Lee reassured Anderson, however, that the matter would be reevaluated after further historical, architectural, and archeological studies. The studies had by this time been extended to cover not only the Franklin House and the ground immediately surrounding it, but also the properties on Market Street. By the early 1960s the researchers at Independence were convinced that significant portions of the Franklin tenant houses, and the buildings adjoining them to either side, survived. Contrary to what the staff had assumed in the 1950s, these buildings had not been demolished to make way for new construction in the mid-nineteenth century. Rather, they had been raised two stories and had suffered extensive alteration. Nevertheless, a considerable amount of original fabric survived.

The first to perceive that this might be the case was Charles Grossman, the resident architect at Independence in the late 1950s and early 1960s. Checking the buildings prior to issuance of a demolition contract in 1959, he noticed hand-split lath and hand-wrought nails in the plaster ceiling of the arched passageway leading to Franklin Court from Market Street. Examining them and the bricks and mortar behind them, he became convinced that the arch was of eighteenth-century construction. Spurred by this discovery, he and Penelope Hartshorne began to probe the buildings' walls. They found that the foundations and party walls were of eighteenth-century construction and that they bore clues to the original arrangement of the buildings.

In March 1961, when the first historic structures reports were completed on the Market Street houses, John Platt composed an eloquent rationale for preserving and restoring Franklin's buildings:

> The remains themselves are intimately related to Franklin and his times. The mode of construction still evident in the scarred walls bears his imprimatur. They stand in mute testimony to his ingenuity. They are tangible remains, conferring on him who knows of them a sense of Franklin's presence and a link with the scene which surrounded him. Through the arched passageway Washington and other members of the Constitutional Convention passed on their way to pay respects and confer with the venerable philosopher.

Platt's eloquence and the interest engendered by the results of the ongoing investigations of Franklin and his property gradually changed the attitude of the National Park Service management. Certainly the acquisition of Franklin Court had been a component of the legislation establishing Independence, but its future development had always had a low priority, and the memorial garden approved in the 1954 master plan, and confirmed by Wirth in 1961, was a modest one. By early 1962, however, although no definitive plan had been accepted, a more ambitious scheme was under discussion. Regional Director Lee reassured Edmund Bacon, the executive director of the City Planning Commission, that the National Park Service agreed with him on retention of the Market Street buildings. However, it was only after several years of further intensive study, and considerable controversy within the park service, that final decisions were reached about the treatment of Franklin Court. After the flurry of investigation in the early 1960s, there was relatively little research at Franklin Court as historians, curators, and architects concentrated on the buildings on Independence Square.

It was not until the master planning process of the late 1960s that definite proposals for the treatment of Franklin Court were again put on the table. The master planning team's draft report, issued in 1968, proposed a tri-theme concept for Independence. The first two themes—"Independence and the New Nation" and "Historic Philadelphia, Capital City"—had always been central to the concept of the park. The third—"Franklin, Man of Ideas"—represented a reassessment of values at Independence over a period of some twenty years. This was in large part due to the accumulation of knowledge through the park service's research. That research, however, coincided with a broader historical interest in Franklin and his affairs that had been engendered by the study and publication of Franklin's papers, then being carried out at the American Philosophical Society and Yale University. Franklin had always remained a towering figure to Philadelphians, and certainly historians had recognized the importance of his contributions to the founding of the nation. Nevertheless, the renewed attention of scholars in the 1950s and 1960s tended to enhance his significance and called for a reappraisal of the property most closely associated with his life.

It was in that context that the master planning draft report not only elevated the Franklin story to a major theme at Independence, but also called for reconstruction of Franklin's house and rehabilitation of the Market Street buildings. This approach had been advocated by the historical sections of the various historic structures reports prepared by the park staff and supported by Superintendent Anderson. It was not, however, universally accepted within the National Park Service. Others supported an archeological interpretation, using a miniature sound and light presentation with the excavated artifacts as props.

In the master plan discussions the antireconstruction forces won out. At a plan review meeting in October 1968, Director George Hartzog refused to approve the plan to reconstruct the Franklin House and build a new interpretive center at Franklin Court. Franklin, he believed, could be interpreted in the Market Street buildings, which were to be restored on the exterior only. The decision did not sit well with many of those who had dealt with the site. Shortly before Hartzog's decision was formalized, one of the advocates of reconstruction, John Cotter, the chief regional archeologist, took what he later termed an "outrageous" step: he sent Hartzog a personal letter protesting against the decision without going through official channels. Although Hartzog had proclaimed that his door was always open to any employee, going to the director without consulting others in the chain of command was virtually unheard of. Cotter, however, had the advantages of a personal acquaintance with Hartzog dating back to the late 1940s and an impeccable professional reputation, both within and outside the National Park Service.

He could afford to take such an action and could expect to have his comments treated with respect.

Cotter based his support for reconstruction on several points. The Franklin House, he believed, represented the personality and history of its builder and occupier in a uniquely intimate way. There were no other tangible memorials to Franklin in the entire country, except for statues. Cotter considered the evidence ample for a reconstruction and refurnishing of the house so authentic that Franklin "could walk in and feel at home," pointing out that many of the building's features and contents represented Franklin's inventive genius. Moreover, he believed that it was quite possible that funding and maintenance responsibilities would be assumed by private interests.

Although Cotter's letter must have reached Hartzog too late to influence the decision at the early October plan review meeting, it did cause the director to reconsider the Franklin House question. At Hartzog's request, Ernest Connally, chief of OAHP, reviewed and evaluated the material in the agency's files and concluded that there was insufficient evidence to justify reconstruction. But Hartzog had also turned to Ronald F. Lee for an opinion. Lee had retired as regional director in 1965, but had remained, as what the park service calls a "rehired annuitant," to advise Hartzog on just such thorny matters. Thoroughly familiar with the situation in Philadelphia, he believed that evaluation of existing files was not sufficient. He pointed out that the *Administrative Policies for Historical Areas in the National Park System* provided that "every reasonable research effort shall be made to exhaust the archeological, architectural and historical evidence" before decisions were made. Yet every report and opinion proffered by those who had done the research had indicated that it was not yet complete. Lee suggested two actions: appointment of a special advisory committee, a device that had served the park service well in the past, and completion of the research.

Hartzog accepted Lee's recommendation, appointing a committee chaired by Lee and consisting of Herbert A. Kahler and Joseph Brew. The committee met for the first time in Philadelphia on March 17, 1969. They were joined by Connally, Cotter, Henry Judd, and Platt from OAHP, Murray Nelligan from the regional office, and Brooks, Kurjack, Sullivan, and Yoelson from the park. After visiting Franklin Court, the group discussed National Park Service policy on preservation, restoration, and reconstruction. Adopting Connally's suggestion that Franklin Court be considered as a complex or small historic district, they agreed that the Franklin House would complete the historical scene and that reconstruction on the original site was feasible. The question of whether there was sufficient evidence for reconstruction remained open. To investigate the matter, the committee recommended formation of a research team consisting of Cotter, Platt, and Judd or a member of his staff.

Connally duly assigned the requested personnel, with Penelope Batcheler as Judd's representative. This task force was joined on a fairly regular basis by Charles Dorman, museum curator, and Marty Yoelson. Their first task was to review all previously assembled materials. In addition, Dorman began compilation of a list of known Franklin furnishings and objects. Beyond the review of existing research notes, Platt's highest priority was a renewed attempt to find the lost Thackara drawing. With considerable difficulty he tracked down Carl Williams, through whose hands the drawing had passed, in New York City. Platt had raised $1,000 in private funds. With this in hand, he made an appointment to meet Williams in New York. The two men talked. Platt was beginning to believe that his mission would be successful when Williams's wife appeared and insisted that her husband had never seen nor had in his possession such a drawing. Platt went back to Philadelphia without the vital piece of evidence that might have convinced the National Park Service management that reconstruction was justified.

In July 1969 members of the research team presented their reports and views in writing. Platt and Cotter still supported reconstruction. Batcheler, who was opposed to reconstruction, submitted not only a written report, but also a series of drawings, annotated to show what was *not* known as well as what was known about the house. In her opinion the evidence, although of a tantalizing quantity and fascinating in its revelations of Franklin's personality and tastes, was too limited to permit anything but a conjectural reconstruction. To illustrate the practical difficulty of reproducing the written evidence in tangible form, she described the many choices an architect would have to make in designing just one feature of the building's interior: a chimney piece as described in an insurance survey. Unknown were the height of the ceiling, the width of the room, the size of the fireplace, the order of the columns and pilasters flanking it, and the design of the moldings and other carvings that had led the surveyor to call the chimney piece "rich."

Cotter, while acknowledging that it was impossible to recreate the Franklin House literally, argued that perfect accuracy was beside the point. What the house was expected to provide was the most appropriate setting for authentic Franklin possessions—his furniture, books, scientific apparatus, and inventions. To the reviewers at OAHP in Washington, however, Batcheler's arguments were more convincing. Robert M. Utley, then chief historian, believed it unlikely that information sufficient to justify reconstruction could be found. Although the special committee had not held its final meeting, it was clear that Connally and his chief advisors had already pre-judged the issue. Connally reported to Lee that although the data permitted "a good literary vision of the house," they were "not enough to support architectural drawings and specifications." Connally went on to describe the practical difficulties that would face the architects, especially in view of the fact that the house was an atypical specimen of its period, incorporating unique features of Franklin's invention. There were so many unknowns that a reconstruction could only be conjectural.

These comments and the discussion that followed at the meeting were set in the context of new administrative policies for historic areas that had been promulgated soon after Connally assumed responsibility for the National Park Service's preservation programs. The park service had viewed reconstruction as an activity to be approached with extreme caution since the 1930s. In so doing it was following a dictum frequently cited, if not originated, by National Parks Advisory Board member Fiske Kimball: better to preserve than restore, better to restore than to reconstruct. Old National Park Service hands like Ronald Lee could still remember the embarrassment associated with one of the park service's early forays into historical areas. Urged on by local interests, the park service had become involved in the erection of a house at Wakefield, the birthplace of George Washington, that proved to be on the wrong site and the design of which had no basis in documentary evidence. The episode left the park service extremely chary of reconstructions. To avoid future Wakefields, it adopted in 1937 its first set of written policies for restoration and reconstruction. In the final analysis, however, these left the decision to the tact and judgment of those making them. The policy promulgated some thirty years later was firmer, deeming reproduction valid only when three conditions were met: it was essential for public understanding of the site's significance; sufficient data existed for accuracy; and the structure could be erected on its original site.

The special committee to consider Franklin Court met in Philadelphia on October 9, 1969. The three committee members were in attendance, as were the researchers who had spent the past year reviewing the Franklin materials. Others around the table were Superintendent Brooks, Assistant Regional Director Palmer, and Regional Historian Frank Barnes, with Joseph Watterson representing OAHP. Platt, Cotter, and Dorman reiterated their belief that sufficient evidence existed to warrant reconstruction of the Franklin House. Dorman made the most persuasive argument. His investigations had convinced him that 30 percent of the building's original furnishings survived, that another 30 percent could be located by intensive search or represented by period counterparts, and that the remainder of a valid furnishings plan could be implemented on the basis of educated conjecture. Lee thought that the amount of furnishings surviving might justify reconstructing the house as the most appropriate setting in which to display Franklin's belongings. Considerable doubt was expressed, however, that institutional and individual owners would part with their Franklin holdings.

Like Connally, the committee ultimately was swayed by Batcheler's arguments that the evidence was insufficient to allow an accurate reconstruction. Convinced of her point of view, Batcheler could be a persuasive advocate. She supplemented her oral and written presentation with drawings clearly illustrating the practical difficulties of reconstructing the Franklin House. In the afternoon she buttressed her arguments with a presentation of an alternative concept for Franklin Court that captured the committee's imagination. Her scheme would use the Market Street houses as a museum and small

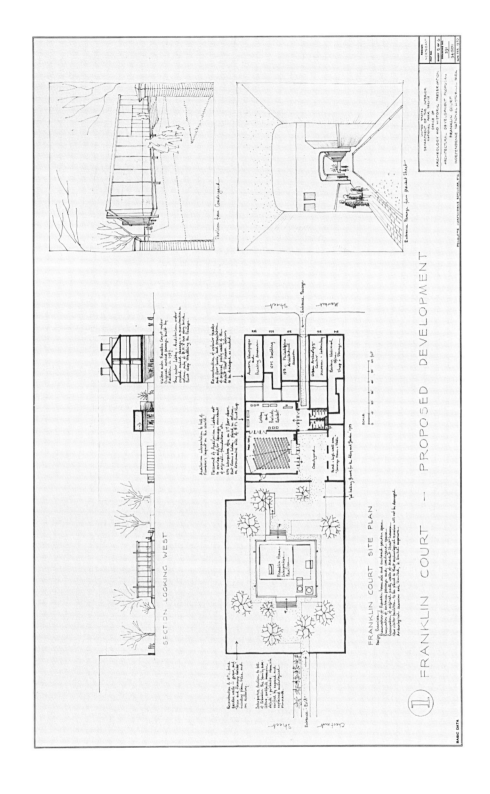

FRANKLIN COURT — PROPOSED DEVELOPMENT

theater showing a movie about Franklin's life. The entrance to the theater would be to the south, so that visitors would first pass through the archway into Franklin Court. The Market Street facades would be treated in a contemporary idiom, perhaps in glass, so that the old party walls would be visible. At the site of the Franklin House, she proposed a glass pavilion in the spirit of her former teacher, Mies van der Rohe. Within the pavilion the house plan would be indicated in the flooring and by partial partition walls inscribed with descriptions of the house from the Franklins' correspondence. Shafts opening into the ground below would allow a view of the archeological remains. She also suggested planting the garden with a mulberry tree and other plants known to have been grown by Franklin. Lee in particular liked the distinction between the surviving original fragments and new construction. It was clear by the end of the meeting that the committee's report would recommend against reconstruction and in favor of further consideration of Batcheler's ideas.

Over the next few months, Batcheler, at Connally's request, further developed her thinking and sketched various alternative schemes for Franklin Court. In late January 1970 she conferred with the Washington staff of OAHP, reaching consensus on a program for the property's development. Most of her original concept remained intact, with the exception of the contemporary design of the Market Street fronts.

It would be a few years before any construction work could be undertaken at Franklin Court. Despite the considerable research already accomplished, more information would be needed before final plans could be drawn. If the Market Street houses were to be reconstructed, for example, the surviving party walls would have to be carefully studied to determine such features as floor levels and the location and size of chimneys. Furthermore, although Powell had thought that no further archeological investigation would be necessary, this had not proved to be the case. Attempts to draw plans for possible reconstruction of the Franklin House had disclosed discrepancies between the written documentation and Powell's interpretation of the archeological evidence. Powell believed that he had uncovered a fragment of the eastern wall of the addition to the house made by Franklin in 1786–87. Instead, he had found the eastern wall of the 1765 construction. The later addition remained to be excavated. A fresh archeological campaign might also assist in the restoration or interpretation of the Market Street houses and other features of the site.

205

Between 1970 and 1973 Barbara Liggett, under contract to the National Park Service through the University of Pennsylvania, conducted a systematic archeological investigation of almost the whole of Franklin Court. The findings established the precise location and extent of the house, unearthed the footings of the retaining wall of the garden, and located the print shop that Franklin had erected for his grandson Benjamin Franklin Bache. Over 2,000 vessels and many more thousands of fragments were retrieved, largely from four privies, a well, and a storage pit that had been sealed at various times between 1765 and 1835. Of special interest were the ceramics and glassware from the period 1690 to 1740, which at the time represented the earliest documented assemblage of artifacts of that period.

Because Powell's and Liggett's investigations were visible to the public, they received considerable attention in the popular press. Heretofore archeology had generally been viewed as something pertaining to aboriginal cultures or lost civilizations, an activity carried out in remote places like Greece or Peru or undeveloped areas like the American Southwest. At Independence large groups of people saw that the past might be uncovered under the streets they walked daily or the buildings they occupied. The work at Independence was meaningful to the professional archeological community as well. It had been assumed that urban sites were too disturbed, too often built upon, to produce verifiable results. Historical archeology in the United States had therefore been confined to rural or abandoned sites, such as Jamestown and Williamsburg in Virginia or Plimoth Plantation in Massachusetts. Powell and Liggett proved that even a site that had been built and rebuilt several times could yield information about its several layers of occupancy. It could provide data about the daily life of the inhabitants, about civic infrastructure, about patterns of trade and international commerce, about industry and building methods. The excavations at Independence, and particularly at Franklin Court, were thus a milestone in urban archeology in the United States.

Obtaining the Funding

Even before he arrived at Independence, Chester Brooks was aware that neither of the major projects called for in the draft version of the master plan—the development of Franklin Court and the creation of a Visitor Center—would come to fruition without additional funding. Appropriations for development at Independence had always lagged behind planning. In the decade beginning in 1956, Mission 66 monies had alleviated the perpetual funding shortage to some extent, paying for the demolition program and work on the Independence Square group and the Walnut Street houses. By 1968, however, the demands of the Vietnam war were adversely affecting the National Park Service budget. When Brooks took command, he learned that the year's construction budget at Independence had been overspent by $70,000. As noted in Chapter 5, he averted an immediate budgetary crisis by dismissing much of the day labor force, but this did not resolve the larger question of financing development of the park for the Bicentennial. By now the Independence project was twenty years old, and some of the first flush of enthusiasm had worn off. Brooks decided that the key to obtaining the necessary funding was to present completion of the park as a fresh program that would again capture the imagination of National Park Service management and the Congress. Because of his sense of urgency and his awareness of the high level of planning that had already gone into Independence, he did not attempt to rethink the project. Rather, he rearranged the priorities and packaged the result as a new five-year program for completion of the park in time for the Bicentennial. Reconstruction of the privy behind the Todd House had been at the top of the list. Brooks shifted it to the bottom, putting tasks related to Independence Hall at the top for the next three years. Once Brooks had established his program, he put a price tag of $30 million on it and persuaded Hartzog to support it. Hartzog was due to unveil the program in a speech at the dedication of the Supreme Court Room in Independence in April 1969. Although Hartzog had to cancel his appearance because of illness, his deputy, Harthorn Bill, delivered the speech with the $30 million program included.

The next step was to win political support. Hartzog and Associate Director Edward A. Hummel refined the program and presented it to Sen. Hugh A. Scott of Pennsylvania in June. Scott had long been a supporter of Independence, always willing to promote legislation favoring the park. Another key actor in winning congressional support for the needed funding was the well-known author Catharine Drinker Bowen. Brooks was introduced to Bowen by Charles E. Peterson at the opening of "See What They Sawed," an exhibit of the park's architectural salvage collection, in October 1969. Bowen, who had recently been appointed to the American Revolutionary Bicentennial Committee, agreed to present the case for Independence to that body. She came back from Washington to report that a fellow member of that body, Rep. Ben Reifel of South Dakota, ranking minority member of the House Subcommittee on Interior Appropriations, had requested slides illustrating the program. Brooks sent the slides and followed up with a call to Reifel, suggesting that Bowen be invited to testify before the committee, which was headed by Rep. Julia Butler Hanson. Brooks believed that Bowen would make an especially appropriate witness. Not only was she articulate and an author with a national reputation, but she was a woman. Brooks's hunch was correct. Hanson, a former teacher of English, was a long-time admirer of Bowen's work. With strong support from Scott in the Senate and Hanson in the House, the Interior budget included a first-year appropriation of almost $2 million for planning at Independence.

With funding assured, it would be possible to begin planning the enormously complicated process of putting the program into effect. The program called for completion of the restoration not only of Independence Hall, but of two other major buildings as well: Old City Hall and the Second Bank. In addition, there would be major new construction for Franklin Court and the Visitor Center, and City Tavern and the Graff House would be reconstructed. Although not as strongly supported within the park service as City Tavern, reconstruction of the Graff House had long been favored by the park's advisory commission. In addition, one large office building, the Irwin Building, along with two adjacent smaller structures, still stood at the northwest corner of Walnut and Fourth Streets. Acquisition and planning for use of the buildings or the site were important components of the program. Finally, the program called for construction of a new maintenance facility.

The Visitor Center

Although reevaluation of the decision not to reconstruct the Franklin House was the first response to the unresolved questions raised by the draft master plan of 1968, Franklin Court was not the first major project to reach the stage of design and construction. Because the approach of the Bicentennial had made the question of how crowds could be handled at Independence appear urgent, priority was given to the selection of a site and design for a Visitor Center. After considerable discussion, a site at the southeast corner of Chestnut and Third Streets was chosen in October 1969.

The National Park Service then moved quickly to select an architect to design the facility. By the 1960s the park service was committed to incorporating modern design of high quality into the parks. Although scattered examples of modern buildings had been erected earlier, the question of design philosophy acquired added importance in the early 1950s as Mission 66 was getting under way. A new generation of park service leadership was dissatisfied with the "Early Alpine" or "Parkitecture" rusticity that characterized most buildings erected in the parks in the pre–World War II era. The park service began to seek out and hire architects with an interest in designing in the modern mode. However, the volume of work generated by the Mission 66 program was so great that it could not be carried out entirely by park service architects. Increasingly in the late 1950s and 1960s, the service turned to outside firms.

Even before the burst of energy produced by Mission 66, the park service had commissioned a major architect to design at least one project: the monument at Jefferson National Expansion Memorial in St. Louis. Seeking excellence and innovative design, the park service sponsored a national competition in 1948. The winner was Eero Saarinen, for a bold, sweeping arch rising over the city's Mississippi River front. However, groundbreaking was delayed until 1962, and it was George Hartzog, then superintendent at Jefferson, who presided over its construction. But Hartzog had little interest in the details of producing a building, and turned over most of the day-to-day dealings with the architect to his chief historian, William C. Everhart, who accepted the assignment with enthusiasm. Everhart, who had been supervising historian at Independence in the late 1950s, had then gone to San Francisco, and later transferred to St. Louis, in part for the opportunity to work with Saarinen. The experience left him with an abiding interest in modern architecture. His promotions in Hartzog's directorate, first to chief of interpretation and then to assistant director, for a time gave him the power to exercise that interest in choosing architects for visitor centers.

Further impetus to the search for excellence in design projects came from the establishment of selection and review committees at the Denver Service Center, instituted in the early 1970s by Connally, then serving as associate director for professional services. Everhart chaired the committee for the Independence Visitor Center, which included some outside experts, among them Edmund Bacon, Philadelphia's chief planner, who pressed for the selection of a Philadelphia architect. According to Brooks, however, no matter what the opinions of other committee members were the choice would always have been made by a majority of one, that one being Everhart. Everhart had first approached the firm of Kevin Roche/Dinkeloo, who had succeeded to Saarinen's practice after his death; they found the budget too limiting. His other choice was the Boston-area firm Cambridge Seven, whose work he had admired at Expo '67 in Montreal and the Boston Aquarium. Cambridge Seven was not merely an architectural firm; its members had produced integrated projects involving films, museum exhibits, and graphics, all of which would be wanted at Independence.

The program for the building presented to Peter Chermayeff, Cambridge Seven's chief designer for the project, was a complicated one. First, the Visitor Center was to provide a new location for the Liberty Bell. For several years the National Park Service had been convinced that the bell would have to be moved out of the stair tower at Independence Hall. As visitation to the park increased, the relatively small space within the tower could no longer accommodate the crowds wishing to see and touch the bell. Moving the bell to the Visitor Center would relieve the crowding at Independence Hall; it would improve general circulation patterns throughout the park by creating another focus of primary interest; and it would encourage visitors to begin their tour at the eastern end of the park, as had been intended ever since preparation of the first master plan in 1954. In addition, the building was to provide a large exhibit and reception area, not only for orientation, but also to accommodate large crowds waiting to see an introductory film that was to be shown on a staggered schedule in two theaters. It was made clear to the architect that he should take the orientation center at Colonial Williamsburg as a prototype for the arrangement of the theaters and the quality of the film.

The shape of the site also influenced the design. Chermayeff gave the building a trapezoidal plan, picking up the straight lines of Chestnut and Third Streets and the rear of the lot and the angle of Dock Street. In relating closely to the park, the building turns its back to the city, presenting a blank brick wall to Chestnut Street. One entrance, facing the First Bank of the United States across Third Street, is largely of tinted glass mirroring the grand colonnaded and pedimented facade of the bank. The doors are approached through a small plaza with a brick bell tower to the left. There is a second entrance, also of glass recessed between brick walls, on Dock Street. The center of the interior is occupied by a large exhibit space or pavilion covered by a saw-toothed glass roof. A ramp leads up from the exhibit space to a bridge across the front of the building, providing entrances to the rear of the two theaters.

Chermayeff understood the program thoroughly, and relations with the National Park Service appear to have proceeded smoothly during the design process. During 1971 there was no reason to believe that Cambridge Seven's work would meet with anything but general approbation. Although Brooks informed the park's advisory commission in February that the Liberty Bell would be moved, the commission appeared to be more interested in other matters. In November park staff explained the reasons for moving the bell to them in some detail. It was then anticipated that 20 million visitors would come to Independence in the Bicentennial year. Brooks, Sullivan, and Yoelson had walked through the park three abreast and determined that there were several areas that would be tight in congested circumstances. Moving the bell would help disperse the crowds focused on Independence Hall. Seemingly convinced, the commission passed a resolution favoring moving the bell either to the Visitor Center or to Independence Square.

The commission's November meeting was also the occasion for the introduction of another new superintendent. Brooks's achievement at Independence had been so substantial that Hartzog had promoted him to regional director, charging him with getting the Bicentennial program moving in the rest of the Northeast. His replacement was Hobart G. Cawood. Handsome, with sparkling blue-gray eyes and a dimple in his chin, Cawood looked as if he had been picked for the part of superintendent by central casting. He spoke rapidly and fluently, with a down-home Kentucky accent and a colorful turn of phrase. Ebullient and outgoing, he was well suited to continue Brooks's method of management by cocktail parties. Nevertheless, Cawood's appointment was something of a surprise, even to him, because of his youth and relatively short service. Yet he had had a range of experience that provided an excellent background for what needed to be done at Independence. He had entered the National Park Service as a historian and then became a planner in the Washington office, where he had caught the eye of George Hartzog. His first assignment to top management, in 1969, was at the Civil War battlefield on the outskirts of Richmond, Virginia. When Cawood arrived, its master plan, dating from the 1930s, had never been implemented. Within a short time he had brought the park from the pre–World War II stage into the Mission 66 era. He had also instituted a summer program for children from inner-city Richmond that combined history,

36. *Hobart G. Cawood, the third superintendent of Independence National Historical Park.*

nature study, and recreation. He did it on a shoestring budget, cajoling the Defense Supply Agency to make a pond available, the Fish and Wild Life Service to stock it, and volunteers to teach the children how to make fishing poles and use them. His background in planning, and in particular his success in interacting with an urban community, a rare experience in the still Western-oriented park service, were undoubtedly important reasons for his selection for the superintendency of Independence.

Brooks knew Cawood well and agreed wholeheartedly with his appointment. Committed to seeing the park completed in time for the Bicentennial, Brooks was supportive of his replacement but never tried to tell Cawood how the park should be run. Although the two lived across the street from one another in National Park Service quarters on Locust Street, there was no confusion or conflict about their respective roles. Because both were open, direct, and communicative, they could solve problems with a minimum of red tape. Like Brooks, Cawood believed in keeping his staff and the park's constituency informed. Where they differed was in decision making. Brooks liked to arrive at decisions by consensus; Cawood, although he canvassed his staff's opinions, felt that only the superintendent could make the ultimate decisions.

There were other differences as well. Despite Brooks's bonhomie and his enjoyment of public appearances, his manner was quiet and relaxed. He intended to control his park, and later his region, but was content to let

211

others, such as Arthur Kaufmann, receive recognition and credit. Cawood was more flamboyant; there was little doubt about who would be at center stage at Independence. His enthusiasm and drive to accomplish things quickly would be valuable assets, but could sometimes be interpreted as brashness or disregard for the opinions of others. These qualities, combined with his youth and relative inexperience, may have contributed to some of the clashes with the park's advisory commission that marked Cawood's early years at Independence. Judge Lewis and M. O. Anderson had always worked quietly together behind the scenes. By the time an issue reached the advisory commission, the superintendent and the chairman usually presented a common viewpoint. Arthur Kaufmann, in contrast, did not always wait to reconcile his own strong views with those of the park's superintendent. Both Brooks and Cawood, unlike Anderson, had considerable experience in planning and management within the National Park Service before coming to Independence and a strong sense of the manner in which their mission at the park should be carried out. Nevertheless, Brooks had managed to achieve a cordial relationship with Kaufmann. By the time Cawood arrived, however, a crisis was brewing. Within a month he was embroiled in a conflict of major dimensions.

The advisory commission's seeming acquiescence in the moving of the Liberty Bell proved to be deceptive. Rumblings of discontent must have been heard even before a special meeting in December 1971, because not only Cawood and Assistant Superintendent James Sullivan, but also Brooks and Ronald F. Lee, Hartzog's trouble-shooter, attended. The purpose of the meeting was to allow Chermayeff to present his designs for the Visitor Center, and it quickly became apparent that several members of the commission liked neither the design of the building nor the idea of moving the Liberty Bell to its tower. Members particularly objected to the roof design and to the starkness of the tower walls. They asked whether Chermayeff could prepare some alternatives for their consideration. They also wanted to review the proposed film while it was still in the conceptual stage. Chermayeff replied that he would be pleased to meet with the commission, but not until the script had been written and reviewed by the park service's historians. Chermayeff was not inclined to compromise on design issues. In his view his client was the National Park Service, not the commission, and the client had accepted the design. His attitude did little to mollify the commission, already annoyed at having been presented with what they saw as a *fait accompli,* rather than being consulted in advance.

To obtain support for his opposition to the Visitor Center, Kaufmann turned to City Hall. Arrangements were made for Kaufmann and Cawood to meet with Mayor Frank Rizzo. In the meantime, the two toured the park with City Representative Harry Belinger. Their reports on the tour diverged sharply. Kaufmann told the advisory commission that Belinger appeared shocked that the bell would be housed in anything but a colonial-style building. Cawood replied that when they approached the site, and he explained the new building's relationship to the First Bank and the compatability of the proposed materials, Belinger's objections appeared to diminish. Kaufmann pressed the commission to take a position on whether the building's design should be colonial or contemporary. Most commission members favored a contemporary expression. In their opinion integration of contemporary and old buildings was working well in Society Hill and could also be successful within the park. Although Kaufmann demurred, the commission passed a resolution approving the building's design.

Moving the Liberty Bell to the Visitor Center was not so easily disposed of. Although the mayor had given verbal approval, Kaufmann claimed that public objections to the projected move were growing. The commission again discussed the question in detail at its April meeting. Representative Belinger attended again, as did R. Damon Childs, executive director of the City Planning Commission. Childs pointed out that technically the bell was part of the contents of Independence Hall, catalogued simply as a "musical instrument." As such it was covered by the cooperative agreement that permitted the National Park Service to care for and display objects owned by the city as it saw fit. Moving the Liberty Bell did not require the city's approval as, for example, did restoration techniques or alterations to the buildings in Independence Square. Nevertheless, the commission members still disagreed about whether the bell should be moved. Judge Lewis, who by this time rarely expressed strong opinions at commission meetings, opposed moving the bell to the Visitor Center. Although he pointed out that the resolution of approval passed at the commission's January meeting was legally binding, he hoped that an alternative location could be found. He reverted to a scheme that the Independence Hall Association had pursued in the 1940s—placing the bell in a bomb-proof shelter behind Independence Hall. However, he could garner no support for his position. Once again the commission voted to support Chermayeff's plan, including the new location for the Liberty Bell.

That should have, but did not, end the controversy. If, as Brooks had noted, Everhart's single vote constituted a majority for the selection of Cambridge Seven, Kaufmann's vote had the same weight on the issue of moving the bell. Kaufmann expressed his opinions not only in the forum of the advisory commission, but also in direct correspondence with Chermayeff and George Hartzog. And he was certainly correct on one score: public opposition to the move was increasing. Isidor Ostroff, who had been so active in lobbying for establishment of the park under the aegis of the Independence Hall Association, brought suit in federal court to prevent the move. Ostroff did, indeed, obtain a temporary injunction, but the case was never completed because it had become moot. Bowing to the strength of local opposition, the National Park Service had begun investigating other possible locations for the Liberty Bell and modifications to the design of the Visitor Center.

The controversy over the Visitor Center had two major roots. One was systemic: the failure of the review process to account for the varied constituencies that wanted a voice at Independence. Chermayeff's design was approved by the Denver Service Center not only without giving the advisory commission a chance to comment, but also without consulting those in Philadelphia who would have to operate and maintain it. The second, perhaps less tangible, cause was the clash of strong personalities. Kaufmann, as vice-chairman of the advisory commission, had observed Judge Lewis being consulted and deferred to during his tenure as chairman. The consultation, if not perhaps the deference, had continued when Brooks became superintendent. Cawood did not solicit Kaufmann's advice as assiduously, in part because he was unaware of past practice, in part because he did not choose to. The situation was exacerbated by Chermayeff's determination not to alter his design. Despite Kaufmann's repeated requests for alternatives, Chermayeff held firm. He had no intention of submitting alternative designs to the advisory commission or, as it turned out, to the National Park Service.

Hartzog eventually became somewhat testy about the manner in which the issue had been handled. Not only was he being importuned by Kaufmann, but the dispute was affecting his usually excellent relationship with Congress. When he appeared before the Senate Subcommittee on Interior Appropriations, the staff produced a sheaf of adverse clippings from the Philadelphia papers. Rather than discussing his budget, the committee inundated him with questions about the Liberty Bell. Finally, his patience at an end, Hartzog announced that he did not much care where the "cotton-picking" Liberty Bell went; he needed a Visitor Center. That broke the tension. After the laughter subsided, the chairman of the committee, Sen. Alan Bible, offered to excise Hartzog's last remark from the record, suggesting that Hartzog was capable of getting into enough trouble without having that appear in print. Although Hartzog continued to back his subordinates, he urged them to avoid future confrontations.

By the time an advisory design review committee met in Denver to reconsider the Visitor Center, the National Park Service had to all intents and purposes abandoned the plan to move the Liberty Bell to Third Street. The committee was chaired by Ernest Connally, who had never been entirely happy with the design for the Visitor Center. Trained as an architect himself, he favored good modern architecture for the parks but thought that it should be subordinate to the historic buildings. The tower, he believed, competed with the towers and cupolas of Carpenters' Hall, the Merchants' Exchange, and Independence Hall. Chermayeff remained adamant, maintaining that the tower was an integral part of the design. He had, however, proposed one alternative that would justify retention of the tower—and, indeed, increase its height. This was to use it as belfry for a Bicentennial bell to be cast by Whitechapel Foundry, the venerable English firm that had cast the Liberty Bell. Chermayeff foresaw a great future for his tower and his bell. The

Bicentennial bell and the Liberty Bell would become a joint focus for the Bicentennial celebration. The enlarged tower would by the twenty-first century become the vertical accent that would tie together an urban fabric consisting of buildings from four centuries. With no trace of false modesty, he proclaimed that the bell tower would become a symbol and presence in Philadelphia, comparable to the impact of great church towers and campaniles on cityscapes in the past.

Others were not as sure that the solution was appropriate. One of the reviewers, J. R. Passonneau, a Fellow of the AIA, wrote to Connally that Chermayeff's description of the tower as the "central pivot point" in the area disturbed him. Should not that distinction be reserved for Independence Hall? Passonneau admitted, however, that he was not familiar with the urban context and was therefore ambivalent. In the end he was persuaded by Chermayeff's eloquence. Cawood also was not convinced, believing that Chermayeff's alternative was simply more of what the advisory commission already disliked.

Cawood also worried about the delays caused by continuing debate about the building's design. He suggested beginning construction without the tower, which could then be added or deleted depending on how the decision went. Connally supported an advisory commission suggestion that bids should be requested for the building with and without the tower. If the bids with the tower came in over the budget, the decision would have been made in the marketplace rather than by the National Park Service. Hartzog, however, decided to ask for only one bid, which included the tower. The bid requests went out in the fall of 1972, and in December a construction contract in the amount of $3.3 million was awarded to Wintz Brothers. Construction got under way in February 1973. Nevertheless, the debate about the tower continued. Kaufmann was pushing his opposition to the tower and the Bicentennial bell, soliciting the support of the Pennsylvania congressional delegation, the newspapers, and the Philadelphia architectural community. In response, Chermayeff came up with further alternatives. Finally, the commission, by a six to five vote, supported the tower.

Meanwhile the concept of the Bicentennial bell was gaining momentum. Chermayeff had taken advantage of an accidental meeting with Secretary of the Interior Rogers C. B. Morton to persuade him of the merits of the idea, which included presentation of the bell as a Bicentennial gift from the people of Great Britain to the people of the United States. Morton was convinced and asked the Department of the Interior's international affairs staff to pursue the project with British representatives in Washington. At the same time, Cawood established contact with staff at the office of the British consul general in Philadelphia and kept them informed of the project's status.

A firm decision could not be expected from the British immediately, yet construction on the tower was continuing, and the question of whether or not it would house a bell was becoming critical, not only because it affected the final details of the design, but also because casting the bell would take considerable time. Because there was no money for a bell in the budget, funds would have to come from an outside source. The National Park Service's Washington office persuaded the Boston-based John Hancock Insurance Company to serve as a back-up sponsor for the bell if the British government failed to approve the project. With funding guaranteed, it was possible to place an order for casting the bell at Whitechapel Foundry. One last issue was the inscription on the bell. The final choice, simple but appropriate, was "Let Freedom Ring."

Cambridge Seven's design, the tower, and the Bicentennial bell were not the only areas of controversy delaying the Visitor Center. The form and content of the interpretive movie were also a problem. The advisory commission had long wanted a film at Independence. Many of its members had been impressed by the orientation center and film at Williamsburg and desired something of equal quality. Hartzog was anxious to have their approval because Arthur Kaufmann had offered to solicit private funding for the film. This was one of his most powerful reasons for urging Brooks and Cawood to cooperate with Kaufmann. Chermayeff, however, had resisted discussing his plans for the film with the commission. The objections to Cambridge Seven's concept came, therefore, not from the commission, which was unaware of what the concept was, but from the park staff. Cambridge Seven had determined that the film would only deal with those events leading up to and culminating in the Declaration of Independence. The park staff believed that the full story of the park, extending at least through the Constitutional Convention, should be told.

In February 1973 Cambridge Seven presented its developed concept to a park service review committee meeting at Harper's Ferry. Despite an expanded time frame that included the Constitutional Convention, the committee gave the proposal a frigid reception. Neither the technique nor the treatment were what they had envisioned. Rather than a technicolor motion picture with actors speaking their parts, Cambridge Seven proposed a series of sepia stills, given animation through movement of the camera over the pictures. Narration and dialogue would be heard as voice-overs. They believed this technique would provide both verisimilitude and a sense of temporal distance from the events. Their proposal also called for a "strong sense of reality" and "sensitivity to its [American history's] human aspects." These would be conveyed by showing such details as the delegates' sweat-stained clothes and the buzzing files in the literally heated atmosphere of the debates over the Declaration of Independence and the Constitution. The quality of social life in Philadelphia would be shown through scenes in drawing rooms and taverns, but also through such images as a dead dog lying in the street, a woman emptying a chamber pot, a delegate walking carefully to avoid an open sewer, and Benjamin Franklin, on his return from England, waving a greeting to the inhabitants of a brothel.

This revisionist view of history was not acceptable to the staff of the National Park Service. Although they were prepared to accept a vision of the founding fathers as something less than godlike, they intended to glorify and celebrate the events at Independence, not follow the radical historiography of the Vietnam era. Cambridge Seven was relieved of responsibility for the film, and Carl Degen of the audiovisual division at Harper's Ferry was charged with preparing specifications to solicit proposals from a new contractor. The document, approved by the regional office and the park, set forth the concept of the film, which was to be a motion picture in full color, with actors speaking their parts. Eleven firms responded to the proposal, and the contract was awarded to 20th Century–Fox in the spring of 1974. An important factor in the selection was the team assigned to the project by the movie company. John Huston would be the director, with Lyman Butterfield of the Massachusetts Historical Society as the historical consultant; the script and the production were in the hands of Joyce and Lloyd Ritter. Marty Yoelson worked closely with the Ritters and Butterfield, guiding them to available materials and checking the script for accuracy. Other members of the park staff were on the scene during the actual movie making, most of which was filmed on location in the park. It was obviously a team effort, but in Yoelson's opinion it was finally Huston's attitude and interpretation that produced a film the park could be proud of. He had captured the sense of almost religious awe that Yoelson believed most visitors to Independence experienced.

Even while the controversies over the Visitor Center and the Bicentennial bell were being resolved, another issue led to contention between Cawood and the advisory commission. Although the Bicentennial was still three years away, the crowds at Independence Hall had increased measurably by 1973. During the height of the visitation season, from April to October, between 4,000 and 6,000 people a day were passing through the building, with the numbers rising as high as 8,000 a day on weekends. These numbers were expected to double in 1976. To protect the building and its contents, and to try to provide a high-quality experience for all visitors, indiscriminate strolling through the building would no longer be allowed. Instead, beginning in March 1973, all visitors would be assembled into groups in the East Wing and taken on a conducted tour. Unfavorable editorial comment in the Philadelphia newspapers and on the radio was echoed by the commission; it violated what many Philadelphians regarded as their sacred right to stroll through the first floor of Independence Hall whenever they wished.

Visitors new to the park either favored the arrangement or accepted it without question. In any event, the objections of the advisory commission now had less force, for its power had been severely curtailed. At the meeting at which commission members voiced their grievances over the new arrangements, Cawood informed them that the Federal Advisory Commission Act of 1973 had defined and reduced the powers of federal advisory commissions.

This act significantly changed the balance of power between National Park Service staff and the advisory commission. Although the advice and counsel of the commission would still be sought for public relations reasons, it was clear that the decisions would be made, depending on their magnitude, by the superintendent, the regional director, or the director of the National Park Service. The commission and its members could still exercise influence, of course, through the normal channels open to private citizens, by appealing to the press or to appointed or elected officials. In the interest of maintaining harmony and ensuring the support of the members of the commission, many of whom were influential for other reasons, Cawood would continue to attend their meetings, listen to their views, and keep them informed of the progress of park development. Gradually, however, the importance of the commission waned, and after 1976 it ceased to meet.

Franklin Court, 1972–75

Before the act was passed, there was at least one major project to which the advisory commission assented almost without a murmur—the design for Franklin Court. What dissent there was took the form of a last hope, expressed by City Representative Belinger and Kaufmann, that the Thackara drawing could be found and the house reconstructed. Kaufmann went so far as to launch a publicity campaign, offering the prize of a trip to Philadelphia and a Franklin medal to anyone who could come up with either the drawing itself or a photograph. Like past attempts to find this elusive view, this proved futile. If the house was not to be reconstructed, the advisory commission was content with the preliminary proposals for the site's development.

Just as Chermayeff's personality influenced the commission's reactions to the Visitor Center, so undoubtedly did the personality of Franklin Court's architect facilitate the ready acceptance of his concepts. The selection of an architect for Franklin Court was concurrent with the controversy over the Visitor Center, and Cawood was determined that a Philadelphia architect would be selected. The actual choice would be made by a design review committee from the Denver Service Center, but the superintendent's wishes would be respected. The choice of a local firm had obvious advantages. Local publicity was apt to be more favorable for one of Philadelphia's own than for an outsider. Communication would also be easier. If the program and design concepts could be developed in cooperation with the park's staff, it was more likely that differences would be resolved before they reached the confrontation stage. For a city of its size, Philadelphia has always had a surprisingly large number of excellent and well-known architectural firms, and the committee had a number from which to choose. At the recommendation of Lee Nelson and Penny Batcheler, they selected the firm of Venturi & Rauch. It was not then one of the city's larger firms, but its principal, Robert Venturi, had a well-established national reputation as an innovative and thoughtful designer.

As had been the case with the Visitor Center building, the park provided the architect with a set of guidelines and requirements, essentially the ones that had been developed in early 1970 after the decision had been made not to reconstruct the Franklin House. The Market Street houses were to be restored fully on the exterior, but treated adaptively for interpretive purposes on the interior. Behind these houses, Franklin's garden was to be recreated, bounded by a brick wall. The house site was to be marked, with a pavilion sheltering the archeological remains, which were to be exposed to view. There would be a visitors' facility within the court as well. Its location had not been decided, but it must not impinge on either the garden or the house site. What was wanted had been established. The question that remained was how it was to be done. Given the relatively short time available, it might have been done well or badly. In the end it was done superbly.

Professorial in appearance and manner, with a willingness to hear the views of others and the patience to explain his own, Venturi proved a perfect choice to carry forward the complicated task of designing and implementing what proved to be a cooperative venture. Because Venturi & Rauch had no experience in the precise form of restoration that would be required for the Market Street houses, John Milner's firm, then known as National Heritage, was retained as a subconsultant. Although one reason for Venturi & Rauch's selection was the firm's proven ability to integrate architecture and exhibition design, specialists in the latter field would also be required. Not only would the project be subject to the normal reviews—by the Denver Service Center, Harper's Ferry, and the Washington directorate—but it would be carried out in close collaboration with the park staff.

Developing interpretive programs for other sites at Independence had been relatively simple because so much of the historical fabric remained intact. At Independence Hall, for example, the main interpretive tool was the accurate restoration and furnishing of the interiors. These could then be presented as the setting for the great events that had occurred within the building's walls. Because the Franklin House would not be reconstructed, the solution at Franklin Court would necessarily be more abstract. Furthermore, the complexity of Franklin's personality demanded a highly sophisticated presentation. In their search for quality, the park turned to outside resources. In June 1972, at the recommendation of Nelson and Batcheler, a gathering of distinguished Franklin scholars convened, under park auspices, for a tour of Franklin Court and a discussion of the interpretive possibilities. The experts included Claude-Anne Lopez, of the editorial staff of the Franklin papers at Yale University, Whitfield Bell of the American Philosophical Society, Lyman Butterfield of the Massachusetts Historical Society, Edwin Wolf II of the Library Company of Philadelphia, Robert Spiller of the University of Pennsylvania, Catharine Drinker Bowen, Edgar P. Richardson,

37. Market Street houses in the 1950s. The arched opening visible to the right of the confectioners' sign is the entrance to the original passageway leading to Franklin Court.

and Charles Coleman Sellers. Robert Venturi and John Rauch attended the meeting, as did David Vaughan, who would be project architect for their firm, and John Milner and Robert DeSilets of Milner's staff. National Park Service representatives included architects Nelson, Batcheler, and Stuart MacDonald (who would later leave the park service and work on Franklin Court for Milner), archeologist Barbara Liggett, historians Platt, Yoelson, and David Dutcher (a recent addition to Yoelson's staff), Dorman from the curatorial staff, Alan Kent from Harper's Ferry, and Harry Pfanz from Washington.

Assistant Superintendent James Sullivan chaired the meeting and opened by apologizing for the absence of the superintendent. Cawood was in Washington receiving the first installment of a $190,000 fund for the furnishing of the second floor of Independence Hall, donated by the National Society of the Daughters of the American Revolution. Almost as soon as the introductions were over, the assembled experts tackled their task with verve and a remarkable degree of agreement. All wished to see the site interpret Franklin the man, not the myth. All agreed that he was a man of many facets—printer, scholar, diplomat, scientist, civic leader, family man, politician, humorist, friend, and neighbor—but that these should not be compartmentalized. Franklin should be portrayed as a whole man, in the context of his times, his city, and a larger stage. Butterfield summed up their appraisal in the phrase "citizen of the world." After viewing Franklin Court, which some of them had never seen, the group began to arrive at some consensus on interpretive devices that would help explain the real Franklin and the site of his home. They suggested reconstruction of his print shop, an archeological exhibit, a museum, and one or two movies. It began to be obvious that the site, and the Market Street houses in particular, might be too small to accommodate the desired program.

Subsequently, there were long, although less formal, discussions of how these ideas could be given physical form. Batcheler recalls meetings at the Venturis' apartment at which the park architects and members of the firm's design team would exchange views. One great breakthrough was the suggestion of Denise Scott-Brown, Venturi's wife and a member of the firm, that the museum be placed underground. This would allow space for the ambitious interpretive program and at the same time free the court for display of the house site and recreation of a garden evocative of the eighteenth century. Franklin Court's most celebrated feature, the "ghost house," evolved from similar discussions. As far back as Grant Simon's designs of 1954, the plan for the court had incorporated the concept of marking the plan of the house on the ground in some fashion. To this Batcheler had added, in 1969–70, some aboveground construction to further define the site. John Cotter traces the germ of the idea to an excavation photograph that he showed Venturi in the course of a conference between the architects and the Independence staff. The photograph had been taken by James Deetz, then working for the National Park Service as a contract archeologist at Wellfleet on Cape Cod. It

38. *Market Street houses after restoration. The party walls of the eighteenth-century buildings had survived and were preserved. Rooflines were taken down to their original heights, and fenestration patterns and details were based on the precedent of contemporary examples.*

showed the foundations and chimney base of a house, above which Deetz had drawn, in white ink, the skeleton frame of the building the foundations might have supported.

Venturi & Rauch produced a design concept with remarkable speed. The Franklin scholars had met in mid-June. In mid-July the architects presented preliminary drawings and a model to the advisory commission. The basic solutions were already in place—the restoration of the Market Street houses, the metal framework to give what was already characterized as a ghostlike impression of the Franklin House, the underground museum and theater, which would be reached by a ramp. There would also be a quiet garden, not a replica, since the design of Franklin's garden was unknown, but one that would evoke the spirit of the eighteenth century. R. Damon Childs, the head of the City Planning Commission, agreed to try to close Orianna Street as a public way so that it could be incorporated into the design.

There were, however, some demurrals when the conceptual plans were reviewed in Denver. Although the National Park Service had been commissioning major modern buildings for at least a decade, Venturi's ideas were a radical departure from the conventional design philosophy. Moreover, there were fears that the budget would be too high—that the park service simply could not afford such a complex project. Cawood and Brooks supported Venturi, but the decisive voice was that of Ernest Connally. Connally put the issue in a national perspective. Other giants of the era had their monuments—Jefferson at Monticello, Washington at Mount Vernon. Although there could be no such great restored house to commemorate Franklin, he deserved a memorial of as high a quality. Connally's eloquence persuaded the group to favor the Venturi scheme.

The relatively ready acceptance of the basic concept for Franklin Court eased what would still be the long and complex task of particularizing the design and the interpretation, constructing it, and bringing it in on time. The architects spent considerable time developing the plan for the garden. Supplied by the park staff with information from Franklin's letters they incorporated elements that were known to have adorned his grounds, such as the mulberry tree. At the same time, they determined that it would not be practicable to reconstruct an archeologically correct eighteenth-century garden. For one thing, the evidence was too thin. For another, the open space that had served as a private garden for a small family in the eighteenth century would now have to accommodate up to twenty thousand people a day. They decided instead to capture the spirit of an earlier garden by using formal and picturesque designs, both of which had been popular in the eighteenth century, but expressing them through heavier and chunkier elements. They combed estate gardens in Chestnut Hill and Germantown, where, earlier in the century, traditional Pennsylvania architecture and landscape had been adapted with an Edwardian amplitude of scale that suited their program for Franklin's garden. The result was a small but complex landscape, filled with references to the past, but also very much a product of its own time.

Fleshing out Franklin Court would require intensive activity on the part not only of the architects and their media consultant, but of the park service staff as well. Yoelson would be responsible for overseeing the interpretive materials on behalf of the park. He would provide the exhibit designers with information, edit scripts, and recommend specific spaces for interpretive purposes. He became, in Cawood's words, the park's "quality control." Because he was fulfilling these functions not only for Franklin Court but also for the Visitor Center and other sites in the park, his staff was augmented. David Dutcher, who had been a historian under Cawood at Richmond Battlefield, became Yoelson's chief deputy at Franklin Court. He also developed an interpretive program for the First Bank of the United States, which was never implemented because of budgetary constraints. Joan Marshall, transferred from the curatorial staff, monitored the reconstruction of the subscription office for Franklin's grandson's newspaper, the *Aurora,* in one of the Market Street houses. Penny Batcheler also put in long hours reviewing the further architectural investigations of the Market Street houses, and consulting with Venturi & Rauch on design issues and on interpretation of architectural and archeological features. She too acquired additional staff, including Mary Mish, who had worked for Barbara Liggett as an archeological draftsman.

Hundreds of small and large decisions were required before the final plans took shape, especially for the complicated multi-media interpretive program that was envisioned. By August 1972 Yoelson had produced a draft report on how space would be allocated in the Market Street houses. Uses included a working print shop, a newspaper office, and a working post office. The interior of the house at 318 Market Street, where the cellar was rich in archeological data, would be stabilized and left open from cellar to third floor so that visitors could see the architectural and archeological evidence on which restoration and interpretation were based. It would also illuminate another aspect of Franklin's life—his role as an owner and developer of property. The upper floors of the other buildings would be adapted for office uses. The rest of the program was less firm. At a meeting in Harper's Ferry, it was agreed that Venturi & Rauch would subcontract various aspects of the interpretive program to a media firm, with Claude-Anne Lopez to be retained as a consultant.

Meanwhile John Milner's firm and National Park Service personnel had been carrying out detailed investigations of the surviving fabric of the Market Street houses. The easternmost of these, at 314 Market Street, had never been owned by Franklin. Documentation showed that a building had been erected on the site about 1720 and entirely rebuilt in 1797. Architectural evidence for its appearance in 1720 was minimal and inconclusive; for 1797 the evidence was excellent, but the building had never existed in that form in Franklin's lifetime. Since the proposed use was for public toilets and offices, Stuart MacDonald, a young architect on Lee Nelson's staff, recommended that what he termed reconstruction not be undertaken, but that a contemporary building be erected. The manager of the historic preservation team at the Denver Service Center agreed with this recommendation.

Yoelson was outraged. He expressed his disapproval in a ten-point memorandum to Cawood. The 1797 building existed; its preservation was recommended in an approved historic structures report. What was planned was not a conjectural reconstruction; it was an exterior restoration. How, since the building was genuine, could the park justify demolishing a historic structure to replace it with a modern one? Furthermore, the cut-off date for the interpretation of the site was not Franklin's death in 1791, but 1800. Cawood backed Yoelson, and after discussion with Denver, Washington, and the regional office, the restoration went forward.

By the summer of 1973, Venturi & Rauch's media consultants, deMartin-Marona Associates, were refining their proposals for interpretive devices. The displays would be the most complex ever installed in a National Park Service facility. In addition to such conventional devices as a gallery displaying some of Franklin's possessions, there would be a mirrored wall with flashing neon lights and two- and three-dimensional images expressing Franklin's multi-faceted personality; a bank of telephones with recorded messages relaying famous people's opinions of Franklin from his era to the present day; exhibits of Franklin's inventions and civic projects in which he had been involved; a film; and a miniature theater in the round, "Franklin on the World Stage." The complexity and ambitious nature of the program overwhelmed Harper's Ferry. Reviewers thought that there were too many "peaks" of experience, and also worried about cost and maintenance. Eventually the proposals were scaled down. Some video displays were omitted, and it was determined that the figures in "Franklin on the World Stage" would be stationary with the effect of movement created through sound and light.

As at the Visitor Center, the park staff did not like the media consultants' first proposal for the film. Although in this case they found the techniques acceptable, the treatment was not. It seemed to pick up the caricature of Franklin that the park service was so anxious to avoid. Again the primary objections appeared to have been voiced by Yoelson. By now Yoelson had been steeped in Frankliniana for twenty years. He believed, and his superiors agreed, that he knew the man intimately and that the interpretation of Franklin should be based on his knowledge. Although time was pressing and changes might disrupt the schedule, the park upheld its commitment to quality. There would be a new film treatment. This time the consultants discussed the concept of the film with, among others, Yoelson, Platt, and Lopez. Yoelson continued to work closely with Mrs. Secondari, who had been retained by deMartin-Marona to produce the film. Also in almost daily contact with deMartin-Marona was Charles Dorman, who had to provide authentic furnishings and props, as well as advising on costumes. Indeed, from 1973 to 1975 Dorman advised on so many National Park Service film productions, not only at Independence, that he began to describe himself in monthly reports as having "gone Hollywood." Dorman also collected authentic furnishings and quality reproductions for display both in exhibit cases and in such reconstructed features as the print shop. This, too, was a massive job done at fever pitch, with hundreds of decisions to be made about individual objects.

Other members of the park service staff also made notable contributions to the finished product. The engraving of quotations from the Franklin correspondence in the paving replicating the plan of the house grew out of discussions between Venturi & Rauch and the park service's architects. Mary Mish then combed the research files for quotations, with Yoelson making the final selection. Mish and Batcheler also worked closely with Milner's firm, which had retained Barbara Liggett as a consultant, on the interpretive features for the interior of 318 Market Street. Batcheler and Venturi prepared the text for the large signs along the west garden wall that describe the evolution of Franklin Court.

In addition to the complex interpretive issues, Franklin Court posed

39. *Visitors of all ages and all walks of life enjoy the sophisticated exhibitry of the museum in Franklin Court. Viewing the miniaturized sound and light show, "Franklin on the World Stage," in July 1976 are Princess Grace of Monaco (in dark glasses left of center) and her family. Superintendent Cawood is to the princess's left.*

tricky technical problems, many of which were solved by the consulting structural engineer, Nicholas Gianopulos, a principal in Keast & Hood. Gianopulos had cut his teeth on historic buildings at Independence, working under Sheldon Keast on Congress Hall and Independence Hall. He was responsible for the structure of the underground museum, for the stabilization of the Market Street buildings, and for the structural system for the skeletal steel ghost frames that would mark the sites of the Franklin House and the print shop that had once occupied the northern end of the court.

Despite the scope and complexity of the project, its design was accomplished with remarkable speed. By August 1973 the project was sufficiently advanced for preparation of cost estimates and a construction schedule. Construction was under way by the summer of 1974, and Franklin Court opened, in time for the Bicentennial, on April 20, 1976. The faith of Brooks, Cawood, Connally, and others in the National Park Service was fully justified on several levels. Franklin Court is the third most popular attraction at

226

Independence National Historical Park; its attendance is topped only by that at the Liberty Bell and Independence Hall. On an artistic level, it has garnered almost universal accolades. It is the only National Park Service project to have won an American Institute of Architects honor award, and in 1985 it received from President Reagan the presidential award for design excellence.

Franklin Court and the Visitor Center were the largest, most expensive, and, with one exception, most hotly debated of the Bicentennial projects at Independence. But they were by no means the only objects of planning and development in the period from 1972 to 1975. The restoration of the second floor of Independence Hall continued into 1972, and the colossal clock on the exterior of the west wall was being reconstructed at the same time. Old City Hall was also undergoing restoration during this period, as was the First Bank of the United States, the Deshler-Morris House in Germantown, and the Thaddeus Kosciusko National Memorial at Third and Pine Streets, a gift to the federal government from Edward J. Piszek. The Second Bank of the United States was also being restored by National Park Service architects and fitted up on the interior as a gallery for the park's portrait collection. Two major reconstructions, City Tavern and the Graff House, were also under way. Although both were based on staff research, the working drawings were contracted to outside architects because the park service's architectural staff could not handle the additional work. John Dickey was selected as the architect for City Tavern, which would be turned over to what the park service dubs a "concessioner" to run as a restaurant. John Milner's firm, with Robert DeSilets as project architect, would design the Graff House. Both would be completed on an accelerated schedule, opening in the fall of 1975.

The National Park Service had never accorded a high priority to reconstruction of the Graff House, but it had always been a favored project of the interlocking directorates of the Independence Hall Association, the Philadelphia National Shrines Commission, and the Independence National Historical Park Advisory Commission. Despite its deletion from the original legislation authorizing the park, members of those various bodies continued to lobby for its inclusion. By 1964 they had succeeded in persuading Congress to authorize acquisition of the property if private funds could be raised to pay for the reconstruction of the building. Judge Lewis gradually cooled, but when Arthur Kaufmann assumed control of the advisory commission, he began to push for the Graff House with great vigor. In 1967 he began to negotiate with the bank serving as trustee of the estate of Emily Balch, who had left several million dollars to establish the Balch Institute and Library devoted to ethnic history. By 1971 the Balch estate had agreed to purchase the corner site at Seventh and Market Streets and sell the portion where the Graff House had stood to the National Park Service for $200,000, the sum authorized by Congress. With Kaufmann's assurances that matching funds to reconstruct the house could be raised privately, there was little the park service could do but acquiesce. Privately, however, some within the park service agreed with those among the Philadelphia historical community who thought that what they termed a "fake" was an unsuitable memorial to Jefferson.

There was additional land acquisition to be negotiated. Authorization for acquisition of the site on which the Irwin Building stood passed Congress in November 1970, but it took several years of negotiation before all its tenants' leases could be terminated and demolition could proceed. This was finally accomplished in early 1974. The legislation for Area F, the site for a proposed parking garage and other park development east of Second Street, came still later. Rep. James Byrnes, a member of the park's advisory commission, introduced it twice in the House, only to see it die in the Senate. Brooks turned to Arthur Kaufmann for help. Kaufmann, whose lobbying efforts on behalf of Independence were prodigious, persuaded the ever-helpful Sen. Hugh Scott to take up the cudgels. Scott was successful; the bill authorizing acquisition was signed into law in November 1974. Kaufmann reported to the advisory commission, with evident relief, that he was glad to be out of the "legislative" business for the first time since he had joined that body in 1949. The legislation, however, provided no appropriation for acquisition or development. Area F therefore would not be planned or developed in time for the Bicentennial.

Moving the Liberty Bell

There remained one development essential to preparing Independence for the Bicentennial. National Park Service management was still convinced that it was necessary to move the Liberty Bell out of Independence Hall. The decision not to incorporate the Liberty Bell into the Visitor Center had thus spawned a new controversy. Where should it be placed? That question had been raised repeatedly, although never so urgently, for fifty years. In the 1920s Jacques Greber had produced a plan for moving the bell to a shrinelike structure across Chestnut Street from Independence Hall, in what would eventually become the first block of the Independence Mall State Park. During World War II the Independence Hall Association had proposed moving the bell to a bomb-proof shelter behind Independence Hall, a solution that Judge Lewis continued to advocate. These locations and others were discussed in the forum of the park's advisory commission during much of 1972 and 1973. This time Brooks wanted to make sure that any decision gained the commission's support. Their assistance would be essential in persuading the city government and the general public to accept the move.

Having won its point and kept the bell out of the Visitor Center, the commission was more than willing to cooperate. At first the commission appeared to agree on a location in the first block of the State Mall. However, this aroused fears that there would be danger to pedestrians crossing Chestnut Street. Although the city's plans called for making Chestnut Street a pedestrian mall west of Sixth Street, the city refused to close it to vehicular traffic east of that intersection. A site in Independence Square was also rejected, despite Lewis's advocacy, because it would require relocation of a statue of Irish-born Commodore John Barry, celebrated as the father of the U.S. Navy. Commission members James Byrnes and Michael J. Bradley, both of Irish descent, were vehemently opposed to this action, as were the Friendly Sons of St. Patrick, representing the Philadelphia Irish community. Clearly such a course would not be acceptable politically.

Bradley undertook the delicate job of negotiating the bell's move with Mayor Frank Rizzo. The mayor was invited to tour the park and see for himself the problems of congestion around the bell's location in the tower stair hall. A meeting was convened in Rizzo's office, including representatives of the National Park Service, the city of Philadelphia, and the commonwealth of Pennsylvania. The group agreed that the first block of the mall would be the most appropriate location, but some problems remained. The mall belonged to the state, not the federal government. The state, however, was prepared to be cooperative. Maintenance of the mall was a strain on the state's resources; relief would be welcome. In late 1973 the Pennsylvania legislature voted to transfer the entire three blocks of the Independence Mall State Park to the federal government.

There was one remaining obstacle. Acquisition and construction of the mall had been funded with development bonds that would not mature until the 1990s. Once again a period of negotiations ensued, this time with the state and the bonding companies. Eventually agreement was reached. Because a portion of the bonds had been paid off, a strip in the center of the mall's first block would be deeded to the federal government in fee in early 1975. This would provide the site for the Liberty Bell Pavilion. The remainder of the mall would be leased to the National Park Service, which would operate and maintain it until the expiration of the bonds, at which time ownership would be transferred.

During these negotiations proposals were solicited for the design of the pavilion. Again Brooks and Cawood felt that it would be politic to select a Philadelphia architect. In early 1974 the contract was awarded to Mitchell/Giurgola, which, although it maintained a New York City office, was perceived by the Philadelphia community as a local firm. The opening of the Bicentennial year was less than two years away, but with careful scheduling the building could be erected and the bell installed in time. Cawood could thus visit Russia as part of a National Park Service exchange team in the belief that the last major impediment to the completion of the park had been removed.

Shortly after he left, the carefully assembled mosaic almost fell apart. Chester Brooks received a telephone call from the mayor's office one morning saying that Mayor Rizzo wished to come down to the park to view the site to which the Liberty Bell would be moved. Brooks met Rizzo, who was accompanied by reporters and television crews, at Independence Hall. The mayor had changed his mind. The bell was not to be moved. Brooks thought fast. He escorted Rizzo into the tower stair hall. As tourists flowed past, he reminded the mayor that the city was predicting that 40 million people would come to Philadelphia in 1976. The National Park Service had estimated that only 2 million could be accommodated in Independence Hall. If the mayor did not want the Liberty Bell moved, the park service would not move it; it would simply tell the remaining 38 million people that they could not see the bell because of the mayor's decision. Having made his point, Brooks quickly shifted to a topic that he thought Rizzo could agree on—the limitations of other locations. He reminded Rizzo that Independence Square was impossible because of the Barry statue. Brooks then shepherded the group out through the front door and across Chestnut Street. Here Rizzo stopped and informed the reporters that this was where the bell would go. With a fine sense of drama and publicity, Rizzo, then considering running for governor, had put his imprimatur on the site that had been carefully and quietly negotiated several months before.

Romaldo Giurgola worked smoothly with the National Park Service in fulfilling its requirements for the Liberty Bell Pavilion. The building must not compete with Independence Hall, but become part of the vista. The bell must remain visually accessible at all times, and within the building the bell must be accessible to the touch. The pavilion must also provide shelter for the bell and for visitors waiting to see it. Giurgola investigated several possibilities for its design including colonnades and arcades. In the end he chose a simple solution—a long, low-lying building with its axis perpendicular to that of Independence Hall. It was roughly dumbbell-shaped, with a large space at the north end in which people could gather and another at the south end to house the Liberty Bell. The two would be linked by a long corridor in which the lines of people waiting to see the bell would form. Large areas of the exterior cladding would be glass. The bell itself would be set against a south wall made entirely of glass. At any hour of the day, passers-by could see the bell. From within the visitor would view the Liberty Bell against the backdrop of Independence Hall. The building thus functioned as a large exhibit case in which the bell would be placed. The design was not universally beloved. Comparisons to subway stations and branch banks were voiced when it was unveiled and have continued ever since. The client and architect, however, were well satisfied. In Cawood's opinion the building's simple and low-keyed contemporary design enhanced the power of the object it was designed to house. Nor did Giurgola resent the comparisons. He had sought a building that would be familiar and without pretension.

Although the design process progressed smoothly, and construction began in the spring of 1975, paying for the pavilion required some ingenuity—indeed creative juggling—on the part of Brooks and Cawood. Only $225,000 had been appropriated for moving the Liberty Bell; the price tag for the building was close to $900,000. Going to Congress for a special appropriation might reopen debate on moving the bell. It would be necessary to find the money elsewhere. Some could be obtained by using funds that had been appropriated for the design of a maintenance building, but this would still be far short of what was needed. Once again Brooks and Cawood appealed to Arthur Kaufmann. True to his commitment, Kaufmann, through the Independence Hall Association, had raised $500,000 for reconstruction of the Graff House. The check, however, had not yet been presented to the National Park Service. On the other hand, money for the Graff House construction had already been appropriated. If Kaufmann consented, the Independence Hall Association's $500,000 would be spent on the Liberty Bell Pavilion, although publicly the association would be credited with funding the Graff House. Kaufmann's willingness to accede to the switch permitted completion of the Liberty Bell Pavilion in time for the Bicentennial. Cawood solicited other Philadelphia institutions and individuals for contributions, obtaining, among others, a major gift from the William Penn Foundation and funds to pay for the oak flooring from the Knights of Columbus.

As it became evident that by a hair's breadth the Liberty Bell Pavilion would be completed by the end of 1975, Cawood began to plan the moving of the bell as a celebration, a great dramatic moment to initiate the Bicentennial year. The successful transfer of the bell from Independence Hall to the new building would thus be cast in a positive light. Cawood viewed the project, in retrospect, as his greatest accomplishment in the intensive and arduous task of preparing Independence for the Bicentennial. He had taken a bell the National Park Service did not own, from a building it did not own to a piece of ground it did not own and erected a building for which there was no design and no funding, in less than a year.

The bell, he determined, would be moved at the stroke of midnight on December 31, 1975 / January 1, 1976. There would be parties beforehand, schoolchildren's choruses, and bands on the mall as the procession followed the bell to its new home, and a brief, dignified ceremony as the bell was placed in its new setting. There would also be ample press coverage, with television recording the event for transmission to homes across the country. In the event, the planning went awry because of circumstances beyond Cawood's control. December 31, 1975, proved to be a night of cold rain and harsh winds. Rain soaked the uniformed children waiting to perform as the bell was moved across Chestnut Street. Gusts shook temporary wiring and interfered with lighting and television transmission.

Nevertheless, as the Centennial bell in the Independence Hall tower sounded the first stroke of midnight, the Chestnut Street door opened and the Liberty Bell began the short journey to its new home. It moved smoothly down a ramp on a special cart, held in a cradle designed for the occasion by scientists at the Franklin Institute. Dignitaries and National Park Service staff accompanied it in procession. Among those marching with the bell was Louise

Boggs. Boggs had gone to work for the city of Philadelphia shortly before the transfer of Independence Square to the custody of the park service. Now a long-time member of the park's maintenance staff, she had cared for the Liberty Bell and other objects in Independence Hall, learning from the curators what cleaning methods and materials to use. Inside the Liberty Bell Pavilion she listened to the speeches and heard the actor Lee J. Cobb read a poem. As the ceremony ended, she stepped forward. Tears mingled with the raindrops on her face. Taking a soft cloth from her bag, she began to dry the rain from the bell she had so often cleaned.

Eight
Celebrating the Bicentennial

Although Judge Edwin O. Lewis began reminding the National Park Service of the approach of the Bicentennial in the late 1950s, it was not until 1969 that upper management began to devote serious attention to the park service's role in its celebration. By late 1970 the park service had begun to plan for the Bicentennial on a national basis, which would spread its resources to satisfy its countrywide constituency. Nevertheless, certain areas were favored: of twenty-five projects in the National Park System accorded Bicentennial priority, five were at Independence, a fact that annoyed some of the regional directors and park superintendents in the West, who were accustomed to getting the largest share of any park service pie. As it gradually became apparent that the celebration at Independence would to a large extent *be* the Bicentennial in the city where the Declaration of Independence had been drafted and signed, the program at Independence acquired even greater urgency.

There was little reason in the late 1960s to think that Independence would be more than a contributing factor, albeit an important one, in the national celebration of the Bicentennial. Philadelphia, remembering its glorious hours as the setting for the Centennial Exhibition in 1876, had determined that this triumph could be repeated, although in a different key, in 1976. In the early 1960s various nonprofit groups met to formulate a "master exposition plan" for Philadelphia. By 1967 these groups had coalesced into the Philadelphia Bicentennial Corporation. The 1876 exposition had been a display of the United States' emerging industrial might. The most popular exhibit, outdrawing even the midway, was the forty-foot-high Corliss engine that powered the fair's machinery. The 1976 celebration, as the Bicentennial Corporation envisioned it, would capture the spirit of the twentieth-century through a three-pronged approach. It would offer the traditional world's fair carnival atmosphere, combined with a celebration of history. At the same time, the exposition had been conceived in the heyday of Lyndon Johnson's Great Society and the civil rights movement. Its third component was therefore a massive urban renewal program, aimed at redevelopment of black, industrial North Philadelphia as well as completion of the still-lagging redevelopment of historic (and by now largely white) Society Hill. Transportation and other elements of the city's infrastructure would be renewed. A further contribution to the economic well-being of the city would be construction of a "megastructure" of permanent exhibition buildings above the Thirtieth Street Railroad Station.

Philadelphia's scheme was ambitious and costly, carrying a price tag of $1 to $2 billion. If it was to be realized, much of the money would have to come from the federal government. Selection of Philadelphia as the site for the national celebration of the Bicentennial would depend, in part, on the recommendation of a thirty-five-member American Revolution Bicentennial Commission, authorized by Congress in 1966. With ten years to go, however, the commission took little action. A reorganization in 1968, when members appointed by Lyndon Johnson resigned and were replaced by Richard Nixon's appointments, did little to hasten its deliberations. It was not until the summer of 1970 that the commission was prepared to hear proposals and make a recommendation. By this time other cities—notably Boston, Washington, and Miami—also were pressing claims to be the centerpiece of the Bicentennial. The commission's means of resolving these conflicting proposals was to support all, or, in a sense, none, since it did not recommend authorizing the almost $10 billion that the four taken together would cost. Briefly, however, it appeared that Philadelphia might still win out. The commission was persuaded to reconsider, probably by the White House, because Nixon wanted to boost Pennsylvania senator Hugh Scott's reelection campaign. A revised recommendation favored Philadelphia as a site for an international exposition, but the other three cities would also receive funding.

By this time, however, the Philadelphia Bicentennial Corporation was crumbling under the combined effects of the dispersion of proposed federal support and internal dissension. Black members walked out of meetings, fearing that their concerns would be ignored when sufficient federal funding failed to materialize. Their pessimism proved justified. By the end of 1970, it was clear that the Department of Commerce did not favor a proposal it viewed as urban renewal in the guise of an exposition.

As the 1972 presidential election approached, it became increasingly clear that Philadelphia would have to scale down its plans. In May the American Revolution Bicentennial Commission recommended that there be no international exposition, citing difficulties in selecting a site as well as the costs. Cynics suggested that with an election approaching, scattering Bicentennial largesse around the country was good politics. Following the inaugural, the Nixon administration proposed, and Congress accepted, abolition of the American Revolution Bicentennial Commission and its replacement by an American Revolution Bicentennial Administration. The latter would exist largely to oversee the distribution of federal grants to all fifty states and to selected cities. Philadelphia would be eligible to receive about $100 million. It was a far cry from the heady proposals of the previous decade. Gradually, under the aegis of a new organization, Philadelphia '76, fresh, if more modest, plans for the Bicentennial began to emerge. They would depend on the city's existing institutions for exhibits, cultural activities, and major sporting events. The historical centerpiece for the celebration would be Independence National Historical Park.

While the Philadelphia Bicentennial Corporation spun its elaborate plans in the late 1960s, the National Park Service drowsed. Bicentennial or no Bicentennial, it went about planning in its usual methodical way. The park service considers its purpose to be the preservation and maintenance, in perpetuity, of the resources with which it is entrusted, either natural or man-made. In that context the several years it may take to produce a master plan for a major park are relatively short. Yet this process is not efficient when the goal is preparing a facility for a specific occasion in a short time. Independence was not galvanized until Chester Brooks's arrival in January 1969; then an accelerated program to prepare the park for the Bicentennial was put into effect. In a little over two years as superintendent, Brooks, with the assistance of his administrative officer, Howard LaRue, set firm schedules for completion of projects already under way, assembled and fought for an adequate budget, and shepherded the Bicentennial program for Independence through the National Park Service directorate and Congress. By the time Hobart G. Cawood assumed the superintendency in the fall of 1971, the framework for what needed to be done was in place. However, executing the program in time for the Bicentennial, and doing it as Cawood wanted, with "class," would require extraordinary dedication and teamwork.

Regardless of the fate of the nation's or Philadelphia's Bicentennial plans, Cawood was determined that at Independence the occasion would be celebrated with style. Cawood believed, and persuaded all those concerned, that no matter what other events were scheduled, on July 4, 1976, the eyes of the world would be on Independence. He had an enormous appetite for work, thriving on a schedule of twelve- to fourteen-hour days, six or seven days a week. His enthusiasm and ebullient personality persuaded others to cooperate in bringing the complicated development plan to a successful conclusion. His blend of friendliness, courtliness, and down-home folksiness were novel but effective in staid Philadelphia. Even Britain's Princess Margaret, known as a stickler for formality and protocol, failed to take offense when Cawood opened the door of her limousine and in a warm Kentucky voice said, "Hi, Princess Margaret. I'm Hobie Cawood." It was more, however, than a matter of charm. Everyone who dealt with him became aware that Cawood genuinely believed that the United States was the best country in the world, that the principles set forth in the Declaration of Independence and the Constitution were sacred, and that showing people the places where those principles had been formulated was a vitally important task.

Those beliefs were an important factor in keeping the Independence development program on target, despite the threats of strikes, material shortages, and budget shortfalls. Thanks, in part, to Cawood's persuasiveness, contractors and workmen wanted to be a part of the Bicentennial effort. At every preconstruction meeting Cawood would deliver a patriotic oration before turning over the floor to Fred Spenser, who would deal with day-to-day construction supervision. If delays were threatened or the quality was not up to the standard he wanted, Cawood would be on the job site to tackle the problem personally.

But the force of one man's personality could never have accomplished the transformation of what Assistant Superintendent James Sullivan called the "park of locked doors" into a facility capable of accommodating 15 million people. When Cawood became superintendent in the fall of 1971, the only buildings that were open on a regular schedule throughout the year were Independence Hall and Congress Hall. Restoration of the Todd House and the Bishop White House was complete, as was reconstruction of the Pemberton House and New Hall, but there was insufficient personnel to staff them on a regular basis. Cawood would have to oversee not only the completion of the construction of the remainder of the park, but also a program to interpret and provide access to all the park's facilities. The effort would require strong teamwork, and Cawood saw his major role as orchestrating and expediting it. He understood the necessity of having good professionals available and taking their advice while supplying them with the community support, the approvals, and the money that they needed to keep the program moving.

There was already on hand at Independence a strong cadre of professionals who were thoroughly familiar with the park and plans for its completion. Yoelson would shift from research to overseeing the content of the interpretive program in terms of both exhibitry and what is known in National Park Service jargon as "personal interpretation." As movie scripts and exhibits were completed and installed in 1975, he and his staff undertook training of the expanded force of interpreters, the people who would guide tours, deliver explanatory talks, and answer visitors' questions. Nelson had left in 1972 to join the staff of OAHP in Washington, but Batcheler remained to assume responsibility for restoration of the interior of Old City Hall and to provide research and design support for the outside architects responsible for the other restoration and reconstruction projects. John Milley would supervise an expanded curatorial staff responsible for furnishing the newly opened facilities and for finally mounting and exhibiting the great collection of portraits, primarily from the hand of Charles Willson Peale, of the leading figures of the revolutionary and federal eras.

More administrative staff was needed to move the construction program forward and to maintain and expand the park's operation. Howard LaRue remained from Brooks's tenure to program construction schedules and oversee issuance of specifications, bid documents, and contracts. In his first two years at Independence, Cawood began to assemble the additional personnel he needed. One of the key slots was that of assistant superintendent. In 1972 Sullivan left to become superintendent of Colonial National Histor-

40. Park personnel are on hand to protect as well as instruct. Here Don Murray assists a young visitor stricken in front of Independence Hall.

ical Park in Yorktown, Virginia. His replacement was Douglas Warnock. More diffident than Cawood in social situations, he assumed responsibility for much of the day-to-day operation at Independence, leaving Cawood free for the public contact at which he was so adept. Cawood could thus carry on public relations, seek political support, and engage in fundraising, knowing that the park would continue to run smoothly.

One of the most important aspects of the expanding park's operation would be dealing with its visitors, especially in view of the enormous crowds expected for the Bicentennial. In the early 1970s projections anticipated that 40 to 45 million people would come to Philadelphia in 1976 and that most of them would visit Independence. Park personnel would be responsible for their safety and also for that of the park and its contents, as well as for ensuring that the visitors' experience was both enjoyable and educational. **237**

These dual responsibilities were the purview of the Division of Interpretation and Resource Management, to head which Cawood recruited Clyde M. Lockwood. Lockwood was possessed of what Cawood characterized as "that old 'can do' attitude," the view that working for the National Park Service is something more than a job or even a career—a service to the parks and to the people. This attitude is instilled in National Park Service personnel, especially in those whom their supervisors expect to rise in management, through example, carefully calculated transfers and promotions, and in-service training sessions. It includes willingness to put in more than a standard number of hours, and to do a job oneself if there is no other way to get it done. In 1974 the Philadelphia Convention and Visitors Bureau instituted a series of candlelight tours of the park and Society Hill. On evenings when the park could not afford to pay guides for the Todd House, it was Cawood and Lockwood who opened the building and showed it to visitors.

When Lockwood arrived in the spring of 1973, he saw his first duty as bringing the protection program at Independence up to National Park Service standards. The twelve men then employed for protection had for the most part been hired locally and had never worked at a park other than Independence. They functioned primarily as guards and night watchmen. During the day they stood guard duty at fixed points; at night they made rounds, recording their stops at various checkpoints with watchmen's clocks. Lockwood oversaw the installation of added portable radio units and computerized alarm systems, so that the protection staff could respond quickly and efficiently when there were indications of trouble. He also added two guard dogs, the first in the park service. Training for the security staff, which would more than double in size in the next two years, fell largely to Richard O'Guin, who was responsible for security under Lockwood. O'Guin had had police experience before joining the National Park Service and had attended the FBI Academy. He sent some of his staff to the Philadelphia Police Academy, saw that all received training in first aid, and worked with them in groups and on a one-to-one basis.

The other aspect of Lockwood's job required oversight of the park's largest staffing requirement—visitors' services. Out of a total staff of 421 in 1976, visitors' services would account for at least 200. This category included all the people, in uniform and in costume, who conducted tours of the park and Independence Hall, greeted visitors at Congress Hall and Franklin Court, gave talks at the Liberty Bell, and operated the desk at the Visitor Center, as well as the projectionists for the movies at Franklin Court and the Visitor Center.

It has always been easier for the National Park Service to obtain funding for acquisition and development than for operations. In 1975 it appeared that the Bicentennial year would be no exception. Citing inflation and budget constraints, Director Gary Everhardt announced that the operating budget for 1975 would be $403.9 million. Congress had earmarked $9.1 million for

Bicentennial activities, which was substantially less than the park service had asked for. Although Everhardt acknowledged that Independence would be the "focal point" of the National Park Service's Bicentennial celebration, it was unlikely that the park would get all that it had requested. By the spring of 1975, the dimensions of the gap at Independence were clear. The National Park Service had received authorization for 50 new positions nationwide; of those, 27 had been apportioned to Independence, but 112 more were needed.

Help came from several quarters. In March a regional directors' meeting, at which Everhardt was expected to be present, was scheduled to take place at Independence. Cawood had always cultivated a cordial relationship with the Philadelphia press. Its support proved particularly useful at this juncture. Hearing about the pending shortfall in staffing, Creed C. Black, editor of the *Philadelphia Inquirer* and a fellow Kentuckian, called Cawood and asked whether the newspaper could help. When the director and regional directors arrived for their conference, each found at his place a copy of the morning paper unfolded to the editorial page. Headed "Independence National Park Cannot Be Starved in '76," the editorial praised the progress of the development program in glowing terms, contrasting it with the disarray of other Bicentennial plans. Under those circumstances, the paper found the failure to supply the park with needed personnel incomprehensible.

This was the opening salvo in a campaign to obtain adequate staffing for Independence. Arthur Kaufmann, who had thought his lobbying days were at last over, once again began to importune members of Congress on behalf of Independence. John O'Hara, managing partner of Price Waterhouse's Philadelphia office, also a member of the advisory commission and the Independence Hall Association, sent copies of the *Inquirer* editorial and other editorials supporting the park to every senator and representative. Other citizens also wrote to their legislators. As an employee of the executive branch, Cawood could not initiate direct contact with members of Congress asking them to contravene the administration's budget request. When he happened to encounter Rep. Joshua Eilberg one day in the lobby of the Bellevue-Stratford Hotel, he felt free, however, to answer in detail Eilberg's question about how things were going at Independence. Eilberg invited Cawood to Washington to brief his staff, and Cawood took the opportunity to visit other members of the local congressional delegation. As always, Sen. Scott was supportive in the upper house. Eventually Independence received almost fifty additional new positions for 1975, for a total of seventy-six, and its full roster for 1976.

In addition to coping with the crowds expected to visit Independence daily, the park would have to be prepared to accommodate an increased number of special events. There would be approximately two thousand of these at Independence in 1975–76, most sponsored by outside groups. In addition, there was an unusually high number of visits from foreign heads of state. The first to come in January 1976 was Israeli Prime Minister Yitzhak Rabin, followed in March by Prime Minister Liam Cosgrove of the Irish Republic, and in April by King Carl XVI Gustav of Sweden. In July, in addition to those present for the official celebrations, Norway's Crown Prince Harald and his princess and West German Chancellor Helmut Schmidt visited the park.

By this time the procedure for escorting heads of state through the park was well established. Other events in which the park participated required extensive advance planning. The first major celebrations inaugurating the Bicentennial were held in 1974, commemorating the meeting of the First Continental Congress in Carpenters' Hall. In September and October Philadelphia '76 and the commonwealth of Pennsylvania, with the cooperation of the Carpenters' Company and the National Park Service, sponsored a series of events. Some were meant to engender a festival atmosphere, including demonstrations of colonial crafts and military maneuvers on Independence Mall, street festivals in Old City and on the Benjamin Franklin Parkway, and movie and concert series. Others were more directly connected with the events celebrated. A lecture series by eminent historians drew overflowing audiences. Pennsylvania's primary contribution was a two-day "reconvening" of the Continental Congress. Fifty-two delegates, including the governors of the thirteen original states, met on September 5 and 6 in Carpenters' Hall. The first day the Carpenters' Company held an evening reception in the long room on the second floor of Independence Hall. The second day concluded with Pennsylvania's dinner for 1,500 people, served under tents on Independence Mall, then still the property of the state. President Gerald Ford was the principal speaker. The festivities ended with a fireworks display. Sadly, these celebrations of the meeting of the First Continental Congress coincided with the final illness of Judge Edwin O. Lewis who died on September 18.

The park's own Bicentennial kick-off was scheduled for October 13 and 14 and revolved around the opening of the portrait gallery in the Second Bank of the United States. This event was the culmination of the work of the museum branch, and in particular of its chief, John Milley. There had been a curatorial function at Independence since the early 1950s, primarily charged with researching, acquiring, caring for, and displaying appropriate furnishings in the restored and reconstructed buildings. At the same time, the National Park Service was well aware that in acquiring custody of the contents of the buildings on Independence Square from the City of Philadelphia, it had assumed stewardship of a major collection of American paintings. These were the portraits by Charles Willson Peale and members of the Sharples family, most of which had been in Peale's museum, which had occupied the second floor of Independence Hall from 1802 to 1828. In the late 1950s and early 1960s, the staff at Independence included a conservator, Anne F. Clapp, whose duties included restoration of the portrait collection. When Clapp left,

41. In accumulating furnishings to interpret Independence Hall and other buildings, Independence National Historical Park has become a treasure house of eighteenth-century Delaware Valley furniture and decorative arts. One of the finest pieces is still known as "Miss Archer's chair" in honor of its donor. This Philadelphia armchair, dating to between 1735 and 1750, is now displayed in Independence Hall.

she was not replaced. Instead, the portraits were sent, a few at a time, to the Fogg Museum at Harvard University for restoration.

In 1959 David H. Wallace, who had joined the park staff as a historian in 1957, became supervisor of the curatorial staff. He began to prepare a systematic inventory of the city's collections, which included approximately four thousand objects, as well as the Peale portraits. Nevertheless, the emphasis continued to be on the furnishings program, which, beginning with the first refurnishing of the Assembly Room in 1955, extended to the Bishop White and Todd Houses, Congress Hall, the other rooms in Independence Hall, and City Tavern. It encompassed the fitting out of fifty period rooms and seventy exhibit areas, and the assemblage of a collection of approximately eighteen thousand pieces.

The acquisition of appropriate pieces was exciting and sometimes frustrating. Purchasing good objects on a limited budget required a thorough understanding of the antiques market and considerable knowledge of the collectors and dealers through whose hands such pieces might pass. Fortunately, two people on the staff during the 1960s and early 1970s knew the antiques business. Fred Hanson's parents had been antiques dealers, and Charles Dorman had worked for a well-known dealer. Money, however, was always a problem. Some acquisition funds were included in the construction budgets, but were never sufficient. At Independence Hall this relative poverty was alleviated by large donations from outside organizations: the General

Federation of Women's Clubs and the National Society of the Daughters of the American Revolution. In other cases owners of appropriate pieces were generous, notably people and institutions related to Bishop White. Another private donor was a spinster from Richmond, Virginia, who wrote to the park offering to contribute some family furnishings with a Philadelphia history. As was routinely done, Dorman replied, asking for further information and photographs. There was no response. Several months later, however, Dorman, who was then placing furniture in the second floor of Independence Hall, was summoned by walkie-talkie. His sometime correspondent was in the park asking to see him. When they met, she told Dorman that a neighbor had offered her a ride to Philadelphia; so she had come, bringing one of the pieces. Dorman accompanied her to the car. There, resting in majesty, was the finest eighteenth-century Philadelphia armchair he had ever seen. With the owner in tow, he returned to Independence Hall, placing the chair in a place of honor in the Governor's Council Chamber. Others of her family heirlooms proved to be of later date and lesser quality, and were gently rejected.

Some cash donations were proffered to enable the park to acquire specific items. When a desk that had belonged to Benjamin Franklin was to be auctioned, the purchase price of $40,000 came partly from National Park Service funds and partly from contributions from the Eastern National Parks and Monuments Association and individuals. Usually, however, there was no time to raise funds when an important piece came on the market. Milley was especially frustrated by his inability to purchase a self-portrait of Charles Willson Peale at auction. Although at the last minute a private donor offered to purchase it for the park, it was too late. Furthermore, there was no budget for conservation, for accessions that would refine the collection, or for exhibits. In 1972 Milley decided that the only solution was formation of a private support group. He began to discuss the concept with a small group of people: Ann Rowland, who had offered to purchase the Peale portrait; Alice Lonsdorf and other members of the Junior League, who had long exhibited an interest in the park through participation in the organization's guide program; and John O'Hara. Assured of interest in such an organization and with Cawood's support, Milley proceeded to draft a constitution and by-laws for what would become the Friends of Independence National Historical Park.

Meanwhile Milley was immersed in plans for mounting the portrait gallery in the great vaulted banking room of the Second Bank of the United States. Milley had come to Independence in 1962. After graduating from Boston University and the Winterthur program at the University of Delaware, he had done further graduate work at Johns Hopkins University and then served for a year as a curatorial assistant at the Abby Aldrich Folk Art collection at Williamsburg. He became curator of paintings at Independence in 1967. This gave him primary responsibility for the eighty-five Peale portraits and the forty-five portraits painted by various members of the Sharples family. The following year he received an internship for a year's study at the National Portrait Gallery, where he expanded his studies of Peale and the Sharples family and became familiar with conservation and restoration techniques.

Milley therefore had an extraordinary interest in the portraits and felt some trepidation at the news that Clement Conger was arriving in Philadelphia to examine them. Clement Conger was curator of the collections displayed in the State Department's Diplomatic Reception Rooms and the White House. He had acquired a formidable reputation for gathering fine furnishings, decorative objects, and paintings, obtained through gifts, loans, and purchases made possible through donated funds, as well as by scouring the collections of other federal agencies, with the full force of presidential backing. Brooks, then superintendent of Independence, and Milley conferred and decided that the latter would show Conger the collection, then in storage. While Milley was conducting Conger through the storage areas, he explained the park's plans for the portrait gallery. Conger meanwhile was making a list. When Milley asked him its purpose, Conger replied that he was listing the paintings he wanted for the White House. He ticked them off—the young Thomas Jefferson, Martha Washington, John Paul Jones, and others—the jewels of the collection. Milley protested that their removal would severely diminish, if not destroy, the proposed portrait gallery. "Oh well," Milley recalled Conger saying, "we shan't treat you too badly." Conger then returned to Washington, confident that the paintings would soon follow.

Conger's confidence evidently stemmed from his belief that the portraits were federal property. They were, in fact, still the property of the City of Philadelphia, although they had been in the custody of the National Park Service for some twenty years. Milley had informed Conger that the proper procedure for requesting a loan of the paintings was to write to the park's superintendent. The letter that came, however, was from the White House to National Park Service Director George Hartzog, who transmitted it to Brooks, and was more a directive than a request. Immediately after it was received, Milley arranged a meeting with the director of the Philadelphia Fine Arts Commission. Milley and the commission had already worked out a loan policy for the paintings that provided that only one at a time would go to any other gallery, for a period of no more than six months. There were no such limits on the order from the White House, which asked for several paintings for an unspecified period. Made aware of these conditions by Milley, the commission, as he had hoped, unanimously refused the loan.

Conger was not easily persuaded that the paintings were not his for the asking. The White House exerted considerable pressure on Hartzog, who transferred the pressure to Brooks. Persuasion as well as pressure were employed. Brooks and Milley found themselves invited to the reception marking the restoration of the Blue Room at the White House, an honor not usually accorded park superintendents or curators. As the pressure intensified, Brooks asked Milley to see whether the commission would reconsider. Milley refused as a matter of principle. At the conclusion of their conversation, Milley recalled Brooks's saying, "John, damn it, you are right. I'm close enough to retirement. I think I can back it up too." To relieve the burden on Hartzog, Brooks wrote directly to Conger, reiterating the commission's policy and agreeing to loans if the White House would accede to that policy. There was no reply, and the incident was finally closed.

Conger attended the party given by the Friends of Independence National Historical Park on the evening of October 13, 1974, to mark the opening of the portrait gallery, and graciously commented, "It's the greatest event in American portraiture I can remember." That accolade must have been particularly sweet to Milley, not only because the quality of the portrait gallery depended in part on the frustration of Conger's attempt to remove its choicest components, but also because it recognized the value of Independence as a museum. Historically, the museum function has been one with which the National Park Service is not entirely comfortable. Objects and fine arts are on display at most park service properties not because of their intrinsic interest, quality, or beauty (although they may possess these characteristics), but because they contribute in some way to the park's interpretive program. Milley found this attitude so unsympathetic that after he finished his museum internship at the National Portrait Gallery, he was undecided about returning to Independence. He believed that collections of the quality of those at Independence required a staff that could care for them properly, perform research, plan for their improvement, and make them known to the museum community and the general public. A meeting with Chester Brooks convinced him that this might be possible at Independence, and that the prospect of developing a museum in the Second Bank was exciting. After his return to Independence, he began to put time and effort into making himself known as a museum professional in Philadelphia, teaching courses in museum methods at Temple University and becoming active in the affairs of the city's Museum Council, including serving a term as its president. He instituted a program that brought students from Temple and the University of Pennsylvania to serve internships in the park. He also encouraged his staff to participate in professional activities in the museum world. To Milley his greatest accomplishment at Independence was establishing a professional museum staff that remains unique among national parks.

The opening of the portrait gallery was the tangible expression of that professionalism. Starting several years before, Milley had planned it down to the last detail. Working back from the target date, he had prepared a large chart, noting when various phases of the restoration of the building must be accomplished, when restoration of the paintings and their frames would have to be completed, when the paintings would be hung, even on what date the invitations would be sent to the printer and when they would be mailed.

The opening was also a triumph for the Friends of Independence National

42. *Portrait of James Madison by James Sharples, Jr., 1796–97. Purchase of this pastel, formerly in the Bristol (England) City Art Gallery and now displayed in the Second Bank of the United States, was made possible by a gift from the Friends of Independence National Historical Park.*

Historical Park, which arranged a benefit dinner for 650 people in the still-unfinished Visitor Center and a cocktail reception for 1,500 at the Second Bank. Guests picked their way to the Visitor Center entrance over construction debris, and the unsheathed walls were hung with bright cloths. The *Philadelphia Inquirer's* society columnist, Ruth Seltzer, said it was a "brilliant strategy. Partygoers felt that they were on the threshold of something new for historic Philadelphia." The Friends' party also symbolized the acceptance of Independence by the social and economic leadership of Philadelphia. It offered renewed hope and confidence. Earlier schemes for celebrating the Bicentennial had failed. The opening of the Second Bank promised that at Independence, and by extension in Philadelphia, the Bicentennial would be a success.

By this time the Friends, under the active five-year chairmanship of Alice Lonsdorf, had more than fulfilled the hopes Milley and Cawood entertained when they encouraged the organization's founding. They were orchestrating social events, such as those associated with the opening of the portrait gallery, with style and grace, generating favorable attention for the park not only in

245

the press, but also in Washington. They sponsored lectures, symposia, and publications that enhanced the park's didactic and scholarly functions. As they gained strength, they would reach out to cooperate with the larger Philadelphia historical community to attract public support for its riches. They started in a small way with a program of special tours called Old Philadelphia Days, focusing on the park and Society Hill. Within a few years it had expanded to a month-long festival of tours and events, justifiably called, since it included the entire city, Philadelphia Open House.

Like most of the Friends' activities, this had a dual purpose: to offer the public an experience of Philadelphia's historical places, and to raise money for the Friends and the participating organizations. The receipts aided the Friends in carrying out one of their primary purposes, to provide funds for the park that would not be available through the appropriations process. Their first major gift was a consequence of Milley's trip to England in the summer of 1972. At the municipal art gallery in Bristol, he saw a pair of portraits of James and Dolley Madison, painted in Philadelphia in 1796 or 1797. Milley found it not too difficult to persuade the museum's director to part with them for $20,000. Emboldened by their success in raising the required funds, the Friends proceeded to more ambitious projects. In 1975 they provided $35,000 to pay for the installation of the architectural and archeological exhibit in the Franklin tenant house at 318 Market Street. In 1981 they were able to purchase for $675,000 the property that would become Welcome Park, the site of the Slate Roof House, and promptly set about raising another $750,000 for its development.

These were, of course, largely volunteer efforts, although as the Friends grew they hired a small staff to organize and coordinate fundraising and other programs. Many of the Friends were involved in more conventional volunteer activities. The group's garden committee provides fresh flowers for many of the park's buildings and also assists in caring for garden areas within the park. The Friends operate a tea garden, just east of the Second Bank, which during the warm months dispenses ice cream and cool drinks. It is staffed partly by students, who are paid, and partly by volunteers, who are not. It is not unusual to find leading businessmen and members of some of Philadelphia's wealthiest families scooping visitors' ice cream cones on a summer weekend. Members of the Friends also serve, after a rigorous training program, as docents at the Second Bank. Many also participate in the Volunteers in the Parks guide program; conversely, most of those in the program generally become members of the Friends.

Volunteers in the Parks is a nationwide program instituted in 1970. Nowhere in the National Park Service has it been accepted more warmly or been more successful over a long period of time than at Independence. The reasons are several. Independence benefits from its urban location, which offers a large pool of potential volunteers. The revitalization of Society Hill has brought good candidates to the park's doorstep, so that volunteers often live within walking distance of their assigned posts. The building stock in Society Hill—rowhouses and apartments—has attracted large numbers of "empty-nesters"—couples who, with children grown and after retirement from business or profession, have chosen to move back to the city. Highly skilled and still seeking activity, many are interested in the opportunities for community service offered by the park. To assure volunteers of their importance to the park, Independence has established a well-organized program. Volunteers are required to undergo training and retraining, both on the subjects of their interpretation and on such matters as emergency procedures. Their work is monitored and checked, just like that of the regular staff. They must commit themselves to at least two four-hour stints per month, and their assignments, complete with breaks and lunch periods, become part of the park's personnel schedule. The corps of approximately 150 volunteers are thus treated like, and expected to behave like, the professionals alongside whom they work. The result has been a reliable cadre of volunteers, with a remarkably low turnover, sharing the National Park Service's "can do" attitude. On one occasion when a large proportion of the staff was scheduled to attend a training session in Boston, the volunteers told the superintendent that they could keep the park open and operating with the skeleton crew remaining. And they did.

Despite the importance of their supplementary assistance, however, an adequate and smoothly functioning staff is essential to provide a meaningful experience to the visitors at any park, especially at periods of peak visitation. At Independence this experience is provided year-round by the park technicians and rangers responsible for interpretation and protection, who are supplemented in the summer by workers known throughout the National Park Service as "seasonals." Many of the latter are schoolteachers, an occupation that is well suited to summer work and also provides a ready-made background in conveying information to groups of people. Many of the seasonals return to Independence year after year and become extremely well informed on all aspects of the interpretive program, sometimes in contrast to the "permanent" staff, some of whom are only at Independence for a relatively brief period before transferring elsewhere within the National Park System.

This was certainly true during the Bicentennial, when the park's staff doubled in two years, with over 200 people assigned to the interpretive function in 1976. Because it remained uncertain whether appropriations for such a large build-up would be forthcoming, finding and hiring had to be done with some haste in the late winter and early spring. Nevertheless, the newly appointed chief of visitor services, Kathleen DiLonardo, refused to compromise on selection standards. The interpreters staffing the park's buildings in 1975 and 1976 differed considerably from their counterparts of the early 1960s. They were no longer "young ladies" dressed to emulate airline stewardesses. There were now men as well as women in the interpreters' ranks, and men and women alike, except for a few who appeared in period costume, wore the standard olive-green National Park Service uniform, with the "Smokey Bear" hat, gray felt in the winter and straw in the summer. The only differentiation was that the women could choose to wear skirts rather than trousers.

It proved to be fortunate that at least some of the increase in personnel at Independence was programmed for 1975 rather than 1976 because visitation to the park began to increase earlier than anticipated. By 1974 the number of visits had risen to 3.4 million from the previous year's 2.2 million. In 1975 it reached 3.9 million. To observers in the park it appeared that many Americans had responded to forecasts of huge crowds of Bicentennial visitors by scheduling their trips a year or two early. The worst period came in February 1976. Approval of the National Park Service budget came late that year, and Cawood did not know until early in the month whether he would be able to afford the year-round and seasonal staff he believed he needed. The process of hiring additional staff had therefore not yet begun when "Presidents' Weekend" hit. This weekend in late February, devoted to the joint celebration of Washington's and Lincoln's birthdays, is always a busy one at Independence. In the depths of the late winter doldrums and faced with a holiday with a patriotic motif, thousands of parents simultaneously decide that it is a fine time to take the children to see Independence Hall and the Liberty Bell. With no seasonals on the roster to handle the extra people, the holiday always places a strain on the park's resources. The crowds in February 1976 were unexpectedly large. Over 200,000 people were counted in the park that month, with over 50,000 at the Liberty Bell on Presidents' Weekend. They seemed to augur a year in which, even with an augmented staff, the park would be overwhelmed.

In the event, the fears proved unjustified. The increased staff was more than adequate to handle the 6 million visits that were clocked at Independence in 1976. Nobody could pinpoint why the 20 to 40 million visitors predicted for Philadelphia failed to materialize. Evidently the predictions themselves had frightened many away, especially when coupled with Mayor Rizzo's forecasts of civic violence. The outbreak of Legionnaire's Disease that struck the American Legion convention in the spring may also have been a factor. Nevertheless, the pressures on the interpreters, the people in the front line, were intense at some locations. During the summer months, groups of 85 to 100 people started a tour of Independence Hall every ten minutes during the eleven hours a day the building was normally open. Often the crowds grew restive waiting in the long lines that snaked into Independence Square from the rear door of the orientation center in the East Wing, where the tours began. In the building itself, however, people tended to be quiet, awed by the almost sacred quality of the events it had witnessed.

On the whole the Bicentennial year was remarkably free of untoward incident, although the beginning of the Fourth of July weekend had some uncomfortable moments. The Fourth fell on a Sunday, with the following Monday also an official holiday. Cawood had decided that Independence Hall and the Liberty Bell Pavilion would be open round the clock from Friday night until Monday. By late Saturday night a large crowd, mostly of young people, had gathered between Independence Hall and the Liberty Bell Pavilion, milling about or sitting on the stands that had been erected for spectators at the following day's ceremonies. Security was tight. Members of the park's supervisory staff, the park's protection force, and a special events protection team brought in from the West were all on patrol. Shortly before midnight it appeared to Chief of Protection Rich O'Guin that the crowd was becoming unruly, and he decided to close the building. Many in the crowd had been drinking, and some began to throw fireworks up at the wood-shingled roofs of the buildings, where O'Guin had stationed rangers with buckets of water to douse incipient fires. As midnight struck on the Centennial clock, the mood of the crowd shifted. Almost with one voice they began to sing "Happy Birthday, U.S.A.," repeating the refrain over and over. Reassured, O'Guin reopened the buildings, and the rest of the night passed peacefully.

The Fourth of July itself dawned bright and relatively cool, a perfect day for a celebration. There were a million people in the park that day, and one observer found them relaxed and amiable. They came to listen to President Gerald R. Ford speak and Marian Anderson sing, to hear music, and to watch fireworks. There were people from all over the country and of all ages, including several governors and justices of the Supreme Court and, catching the crowd's particular attention, the movie actor Charlton Heston. There was one tense moment around four o'clock in the afternoon when the crowd began to show signs of restlessness. O'Guin asked the Philadelphia chief of police, who was on duty near Independence Hall, to move the crowd back. The police proceeded to do this, with the assistance of a providential brief rain shower. Again the moment of potential trouble passed quickly.

Even with the Fourth of July behind them, there was very little rest for those responsible for protection at Independence. For on Tuesday, July 6, the queen of England was scheduled to visit the park. Once again large crowds were anticipated, and this time an untoward incident could have international implications. As always when a visit from a head of state was planned, responsibility for security would be shared not only by the Philadelphia police, but also by the FBI and the Secret Service. Nevertheless, the occasion would put additional strain on a security force already suffering from lack of sleep.

Knowing that their schedule at Independence would be a prelude to exhaustion, Cawood and O'Guin had earlier accepted an offer from security personnel in the regional office to send special protection teams to assist the park staff. The team that had come in for the Fourth of July departed. The new team that came in on the night of July 5 had been assembled from many regions for special assignments over the Fourth. Like the security force at Independence, its members had been on duty through the long weekend, and tempers soon frayed. Hot and tired, the newly arrived team objected strenuously to Cawood's directives that the summer uniform at Independence included neckties and that firearms would not be worn during the daytime. This had not been the case at Fort McHenry, from which they had just come. Fort McHenry is close enough to Baltimore that urban crimes, such as mugging and pickpocketing, pose problems for the security force. However, it is more isolated from the city than Independence, and cannot expect the type of cooperative arrangement with the metropolitan police force that Independence has long enjoyed. Having worn their guns, but not their neckties, in Baltimore, the team intended to behave the same way in Philadelphia.

Telephone wires began to hum, as some of the men called their regional directors, who in turn called National Park Service Director Gary Everhardt. As the news of their attitude, and the phone calls, filtered back to Regional Director Brooks and Cawood, it became evident that firm action would be needed. Accordingly, Brooks and Cawood met with the group on the morning of July 6. Cawood had already been in consultation with the Secret Service and the Philadelphia police, both of which had assured him that they had more than enough firepower to handle any situation that might arise. He relayed this to the men, pointing out that he expected them to abide by his decision in the park in which he was in control. Most followed his directive, although some persisted in wearing their guns.

The question of firearms, and indeed Cawood's handling of the issue at Independence, came up in the course of a study, undertaken over the following few months, of law enforcement in the National Park Service. Crime was a topic to which the park service was being forced to address itself. For the first sixty-five years of the agency's existence, law enforcement had played a minor role as it dealt with a predominantly middle- to upper-middle-class clientele that visited the parks to see the wonders of the West or commune with nature. The visitors and the rangers shared common attitudes toward preservation and care of the parks' resources, as well as a common respect for rules and authority. As the ability to travel became more widespread, and as more parks were established in or relatively accessible to urban areas, the pressures on their use intensified. Crowd control began to be a problem, not only in the distinctively urban parks such as Independence or those in New York City, San Francisco, and Washington, but in some of the western parks as well. The situation was exacerbated by the antiestablishment stance adopted, especially by many young people, as a protest against the Vietnam war and the Watergate scandal.

The first major episode of violence occurred at Yosemite in 1972. What many both inside and outside the National Park Service regarded as an invasion of hippies began to camp in the valley. Drinking, noise, and behavior considered inappropriate to the pristine beauty of the setting led to a bloody confrontation between the young people and park personnel. By 1974 crime in the parks had led to the assignment to law enforcement of as much as 25 to 30 percent of the personnel at some major parks. Park police, long a feature in Washington's parks, which were under the jurisdiction of National Capital Parks, a component of the National Park System, were being transferred to Gateway in New York and Golden Gate in San Francisco. The tension had not abated by the Bicentennial. The Weather Underground, a radical group, had threatened to "bring the fireworks" to Washington. Park police spent the spring of 1976 practicing their response to such situations as a bomb threat at the Lincoln Memorial, a sniper firing from the top of the Washington Monument, and the imprisonment in the monument of ninety hostages. Although none of these dire possibilities were realized, debate about law enforcement within the National Park Service intensified. Rich O'Guin disagreed with Cawood's stricture against firearms in the daytime, although he honored it during his time at Independence. In his view the potential for violence against persons was always present in urban settings. Properly trained law enforcement personnel should be prepared to protect themselves and others by use of firearms if necessary. Besides, O'Guin believed that the presence of armed personnel was reassuring to the public.

It was this view that prevailed. In October 1976 Congress passed a General Authorities Act, defining the law enforcement responsibilities of National Park Service personnel. Among other provisions, it authorized the bearing and use of firearms. To implement the law, the director of the park service issued a policy statement making the bearing of sidearms by park protection forces mandatory. Independence protection personnel began to carry sidearms on their hips, as well as the ubiquitous walkie-talkies with which they communicate with their central office and the park's several districts.

For the queen's visit, however, Cawood's sanguine predictions proved accurate. Once again the weather was beautiful, although warmer than on the Fourth, and so was the mood of the crowd. Royalty was to pay a long visit, and the arrangements for it had been worked out far in advance and in considerable detail. Starting in the spring representatives of security forces from the British Embassy, the Secret Service, and the Philadelphia police department met regularly with the park's management and protection forces. To aid their planning, the park's maintenance division created a map showing the exact route the queen would follow, where barricades would be placed to control crowds, and how the seats would be arranged for the ceremonies at the Visitor Center. There the queen would present the Bicentennial bell, for which Parliament had voted funds, as a gift from the British people to the American people. By the time the event took place, every participant would know exactly where he or she and everyone else involved was to be at any given moment. The preparations covered not only security arrangements, but

43. Queen Elizabeth and Prince Philip visiting the Assembly Room on July 6, 1976. Accompanying them are Secretary of the Interior Thomas F. Kleppe (center) and Mrs. Kleppe.

also protocol. About a week before an important foreign visitor is expected in the park, the State Department sends a briefing book to the superintendent's office with information about the visitor's country and the special interests of members of the party, as well as forms of behavior that may or may not be acceptable to them.

Queen Elizabeth and Prince Philip arrived at Penn's Landing on the royal yacht *Britannia* at nine o'clock on the morning of July 6. At ten o'clock they left to call at City Hall and pay their respects to Mayor Frank Rizzo. By eleven they had arrived at the park, where Cawood, Assistant Superintendent Warnock, and Secretary of the Interior Thomas S. Kleppe and Mrs. Kleppe were waiting to escort the party to the Liberty Bell. The queen's party proceeded to the observation deck atop the Penn Mutual Tower and then returned to the yacht for luncheon. At three o'clock they were back in the park for the dedication ceremony at the Bicentennial bell. A high school band from Bethlehem, Pennsylvania, entertained with stirring music, and then the queen made a brief and gracious speech. Ruefully acknowledging that her ancestor, George III, had been mistaken, she expressed gratitude to the founding fathers for having taught the British "to respect the right of others to govern themselves in their own way." That lesson had enabled Britain to turn an empire into a commonwealth. The speech has been inscribed on a bronze tablet set into the wall of the tower that houses the Bicentennial bell at the Visitor Center.

From the Visitor Center the royal party began a tour of Independence that lasted an hour and a half. They formed a procession led by the queen with Secretary Kleppe on her left and Cawood on her right. Behind them came Prince Philip, escorted by Mrs. Kleppe and Warnock, with the rest of the royal entourage following. Progress was slow because the queen stopped to shake hands and chat with groups and individuals along the way. The first stop was Carpenters' Hall, where members of the Carpenters' Company were assembled to greet them. Charles E. Peterson, serving as the company's historian, presented the royal couple with a specially bound copy of its Bicentennial publication, *Building Early America.* The group then proceeded to the Second Bank, where John Milley provided a brief tour of the portrait gallery. The last stop was Independence Hall. At the conclusion of the tour, the queen and her party returned to the *Britannia,* where they hosted a reception for a stream of dignitaries. Cawood and Warnock were among those in attendance. That night the city sponsored a gala dinner at the Philadelphia Museum of Art. For Cawood it was the capstone of a perfect day. He had not only had the opportunity to introduce his wife to the queen, but had also met the actor John Wayne, whom he had long admired.

The four days embracing the Fourth of July weekend and the queen's visit were the culmination of eight years of planning and frantic preparation, all targeted toward that period of ninety-six hours. The remainder of the summer at Independence continued to be busy, although the crowds were never as large as had been anticipated. Because the level of staffing was adequate, the park was able to provide an experience of unusually high quality. The audiovisual presentations and other exhibitry were the most extensive that had ever been available in a national park, and except for exceptionally crowded weekends, there were plenty of staff members to answer visitors' questions and supplement the displays with personal interpretation.

After Labor Day, however, the crowds dwindled precipitately. In the superintendent's office, the phone once constantly busy with calls to and from contractors, the press, City Hall, the White House, and the British Embassy rang far less often. The stacks of mail were no longer piled high on the desks. Now that the task was accomplished, the goal reached, there was a sense of let-down among those who had worked at fever pitch for so long. Chester Brooks had anticipated the change. On July 4, accompanying the director of the National Park Service on a helicopter flight to Independence from Valley Forge, he requested a transfer from the regional office back to superintendency of a park. The management team at Independence gradually broke up. Warnock, Lockwood, and O'Guin all sought and received transfers back to western parks. Cawood remained. For a man with his energy and drive, it was a difficult period of adjustment to a different type of superintendency.

All parks pass through three phases—planning, development, and operation. Each of the phases embraces aspects of the others, but in successive stages one element predominates. At Independence, planning had been the preoccupation for over twenty years, beginning with the Shrines Commission's report of 1947 and culminating in the master plan of 1971. Development had also proceeded during those years, albeit at a leisurely pace, and then been virtually completed, during Cawood's tenure, in a remarkably intense five-year period. From the time the National Park Service took possession, of course, the park had also been operated, beginning with the buildings on Independence Square and gradually expanding as other facilities were completed. By the Bicentennial the operations had been tuned to a fine pitch, capable of exhibiting Independence as a showplace to anyone from the queen of England to the millions of ordinary visitors from all over the United States and around the world. Now maintaining the park's precious physical resources and the quality of the visitors' experience would be the staff's task for the foreseeable future.

There were still a few development projects to accomplish. Construction of a maintenance facility had been deferred in the interests of preparing the park's display facilities for the Bicentennial. By 1979 it would be built on park-owned land at the corner of Fifth and Manning Streets. A garage was also slated for construction, to be owned and operated by the city on park land in Area F east of Second Street. With funds raised by the Friends of Independence National Historical Park, Welcome Park, a vest-pocket open space planned, like Franklin Court, by Robert Venturi's firm, was developed adjacent to the garage.

Cawood would continue to use all his political skills to obtain adequate funding for continued preservation of the park's historic resources and maintenance of its high level of visitors' services. In 1981 Penelope Hartshorne Batcheler transferred from the staff of the Denver Service Center to that of the park to prepare a twenty-five-year cyclical maintenance program for the park's buildings. The most dramatic manifestation of the program was the erection, in 1982, of scaffolding so that the tower of Independence Hall could be repaired and repainted. And the public continues to visit Independence. Visitation declined dramatically immediately after the Bicentennial and then began to rise again. By 1985 it was again approaching the level of 1976. It will undoubtedly rise even higher when a second Bicentennial, that of the Constitution of the United States, is celebrated in 1987.

The creation of Independence National Historical Park culminated in 1976. But the story of Independence has no end. As long as American democracy survives and remains the envy of the people of the world, Independence will be a place of pilgrimage, a destination for the millions who want to see for themselves the place where liberty was born.

Nine
Epilogue

During the almost half-century of planning for the creation and development of Independence National Historical Park, the project reflected and also influenced the philosophy and practice of historic preservation in the United States. The vision of a major park centered on Independence Hall and other nearby historic buildings was conceived, and to a large extent brought to fruition, by men born and educated in the nineteenth century. Their thinking was shaped by Beaux Arts classicism and the City Beautiful movement, by the wish to impose order on a grand scale on urban areas that had developed in a haphazard and untidy manner. Judge Edwin O. Lewis, the most powerful force behind the creation of Independence, often spoke almost wistfully of the broad boulevards and fountain-bedecked greenswards of the formal parks he had seen in Europe. He sincerely believed that formal landscaping, fountains, and statuary would be fitting enhancements for the historic monuments a park would preserve. Fittingly, his permanent monument at Independence is the Judge Edwin O. Lewis Fountain in the second block of Independence Mall north of Independence Hall. This mall is now administratively part of Independence National Historical Park, but the National Park Service had no part in its planning. It was financed by the commonwealth of Pennsylvania and designed for the state by Roy Larson of the firm of Harbeson, Hough, Livingston, and Larson. More directly than the areas of the park for which the National Park Service was responsible, its formal vistas and symmetrical arrangement reflect late nineteenth- and early twentieth-century concepts of urban design and beautification.

Judge Lewis's vision was not a fresh beginning, but the culmination of earlier formalistic approaches to an appropriate setting for Independence Hall. In 1915 the solution proposed by architects Albert Kelsey and D. Knickerbacker Boyd would have created a formal plaza across Chestnut Street from Independence Hall, backed by a Colonnade of the Signers, a Palladian five-part construction with a central pavilion linked by curving passages to smaller end pavilions. In the 1920s more ambitious plans were put forward, linked with the creation of the most prominent Beaux Arts contributions to Philadelphia's cityscape, the Benjamin Franklin Parkway and the Benjamin Franklin Bridge and its approach. Paul Phillipe Cret, designer of the parkway, proposed a modest but formal plaza in the same location that Kelsey and

Boyd had suggested. His associate on the design of the parkway, the French landscape architect Jacques Greber, drew more ambitious schemes, commissioned by the city. These envisaged a monumental mall from Chestnut to Market Street. It would contain a "Great Marble Court," surrounded by Neo-Palladian buildings, with the Liberty Bell presented as an icon on an altar at its center. In the 1930s Roy Larson expanded on these schemes, omitting the buildings but extending the mall north to the approach to the Benjamin Franklin Bridge. At the same time others were propounding the concept of a mall linking Independence Hall with the historic buildings to its east. During and after World War II, Judge Lewis and his associates in the Independence Hall Association adopted and combined these ideas, all calling for massive clearance of existing buildings and creation of monumental open spaces, focused on, if not necessarily related in scale to, the historic buildings.

These early schemes fell rather more into the category of urban planning through redevelopment than that of historic preservation, although all embraced retention of the buildings on Independence Square, Carpenters' Hall, and a handful of other eighteenth- and early nineteenth-century buildings. The preservation philosophy to be applied to these buildings was one that had been practiced in the United States since the mid-nineteenth century. They would be displayed, like the Liberty Bell on Jacques Greber's altar, as venerated but isolated artifacts, without regard for the nature of their original setting. By the time plans for Independence were actually being formulated in the late 1940s and early 1950s, however, other approaches to historic preservation had come to the fore. Primary among these was the example of Colonial Williamsburg. In this prerevolutionary Virginia capital, Rockefeller money had made possible the preservation and restoration of an entire town. Williamsburg was still in the process of being recreated as it had stood in the eighteenth century, a process that incidentally included the ruthless excision of the physical remains of its later history. Standing eighteenth-century buildings were being restored, with accretions representing the changing tastes of later generations removed; lost buildings were being reconstructed; and the historic ambience of the town was being recaptured through the recreation of antique streets, gardens, and public spaces.

Massively publicized, Colonial Williamsburg captured the imagination of the American public in the 1930s with an appeal to which the National Park Service, itself newly launched in historic preservation, was not immune. Indeed, many of the historians, and at least one of the historical architects, who helped formulate preservation philosophy and practice within the park service, had worked in geographical and associational proximity to Williamsburg at Jamestown and Yorktown. Like the managers of Colonial Williamsburg, the National Park Service in the 1930s thought in terms of "cut-off dates." If Williamsburg was to be recreated as an eighteenth-century town, no nineteenth-century remains could intrude. So, too, at the few National Historical Parks developed during the period, notably Colonial and Morristown, buildings and their landscapes would be returned to their appearance during the period in which they had acquired historical significance, and later buildings would be removed. Similar views influenced other preservation-related activities within the National Park Service. The National Survey of Historic Sites and Buildings, established by the Historic Sites Act of 1935 to identify potential additions to the National Park System, was charged with examining sites related to the broad stream of American history but categorized its subjects by themes and periods of significance. The Historic American Buildings Survey, more focused on architecture and aesthetics than on history per se, nevertheless operated with an arbitrary (although occasionally exceeded) cut-off date of 1830.

Yet another strain of preservation-related activity originating in the 1930s would influence some of those involved in the planning and development of Independence. Concomitant with the introduction of zoning plans, a few cities, with Charleston and New Orleans in the vanguard, instituted preservation districts. Because these encompassed not only major monuments, but also lesser buildings and entire streetscapes, their proponents were more accepting of diversity and change over time than more traditional preservationists. The rationale behind the creation of these districts was not strictly the memorializing of particular personages, events, or historical periods, as was the case at museum houses and villages, including sites administered by the National Park Service. History was important, but so were the aesthetic effects and quality of life represented by the past. Districts were also viewed as presenting an opportunity for achieving civic purposes, as tools for not only preserving, but also revitalizing older urban areas. The potential of historic areas as keys to urban rebirth was one factor in garnering support for the establishment of Independence. Isidor Ostroff, who played an important early role in obtaining congressional support for the project, had tried as early as 1938 to persuade the realtor Albert M. Greenfield to spark a rebirth in the area of Independence Hall by constructing new moderate-income apartments there. Although he failed, he used their common interest in the neighborhood to enlist Lewis's aid in working for state legislation enabling creation of a Philadelphia Redevelopment Authority, a vital step in providing financing for revitalization. By the time the creation of the park was under serious consideration in 1949, the Philadelphia City Planning Commission was committed to rehabilitation of the residential area south of Walnut Street, now known, as it was historically, as Society Hill. Although their plan called for considerable new construction, some of it on a large scale, it also envisioned retention and restoration of hundreds of eighteenth- and early nineteenth-century rowhouses. These would be interconnected through small-scale greenways. Edmund Bacon, the city's chief planner, saw the presence of a federal park north of Society Hill as a key factor guaranteeing long-term commitment to its stabilization and improvement. At the same time, he hoped that planning for the park could be integrated with that for Society Hill and another proposed city project at Penn's Landing.

Still other voices would comment on and attempt to influence the park's planning. By the early 1950s younger critics and scholars were beginning to challenge the fly-in-amber view of history and preservation epitomized by Colonial Williamsburg. Like Judge Lewis, many of them had been influenced by European cities, during wartime service or study afterward. What they admired, however, was far different from what had so impressed the judge. Although they could appreciate the order and majesty of the boulevards of Napoleon III's Paris or Bismarck's Berlin, they also liked the diversity and complexity of the many layers of Rome and the byways of London, the delight of the surprising vista opening at the end of a narrow alley, and the contrast produced by the random juxtaposition of buildings of different periods. Articulate and organized through professional and scholarly associations, they were not hesitant about commenting on the planning for Independence. Nevertheless, their influence was slight in the early years of the planning process. Their criticism of the Williamsburg approach was not widely shared, even among professionals. To many within the National Park Service, and certainly to the layman, Williamsburg remained an excellent model. The advisory commission for Independence National Historical Park often cited it as an exemplar; in the late 1960s and early 1970s, that body was still advocating provisions for visitors' orientation and an introductory movie based on similar facilities at Williamsburg.

As plans were developed in the 1950s for the major portion of Independence National Park east of Independence Square, the National Park Service assumed full control over the outcome. The Philadelphia City Planning Commission, courted and consulted during the planning that preceded congressional authorization of the park, was virtually ignored during the long master planning debates. Other than the advisory commission, which acted with considerable independence, there was no established channel of communication between the National Park Service and city agencies. Whatever discussion with the city took place was generally conducted by Superintendent Melford O. Anderson or Judge Lewis, and their deliberations and conclusions were not recorded. Preoccupied with their own ambitious plans for Center City, Society Hill, and redevelopment of the blocks facing the state's mall, city officials rarely commented on plans for Independence except to complain about the slow pace of development. When they did protest against a decision, they were politely but firmly told to mind their own business, as when the planning commission objected to construction of a maintenance building on Marshall Street. The National Park Service was forced by political pressure to pay more heed to the Philadelphia Fine Arts Commission's wish to be heard on design issues, much to the annoyance of Director Conrad Wirth, but it avoided accountability to the city's commission by appointment of its own architectural advisory committee.

Nor was heed paid to the scholars and critics who hoped to see more buildings, more of the urban fabric, preserved. Although demolition was delayed largely because of the advocacy of the chief internal proponent of this viewpoint, Charles E. Peterson, the wholesale clearance of later buildings demanded by Judge Lewis prevailed. In part this decision reflected the National Park Service's premise that preservation was a tool for interpreting particular historic periods and events.

Although Lewis achieved a large part of his goal, the creation of an open park with the historic buildings displayed like individual gems in a setting of lawns and trees, Independence escaped becoming a formal set piece adorned with fountains and statuary. (Three statues, already in place, survived the creation of the park, that of President George Washington in front of Independence Hall, that of Commodore John Barry behind Independence Hall, and that of Robert Morris, relocated behind the Second Bank of the United States; a fourth, an idealized signer of the Declaration of Independence, a gift of the Independence Hall Association, was erected in 1982 at the corner of Chestnut and Fifth Streets.) In the ultimate design, a preservation plan derived from Williamsburg prevailed. Historians and architects argued for a philosophy that would suggest, and to some extent reproduce, the ambience of eighteenth-century Philadelphia. Old street and sidewalk patterns and materials were carefully reconstructed. Contouring suggested early land forms. Reconstructed buildings recreated the sheltered character of Carpenters' Court. On Walnut Street, the early master plan had called for the restored Bishop White and Todd Houses to stand in splendid isolation. By the end of the decade, the plan had been amended to permit rehabilitation of additional historic houses and reconstruction of others. The emphasis had shifted from the restoration of individual buildings to the recreation of an eighteenth-century streetscape. This view of the past, heavily influenced by Colonial Williamsburg, was one with which the National Park Service was comfortable. Reconstruction, especially if it served the purposes of interpretation, was generally accepted, as long as the documentation of the historic appearance of the building was adequate. Had funding been available, additional buildings, such as Norris's Row at the corner of Fifth and Chestnut Streets, might well have been reconstructed in order to provide visitors with more of the flavor of the colonial city.

Financial strictures also led the park service to give more consideration to the uses of buildings than had ever been necessary before. The decision to demolish such structures as the Jayne and Penn Mutual Buildings was made largely on interpretive and aesthetic grounds. Once the park's cut-off date was set at 1800, there was no defensible historical rationale for their presence. But the cut-off date was clearly flexible. Preservation of two early nineteenth-century buildings—the Merchants' Exchange and the Second Bank of the United States—was mandated in the legislation establishing the park. The essential difference was that in the 1950s these classically inspired buildings were generally admired; the more flamboyant later structures were not. Nevertheless, a strong undercurrent in the decision making was economic. There were no mechanisms available through which the National Park Service could preserve additional buildings and lease them for the commercial uses for which they were most suited.

Although no solution was found for the later nineteenth-century buildings, the park service was compelled to find suitable uses for a greater number of historic buildings than at any other of its holdings. The first interpretive program visualized most of these as museums, a decision that would have imposed impossible staffing and budgetary burdens. As the planning process continued through the decade, and the number of buildings to be maintained expanded, an increasing variety of adaptive uses was considered, including staff quarters, administrative and other park service facilities, libraries, and museums or headquarters for other institutions. Some decisions on use were made because space was available at Independence. The move of the regional office to Philadelphia, and its location in the Merchants' Exchange, occurred in part because the building was there and the park service was required to preserve it. Individually none of the uses was particularly innovative. Staff quarters and park administrative offices had been located in lesser historic buildings at other parks. At Independence, however, the range and scale of adaptive use was greater than had previously been attempted. Much of this was accomplished by stretching the device of the cooperative agreement to its limit, with outside organizations occupying and maintaining the buildings at Carpenters' Court and many of those on Walnut Street. Independence demonstrated that it was feasible for the National Park Service to become a landlord in order to preserve buildings that were not needed for park activities. In a decision that came far too late to save structures like the Jayne and Penn Mutual Buildings, the park service in 1980 was given authority to lease buildings within parks to private profit-making enterprises for preservation purposes, although no leases have yet been signed.

The change during the 1950s in the proposed treatment of the major portion of Independence, from preserving individual buildings in an alien setting to attempting to recreate the ambience of a particular period, reflected a shift in the philosophies of both preservation and urban design. Yet even as construction of the park began, scholars and preservationists were questioning the premise of erasing part of the urban fabric in order to recapture a moment frozen in time. Like contemporary historians, who were beginning to look at the past as a seamless web rather than as an accretion of discrete periods, younger preservationists viewed historic buildings as inextricably bound to their surroundings, acquiring added significance from the buildings around them, and from the process of change in that fabric. These ideas were embodied in the creation of the National Register of Historic Places under the National Historic Preservation Act of 1966. First proposed by Ronald F. Lee in 1960, the National Register expanded the Historic Sites Survey established in 1935. It recognized the importance of places of state and local, as well as national, significance and afforded them a measure of protection from federally funded or assisted projects. To the individual sites and building complexes covered by the older law it added recognition of historic districts. Two of those who would be instrumental in overseeing implementation of the new law and the programs it established had received their National Park Service initiation at Independence in the early 1950s. Dr. Ernest Allen Connally became chief of the Office of Archeology and Historic Preservation, while Dr. William J. Murtagh became the first keeper of the National Register. Both had undergraduate degrees in architecture as well as doctorates in architectural history. Both had been recruited for HABS teams at Independence by Charles E. Peterson. Both had witnessed and been disturbed by the clearance of nineteenth-century buildings that had marked the first stage of the park's development.

At Independence the impact of a new preservation philosophy was demonstrated most strongly in the treatment of Franklin Court. In 1954, when plans for its development were first broached, Peterson pleaded in vain for retention of the historic fabric along Market Street. Instead, considerations of cost, and lack of knowledge about the buildings, led to a decision for demolition. No action was taken, however, and by 1960 the National Park Service had begun to agree with the City Planning Commission that the buildings should be saved. With passage of the National Historic Preservation Act of 1966, their preservation was virtually ensured. The debates over other aspects of Franklin Court pitted the newer preservationists' philosophy against the views that had prevailed in the 1930s, epitomized by Colonial Williamsburg. The objective was now to preserve and rehabilitate what existed, not to recreate a vision of the past. The latter was considered false historicity, devaluing the genuinely old by surrounding it with meretricious copies. The park service had always been chary of reconstruction because of the possibility of error; now reconstruction would be viewed with even less favor as inherently deceptive. Where infill in a historic area was required, the new preservationists advocated compatible contemporary design.

These attitudes influenced the final shape of Franklin Court, although there were compromises. They proved most telling in the treatment of the sites of such vanished features as Franklin's house, his print shop, and the surrounding garden. The Market Street houses, however, were not interpreted in a modern idiom but were restored in a manner so conjectural as to be tantamount to reconstruction. Nor did the pendulum swing all the way in cases where other factors militated against purism. City Tavern and the Graff House were both reconstructed in the 1970s, the former because it had been a key element in the interpretive plan since the early 1950s, the latter because it had long been a favored project of the Independence Hall Association, which garnered political and financial support for its authorization and construction. That organization and the closely related advisory commission never adopted new attitudes toward preservation, maintaining a preference for individual "shrines" in well-landscaped grounds.

If Independence's preservation planning was reactive rather than initiative, this was not the case with its handling of major historic buildings. National Park Service architects, with Charles Peterson in charge during the formative years, built on the foundations of thorough documentary and physical research and use of historic precedent established at Williamsburg and other restorations of the 1930s. To these they added, as became clear during the controversy over whether the buildings on Independence Square should be reframed in steel, the principle that all of the historic fabric of a building, even that which was hidden from sight, was worthy of respect. Contrary to the Williamsburg precedent, where the entire interior structure of the so-called Wren Building was rebuilt in steel and concrete, they argued successfully that the old timbers should be retained and reinforced. As the architects worked on the restorations at Independence, they developed, sometimes through trial and error, procedures and techniques that became standards for building restoration in the United States. Paint and mortar were analyzed not only for information about the original appearance of finishes, but also as aids in dating original fabric and subsequent alterations. Building technology and the history of such building components as nails were studied for the same purpose. Peterson also insisted on leaving intact the physical evidence on which conclusions were based, as well as maintaining a written, graphic, and photographic record.

That these advances in restoration practices did not become merely local or National Park Service "arts and mysteries" was due largely to Peterson's fervor and persistence. A teacher by instinct—indeed, a militant evangelist in the cause of old buildings—Peterson also had what Lee Nelson termed a strong sense of accountability. He believed that the public should know how its money was being spent on historic buildings, and what was being learned through that expenditure. From his earliest days in Philadelphia, in contrast to most of those on the park's staff, Peterson made a point of becoming known among the local historical and architectural communities. He already had a wide acquaintance among scholars and those engaged in preservation and restoration around the country. These contacts would serve him well as he proceeded to construct a restoration "academy" in Philadelphia, a center in which architects, scholars from other disciplines, and craftsmen could come together to learn from one another. To staff it he would depend in part on academics and architects from across the country, who would recommend bright young people for temporary or longer-term employment on the Independence restorations.

One of Peterson's earliest steps was to revive HABS, which he had designed in 1933. Although one of its primary Depression-era functions had been to provide work for unemployed architects, Peterson had always viewed it as having a strong didactic purpose. HABS had virtually ceased to operate during World War II and had no budget account within the National Park Service thereafter. Peterson saw a fresh opportunity for the program at Independence, where measured drawings were needed as a basis for the restoration work. He recruited the first of a series of summer teams in 1952, paying them from the park's budget. They would provide drawings at a low cost to the park service. At the same time, they would be educated in drafting skills that were no longer taught at most architectural schools. Peterson believed that the production of measured drawings was one of the best means of understanding old buildings. Students trained through this process would form a cadre of professionals with respect and sympathy for historic buildings, whether or not they actually became restoration architects. Peterson provided other educational opportunities as well, including a series of informal talks by academics from the University of Pennsylvania or other Philadelphia institutions, local practitioners, and visiting scholars and experts. Peterson was generous in inviting students and young professionals on the park's staff to join him and a fairly steady stream of distinguished visitors for lunch. When Peterson moved from the Independence staff to EODC, he seized the opportunity to expand HABS activity at other parks. A few years later an appropriation to reinstitute HABS outside the parks was approved as part of the Mission 66 program. With the organization of OAHP in Washington after passage of the National Historic Preservation Act of 1966, HABS once again became a national program.

HABS was not the only vehicle through which Peterson sought to arouse interest in and expand knowledge of historic buildings. Always anxious to see the fruits of new research in print (he was for many years editor of "American Notes" in the *Journal of Architectural Historians*), he was one of the moving forces behind the 1953 publication of the special edition of the *Transactions of the American Philosophical Society* published as "Historic Philadelphia." The volume brought together the latest information on Philadelphia buildings in and outside the park in a series of essays written by park staff and scholars from other institutions. To foster the cooperation that made such a venture possible, Peterson encouraged members of his staff to attend meetings and address scholarly and professional groups. In addition to fostering attendance at such formal gatherings, Peterson in the mid-1950s organized a series of monthly luncheons at the now defunct Hotel Edison. At these, National Park Service architects and historians would meet with professional staff from Philadelphia's historical and cultural institutions. There would be opportunities for informal discussions over lunch. Afterwards members of the group would make brief presentations on discoveries at the park, their research, or interesting material in their holdings. These meetings provided an important forum for the exchange of information and also helped to create an atmosphere of cooperation between the park service and Philadelphia's venerable institutions, which in that era could still be cool to outside researchers.

Somewhat later phenomena were the Carpenters' Carnivals, annual affairs more formally known as Historic Structures Training Conferences. Peterson organized three of these before he left the service in 1962. These were more structured affairs than the Edison Hotel lunches, with prepared speeches and demonstrations of building crafts. Those attending included not only National Park Service personnel, but outside architects and architectural historians, historians, and builders. Members of the staff were assigned to contribute. Penelope Batcheler's pamphlet on paint analysis and Lee Nelson's on nail chronology, both still important items in the restoration bibliography, grew out of papers presented at a Carpenters' Carnival.

This sense of obligation to make findings comprehensible to the public outlasted Peterson's tenure in the National Park Service. Throughout the long restoration process at Independence Hall, Nelson and Batcheler regularly mounted small exhibits explaining their activities and findings to the visiting public. In 1969 Batcheler organized a major exhibit in the First Bank, entitled "See What They Sawed," using items from the park's architectural study collection to explain early building practices. More recently she has arranged a series of smaller exhibits in that building's basement, illuminating various aspects of early building technology.

Independence from the late 1950s through the early 1970s became a national center for restoration for a variety of reasons. The major attraction, of course, was the restoration of a score of buildings, among them the most historically important building in the United States. Because of the associations of Independence Hall, its restoration attracted the attention of the popular press, enhancing public awareness of restoration processes and of what constituted authenticity. As the work on the buildings progressed, the park became a laboratory in which the most advanced techniques for investigating and rehabilitating historic buildings were developed and tested. In the process, and through the host of allied activities for which Peterson was the catalyst, a cadre of professionals received their training and formed their attitudes. Some of the students and young professionals he hired remained in the National Park Service to become leaders in its emerging preservation activities. Through requirements for federal undertakings, and through grants-in-aid and tax incentives available to those outside the government, they codified and promulgated nationwide preservation standards. Others who worked at Independence—not only staff, but also consultants, architects, structural engineers, and contractors—became principals in private firms specializing in restoration. As these people moved on from Independence to other park service posts, to the burgeoning restoration scene in Society Hill, and to other areas in the country, they carried with them the principles they had absorbed: careful research, respect for the integrity of a building's historic fabric, and the necessity of leaving a record of what they had done. Independence thus became the testing ground at which American restoration came of age.

It was not, of course, only preservation policy and practice that changed during the years of Independence's creation. Because of its size and importance as a historic site, Independence became the focus for new and sometimes experimental programs. The recruitment of women to serve as guides and interpreters, however sexist its original premises, opened the way to increased employment opportunities for women in the National Park Service. The need to tell the park's story to large numbers of people, especially as the Bicentennial approached, encouraged the park service to institute imaginative interpretive programs that went well beyond the guided tour or campfire talk to sophisticated audiovisual devices, live drama, and participatory activities. Stewardship of the extraordinary collection of American portraits led to strengthening of the park service's museum function. In the 1970s policies directed toward enhancing the National Park Service's presence in urban areas, combined with the personalities of the park's superintendents, Chester Brooks and Hobart Cawood, produced closer integration with the surrounding community. Independence, which had remained studiously aloof from the city in which it was located while plans for its development were formulated, became communicative and cooperative. National Park Service personnel worked closely with the City of Philadelphia and local groups in fighting for a design for Interstate Highway 95 that would minimize damage to Society Hill and other historic areas along Philadelphia's waterfront and in planning for Philadelphia's celebration of the Bicentennial of the Declaration of Independence. As for the succeeding Bicentennial, that of the Constitution, Cawood became the chairman of the city-wide committee overseeing its celebration. By now Independence, while maintaining its national importance, has also become a cherished Philadelphia institution. Its support group is the envy of other components of the National Park System and has reached out to assist other historic sites in the Philadelphia area.

There will never be another National Historical Park like Independence. For one thing, no other site, except perhaps the Statue of Liberty, alone on its island, is so meaningful to the American people. For another, the National Park Service can never again destroy so much of the historic fabric of a city in order to create an artificial vision of the past. Even if such an approach were desired, legislation passed during the creation of Independence would forbid it. Neither the National Historic Preservation Act nor the National Environmental Protection Act would permit the wholesale demolition that attended the creation of Independence. Newer National Historical Parks, such as Boston and Lowell in Massachusetts, are very different, preserving their historic monuments within an existing context. Their buildings and areas, some older, most newer, than the sites at Independence, are not set apart but are integrated with the city around them, physically as well as socially. Yet they are, in a sense, the children of Independence, the heirs of philosophies and policies aired and argued in the years of its conception, birth, and maturation.

Notes on Sources

F or those who may wish to check specific sources related to events recounted in this work, an expanded and fully annotated version is available at the Independence National Historical Park Library.

The major sources for this book fall into four categories. The first is written primary material generated by the National Park Service and held in several federal repositories: Independence National Historical Park Library and Archives, the Federal Record Centers at Wissahickon, Pennsylvania, and Suitlands, Maryland, and the National Park Service's Office of Archeology and Historic Preservation and Office of History in Washington, D.C.

Among the collections of papers that were of particular usefulness because of their long-term coverage of the development of the park are the monthly reports filed by the historians and interpreters. Although the office from which they were generated reflected organizational changes in a sequence of names, these are generally referred to as the Interpretive Division Monthly Reports (hereafter IDMR). A nearly complete set of these reports is available in the park's archives. Although the superintendent's office also filed monthly reports, preservation of these (at Wissahickon and Suitlands) has been fragmentary, and their contents are not as extensive. The second major source for the park's chronology consists of the Minutes of the Advisory Commission for Independence National Historical Park (hereafter ACM), copies of which are in the park's archives and headquarters. This group met at least quarterly, and often more frequently, from 1949 to 1976. The reports made to the members of this body, and their reactions and comments, illuminate most of the major issues in planning and development.

One large group of useful records has unfortunately disappeared within the past three years. It comprised the park's copies of minutes, memoranda, and correspondence sent, as well as some original correspondence received, from the 1950s through the early 1970s. However, notes on these, as well as copies of many documents, are in the author's files, which have been deposited in the park's archives. It is possible that duplicate copies of some material may exist in the files of the Washington office, at the Federal Record Center at Suitlands, or in regional files at the Federal Record Center at Wissahickon.

For activities leading up to the establishment of Independence as a National Historical Park, the most important sources are the papers of David Knickerbacker Boyd, Judge Edwin O. Lewis, and the Independence Hall Association, all of which have been deposited at the park's archives.

Other important groups of papers include the voluminous reports generated during the creation of Independence National Historical Park. These, along with the files of the historians, curators, archeologists, and architects, as well as press clippings and reports of special events, are also in the park's archives. Additional architects' files and day books maintained during the investigations of the buildings are in the architects' office at Independence.

The second major source of information was the memories of the participants. Three major series of interviews related to Independence have been conducted and tape-recorded. The earliest was undertaken by the Columbia University Oral History Project (hereafter CUOHP) and focused on the events leading up to the establishment of the park and on the early years of its formation. Transcripts of the interviews have been deposited in the park's archives; the tapes are held by Columbia University. The second set of interviews was conducted by George A. Palmer (hereafter GAP), who retired as deputy regional director of the Mid-Atlantic Region in 1973, having served in the Philadelphia regional office since 1955. Thoroughly familiar with the development of Independence, Palmer undertook his oral history project in 1976 and 1977, when the preparations for the Bicentennial and the events of its celebration were fresh in the minds of the participants. Copies of transcripts and tapes of Palmer's interviews are at both the Independence archives and the National Park Service Archives at Harper's Ferry, West Virginia. The author (hereafter CMG) carried out a third series in preparation for this book. It consisted of formal, taped interviews and informal consultation on particular questions. Tapes of the formal interviews, as well as transcripts of most of them, have been deposited in the archives at Independence.

A third source for the development of Independence is the graphic record. Several thousand drawings detail the master planning process, the landscaping, and the construction, rehabilitation, and restoration of buildings. Prints of many drawings are in the files of the Mid-Atlantic Regional Office in Philadelphia, while originals are at the Denver Service Center. Drawings are also available on micro-fiche at the Mid-Atlantic Regional Office and, for buildings, in half-scale copies at the park architects' office. The progress of clearance and demolition and the park's subsequent development, as well as personnel and major events, are pictured in photographs taken by members of the staffs of the park and the Eastern Office of Design and Construction and by professional photographers. There are also a few reels of amateur and professional motion pictures. All are available through the park's library.

Finally, some published sources were of help in defining the background of preservation and National Park Service philosophy that influenced the development of Independence National Historical Park. Particularly useful were the following: Charles B. Hosmer, Jr., *Preservation Comes of Age* (Charlottesville: University Press of Virginia, 1981); Ronald F. Lee, *Family Tree of the National Park System* (Philadelphia: Eastern National Park and

Monument Association, 1974); and Conrad L. Wirth, *Parks, Politics, and the People* (Norman: University of Oklahoma Press, 1980).

Particular sources for each chapter are described in more detail below.

Chapter One

Chapter 1 is based on personal observation, park interpretive materials, historic structures reports on individual buildings and areas, and interviews with park personnel, in particular Superintendent Hobart G. Cawood and Assistant Superintendent Bernard Goodman.

Chapter Two

Information on the development of the neighborhood of Independence National Historical Park was based on historical maps and views; contemporary descriptions of the eighteenth- and nineteenth-century city, many of which can be found in the research cards assembled by the park's staff; nineteenth-century guide books; and later published sources, including Carl Bridenbaugh, *Cities in the Wilderness* (New York: Roland Press, 1938); [Carroll Frey], *The Independence Square Neighborhood* (Philadelphia: Penn Mutual Life Insurance Company, 1926); *Historic Philadelphia* (Philadelphia: American Philosophical Society, 1953); Thomas J. Scharf and Thompson Westcott, *History of Philadelphia: 1609–1884* (Philadelphia: L. H. Everts, 1884); Martin P. Snyder, *City of Independence: Views of Philadelphia Before 1800* (New York: Praeger, 1975); Sam Bass Warner, Jr., *The Private City: Philadelphia in Three Periods of Its Growth* (Philadelphia: University of Pennsylvania Press, 1968); J[ohn] F[anning] Watson, *Annals of Philadelphia*, rev. and ed. by Willis P. Hazard, 3 vols. (Philadelphia: Leary, Stuart & Co., 1909); and Edwin Wolf, 2d, *Philadelphia: Portrait of an American City* (Harrisburg: Stackpole Books, 1975).

For activities leading up to the establishment of Independence National Historical Park, the major sources are: the historic structures report for Independence Hall; plans for early schemes for enhancement of the Independence Hall area in the photographic files at the Independence National Historical Park Library; Lewis, Boyd, and Independence Hall Association papers; interviews with Roy E. Appleman, Edmund Bacon, Michael J. Bradley, Roy Larson, Edwin O. Lewis, Isidor Ostroff, and Charles E. Peterson (CUOHP); interviews with Elizabeth Boyd Borie and Charles E. Peterson (CMG); and *Independence Hall and Adjacent Historic Buildings: A Plan for Their Preservation and the Improvement of Their Surroundings* (Philadelphia: Fairmount Park Art Association in collaboration with the Independence Hall Association, 1944); Roy E. Appleman, Report on Tour of Duty in Philadelphia, May 23–June 18, Philadelphia Shrines National Park Commission, September 30, 1947, Appleman File, Federal Record Center Wissahickon, RG79 Box 64; Charles E. Peterson, a Preliminary Report—June 1947: The Philadelphia National Shrines Project, author's files; Philadelphia National Shrines Park Commission, "Final Report to the Congress of the United States," December 29, 1974, Independence National Historical Park Library.

Chapter Three

Sources for this chapter include the Lewis Papers; newspaper clippings; interviews with Edward M. Riley, Edwin O. Lewis (CUOHP); interviews with Melford O. Anderson, David A. Kimball, George A. Palmer, Charles E. Peterson, Conrad Wirth, Martin I. Yoelson (CMG); ACM, November 1949, April 1950; Superintendent's Monthly Report, February 13, 1951, Federal Record Center Wissahickon, RG 79 Box 64. This first official report from Independence summarizes activities for the previous fifteen months.

Chapter Four

Much of the information for this chapter came from memoranda, correspondence, and minutes of meetings in files at the Federal Record Center, Wissahickon, the architects' files in the Independence archives, and the now-lost files formerly stored at park headquarters. Also useful were the Lewis Papers; the IDMR for January 1951 and December 1951 through November 1952; and the ACM for November 1955, January 1957, April 1957, November 1957, and September 1959. Master plan drawings also contain important information, especially those numbered (with the preface NHP-IND) 2001, 2006A, 2495, 3018, 3018A, 3018B, and 391/60,002. Information also came from interviews with Hobart G. Cawood, William C. Everhart, Nicholas Gianopulos, George A. Palmer, Charles E. Peterson, Conrad Wirth, and Martin I. Yoelson (CMG). Other important sources included: Charles E. Peterson, "Philadelphia's New National Park," *Proceedings of the Eightieth Annual Meeting of the Fairmount Park Association* (Philadelphia: Fairmount Park Association, 1952), pp. 32–36; Recommendations for Proposed Redevelopment East of Third Street, draft, August 10, 1951, in the Office of History files in the park's archives; Master Plan Development Outline, Independence National Historical Park (Project), 1954, Project Area A, formerly in files at park headquarters; Revised Master Plan, July 21, 1955, and Mission 66 Prospectus, Independence National Historical Park, April 22, 1957 (revised May 10), both at the Independence National Historical Park Library; and Lewis Mumford, "The Sky Line: Philadelphia," *New Yorker,* November 17, 1956, pp. 132–42; February 9, 1957, pp. 98–106; April 6, 1957, pp. 120–29; and April 13, 1957, pp. 143–50.

Chapter Five

Probably no American building has been as thoroughly researched as Independence Hall. The fruits of that research are preserved in several forms: the multi-volume historic structures report and historic furnishing report, covering almost every aspect of the building, room by room and feature by feature, drawings and photographs, and the daily log books kept during the physical investigation, all of which are available in the architects' office at Independence. Similar although less voluminous materials exist for the Bishop White House, including a historic building report, historic structures reports, and the historic furnishing report and George L. Wrenn III's day books on research and restoration at the Bishop White House, Todd House, and Hibbard-Griffiths House. Other reports shed light on research and restoration practices before the production of historic structures reports became standard. These include John B. Lukens's report on work carried out on Independence Hall in 1951; William Campbell's notes on early research at the Bishop White House; Paul J. F. Schumacher's notes on his archeological work at the Bishop White House; and William J. Murtagh and Samuel Edgerton's report on their investigations of the Merchants' Exchange. Helpful in illuminating the development of attitudes toward restoration are meeting minutes and memoranda, especially those in the architects' files in the park's archives and architects' office. Additional information on these issues, as well as the progress of architectural research and restoration, came from interviews with Penelope Hartshorne Batcheler, Chester A. Brooks, William Campbell, Ernest Allen Connally, Charles G. Dorman, James C. Massey, William J. Murtagh, Lee H. Nelson, Charles E. Peterson, and Martin I. Yoelson (CMG). Other important sources included Charles E. Peterson's memorandum to Conrad Wirth, February 14, 1962, setting forth his reasons for resigning, author's files; *The Restoration and Refurnishing of Independence Hall, 1953–1963* (N.P.: National Park Service, 1963); James M. Mulcahy, "Congress Voting Independence," *Pennsylvania Magazine of History and Biography* 80 1 (January 1956): 74–92; Penelope Hartshorne Batcheler, "Independence Hall: Its Appearance Restored," and Lee H. Nelson, "Independence Hall: Its Fabric Restored," in *Building Early America* (Philadelphia: Chilton, 1976).

Chapter Six

Valuable material for this chapter came from the IDMRs, in which are recorded not only the work accomplished, but often the historians' opinions on current issues as well. Also useful were the special events files and newspaper clippings in the Office of History files at the park's archives. Other special events and, in particular, the sound and light presentation are covered in the ACM for November 1955, September 1959, March 1960, June 1960, December 1960, October 1961, February 1962, July 1964, April 1966, and March 1969. Information on the research and interpretive programs in the 1950s came from priority lists, plans, and analyses in files at the Federal Record Center, Wissahickon, and reports entitled "Research Program, Independence National Historical Park, for Fiscal Year 1959," and "Interpretive Survey, Independence National Historical Park, 1959," both in the park's archives. Material on the hiring of women as interpreters can be found in Roy Appleman's report to Ronald F. Lee of September 26, 1960, in "A Report on the Employment of Women as Guides at Independence National Historical Park," June 11, 1962, in an untitled manuscript by Pearl Millman, and in related correspondence, all in the park's archives. Further information came from interviews with Dennis Kurjack and Edward M. Riley (CUOHP), Charles G. Dorman, William C. Everhart, George A. Palmer, John D. R. Platt, and Martin I. Yoelson (CMG).

Chapter Seven

The complicated chronology of new development in the late 1960s and early 1970s— the Visitor Center, Franklin Court, and the Liberty Bell Pavilion—is clarified through the ACM, especially for November 1967; March, June, and October 1968; November and December 1971; January, April, and May 1972; March and June 1973; January, April, and August 1974; February and October 1975; and March 1976. As always, files at the Federal Record Center, Wissahickon, and those formerly at park head-quarters supplied additional information. Of particular importance for this chapter were files in the architects' office at Independence and the Office of Archeology and Historic Preservation in Washington. Also extremely interesting are the tapes of a meeting on Franklin Court held on the afternoon of October 9, 1969; the transcript of a meeting of Franklin scholars held at the park in June 1972; and the tapes and transcripts of a program entitled "Architects in the Park," held February 24, 1979, at which Peter Chermayeff, Romaldo Giurgola, and Robert Venturi spoke about their respective projects at Independence. Among the participants and observers interviewed were Penelope Hartshorne Batcheler, Hobart G. Cawood, John L. Cotter, John D. R. Platt, and Martin I. Yoelson (GAP and CMG); Chester A. Brooks, Ernest A. Connally, Charles G. Dorman, David Dutcher, William C. Everhart, Arthur C. Kaufmann, David A. Kimball, and George A. Palmer (CMG); Louise Boggs, Howard LaRue, and James R. Sullivan (GAP). Other important sources included the IDMR for February and October 1961, September 1963, August 1973, March and April 1975; historic structures reports and reports on archeology and furnishings at Franklin Court; Barbara Liggett, *Archaeology at Franklin Court* (Philadelphia: Eastern National Parks and Monuments Association, 1973); and Carleton Knight III, "The Park Service as Client: II," *Architecture* (December 1984): 48–55.

Chapter Eight

Preparations for and celebration of the Bicentennial at Independence were carried out at such an intense and rapid pace that written records are relatively slim. This chapter therefore depends heavily on oral history, including interviews with Hobart G. Cawood and John C. Milley (GAP and CMG); Genevieve M. Bell, Mary Borov, Howard LaRue, Clyde M. Lockwood, Richard O'Guin, James R. Sullivan, and David H. Wallace (GAP); Adelaide W. Cawood, Chester A. Brooks, Charles G. Dorman, Bernard Goodman, and George A. Palmer (CMG). Magazine and newspaper articles in the park's clipping files were also useful, as were the ACM, particularly for March 1968, October 1970, August 1974, February 20, 1975, and April 1975.

Index